AMERICAN DEMOCRACY:

SUICIDE OR REVOLUTION?

The Life and Death Struggle

Between Democracy and Despotism

Robert T. Latham

ISBN: 978-0-578-60310-0

Published by MythingLink
Printed in the USA

ACKNOWLEDGEMENTS

My appreciation to:

Brooke Maddaford of Word Hawk Editing, LLC for her initial developmental editing and suggestions.

Nancy Blanton and Andrea Patten of Amelia Indie Authors for the cover design, final developmental editing, and expert guidance through the self-publishing process.

I owe them all immense gratitude.

Robert T. Latham

To Cynthia
Companion on the Journey

Many forms of Government have been tried, and will be tried in this world of sin and woe. No one pretends that democracy is perfect or all-wise. Indeed, it has been said that democracy is the worst form of Government except for all those other forms that have been tried from time to time...

Winston S. Churchill
Parliament Speech
1947

CONTENTS

INTRODUCTION

PART I

DEMOCRATIC MODELS

PART II

INTERNAL NECESSITY AND THREATS

PART III

A DESPOTIC MODEL

PART IV

THE BATTLE ENJOINED

PART V

HOW DO WE KNOW?

PART VI

WE THE PEOPLE

PART VII

THE CHOICE AND BECOMING

EPILOGUE

INTRODUCTION

AMERICAN VISION AND DESTINY

The American citizenry has been compelled to choose between two styles of governance that have battled for citizenry allegiance since the country's birth. This has caused the nation to see with a distorted double vision that invites the suicide of democracy.

Double Vision Malady

Double vision is a sight malady. It is misalignment of the two eyes. It is the inability to gain a single focus. America was born with political double vision—one eye focused on democracy and one eye focused on imperialism. The eye out of which it was colonized was British economic imperialism. This eye's vision is a singular devotion to profit making. The eye which prompted its birth as a separate nation was democracy. This eye's vision is devoted to citizenry equality and their common good.

This political malady has made it impossible for the populous to give full focus to either way of governing. An image metaphor of this national malady is that of the face of the Statue of Liberty with unfocused eyes—one eye reflecting the vision of Old Glory and one eye reflecting the vision of the dollar $ign.

The result is a conflicted patriotism. Patriotism is the people's commitment to the nation's political vision. Countries normally share a common political view which unites them. However, America has competing patriotisms that reflect the double vision of democracy and economic imperialism. These views draw opposing conclusions about national purpose and direction.

This means that the conflicts that consume citizenry energy are less

1

about how to apply democracy than they are about how to reconcile the incompatible and competing goals of these different ways of seeing. The citizenry is forced to accommodate to opposing governing perspectives in order to make sense of their existence—perspectives that cancel each other's devotions. The end result is a double-bind commitment which invites the suicide of vision paralysis.

The Problem and the Danger

The problem the nation faces is that in order to accommodate to these radically different ways of seeing the citizenry must compartmentalize its existence. It must live a schizophrenic life-style with a divided focus. This makes for a blurred vision that can only see that which is closest. Thus, its lifestyle is always reactive to what is in front of it without the capacity to see beyond. It cannot envision the bigger picture.

The danger is that if this is the basic lifestyle of the majority of the citizenry then it may be viewed as reality. The consequence is that a culture trying to make such an impossible accommodation will lose its capacity to see beyond the immediate. It can never envision the future. It can only react to now.

The alternative is for one or the other of these two views of reality to capture the citizenry's focus and full allegiance. In this case the issue is whether democracy wins or economic imperialism wins. If economic imperialism wins then democracy dies.

The Threat

This is the imminent threat that confronts the American people. Currently, economic imperialism has gained the upper hand in this battle, having captured the empowering structures of American government. The nation is in peril of losing its vision to that which it rebelled against in order to be born. It is a destiny determining moment which is as consequential as that which initiated the American Civil War. And it will go the direction chosen by the citizenry. But the issue can only be engaged deliberately if the citizenry understands with clarity the choice it must make. At this moment, America is unwittingly drifting toward democratic suicide.

The Urgency of Revolution

The only thing that can save democracy is a citizen revolution. This revolution need not be physically violent. It need only be socially transforming. This transformation can only happen by voting into office those who are totally committed to the democratic eye so that its vision will inform all decision-making. To make such a revolution happen would require that the citizenry know:

- How to distinguish between democracy and economic imperialism.

- The two primary threats that feed economic imperialism and imperil democracy.

- How economic imperialism has expressed itself in American history.

- How to measure the success and failure of each governing vision.

- How democracy can win this battle of competing visions

The following provides this knowing. The populous must engage this knowing or American democracy will die. There is no alternative. It is revolution or suicide.

VISIONS AS DIFFERING GOVERNANCE

The democratic and despotic visions are deadly enemies. And both can be expressed in different ways of governing.

Democracy

The word democracy refers to the common people. In a democracy it is neither its structures nor its officials who are responsible for success or failure. It is the people for which these structures and officials work. There are two kinds of democracies. In a direct democracy all the people of a nation consider and vote on the issues of governance. The problem with this version is the overwhelming number of people participating and their incapacity to be informed. In a representational democracy it is the officials the citizenry elect who consider and vote on their behalf. The problem with this version is those who are elected remaining true to those who elected them.

Founding father Thomas Jefferson sums up the baseline of responsibility:

Every government degenerates when trusted to the rulers of the people alone. The people themselves therefore are its only safe depositories.

Whether it is a direct or representational democracy, it is the people who are responsible for its success or failure. It is of them, by them, and for them.

Despotism

Despotism refers to rule by absolute power. It is about unlimited authority. It can be one person or a small group of persons. This form of government has dominated human history. Its titular heads have been known by many names such as queen, king, pharaoh, czar, emperor, president, chief, leader, and chairman. Whatever the title, despots normally rule in a suppressive manner for their own benefit. The people are tools to fulfill their goals. As Mecha Constantine, author, poet, teacher, and activist of Kenya Africa, reminds us:

> *In despotism the systems are there to protect the privileged and suppress the underprivileged.*

The term fascism originated in Italy during World War II. It designated a group that took over the country under the despotic leadership of Benito Mussolini. It referred to total obedience to a single authority. Mussolini gave it meaning:

> *The definition of fascism is the marriage of corporation and state.*

This is an apt definition of economic imperialism. In America it is the marriage of capitalism to democracy—business and government. It reverses roles by making democracy the servant of capitalism. Profit takes precedent over people. What applies to despotic fascism applies to economic imperialism. The only thing that separates the two is the thin membrane of language. Economic imperialism is rule by economic despots for the purpose of profit-making. The economic imperialist can use any organization or adopt any name to accomplish this purpose, including democracy.

The Problem

The problem is that democracy and despotism are so finely interwoven in American culture that it is difficult for the citizenry to distinguish between them. This means that, more often than not, they assume the two are partners rather than enemies. It is this assumption that invites democracy's suicide.

5

PART I

DEMOCRATIC MODELS

1

PRIOR DEMOCRATIC MODELS

The Athens Experiment

The first large scale attempt at democratic rule in western civilization took place mostly during the fifth century B.C. The site was the small city state of Athens in lower Greece. Its total population was between 250,000 and 300,000 during the hundred years it engaged the experiment. The majority of this population was women, children, foreigners, slaves, and freed slaves. The adult male population eligible to vote numbered between 30,000 and 50,000—a maximum of a little over 15% of the total.

For almost the first half of Athens' democracy only those who had property wealth were allowed to vote. Eventually, the less wealthy were granted the privilege. At this time the term democracy came into vogue, a Latin reference to rule by the common people.

Why the Experiment Failed

With thousands of citizens voting directly on issues, the primal concern was to reduce voting from mob rule to some form of sane decision making. Despite the organizational schemes devised to achieve this goal the government was never able to solve the problems posed by the multitude of voting participants. Eventually, the experiment failed.

What caused Athenian democracy to fail? The overall reason was that it was direct rather than representational in its process. It was overwhelmed by the number of people voting and their incapacity to be fully informed and have meaningful dialogue. Here are some of the specific issues:

- **Education and Wealth Inequality**
  The meetings were a mix between those whose wealth allowed their votes to be informed by education and relevant news and those whose lack of wealth prohibited such contributions. This inequality of perspective often caused the end result of issue dialogue to be contentious and counter-productive.

- **Political Corruption**
  The government's system of justice offered little protection for those accused of various crimes. Because of this deficiency, the lucrative role of being a professional accuser flourished. Bribery became a way of life. This caused the system of justice to become less about justice and more about politics and private goals. This corrupted the entire democratic structure. It invited false accusations to be used to undermine honest debate and the integrity of those involved. This brought into constant question the validity of leadership and what it proposed.

- **Expansive and Expensive Wars**
  There was disagreement about the necessity of empire expansion versus consolidation with imperialism often winning the day. Much of the city state's treasury was spent fighting wars. This required increased tribute from conquered provinces, fostering discontent and rebellious attitudes. Governing focus easily shifted from democratic fulfillment to maintaining national solidarity.

- **Institutional Instability**
  The issues that faced such a large population engaged in direct voting were unsurmountable. Despite its attempts, Athens was never able to create the institutional processes necessary to stabilize efficient democratic debate and satisfactory outcome. These procedures remained ragged and ineffective.

- **Lack of Professionalism**
  Given the radical differences in education and perspectives of the voters there was never sufficient professionalism to keep the democratic attempt on even keel. It became overburdened with amateurish leadership, behavior, and facilitation.

- **Disproportionate Capacities**
  With inadequate technology and forced timing of votes, the meetings of thousands of people to determine issues became dominated by those few who had sufficient eloquence, projecting vocal capacities, and behind the scene influence to sway large unruly assemblages to their viewpoint. Such did not allow for considered voting and often important decisions made had dire consequences which were looked on in retrospect with deep regret. There was little group wisdom because there was neither time nor process to gain such a focus.

The End of Athenian Democracy

After a hundred years the experiment simply bogged down in its inability to solve the problems posed by citizenry direct voting. And toward the end of the experiment it sometimes resorted to despotic means in its attempts to resolve the issues it confronted. Eventually, a weakened Athens was absorbed into the Roman Empire and reduced to a limited state of self-government.

The Lesson

The lesson of the Athens experiment is that while a direct democracy may work well in a small community, the larger the population the less effective it becomes.

Other Democratic Attempts

Democracies come into being in many different ways and take varied structural forms. Whatever their form, they are required to adapt to the peculiar cultural history from which they rise which makes them all unique creations.

Great Britain

Great Britain is an example of a country with a thousand year history of transition from monarchy to democratic governance. The seedbed for this transition was the creation of the Magna Carta in 1215 which expanded citizen rights and their representation in government. In the mid-thirteen hundreds the House of Commons came into being which broadened Parliamentary representations from various constituencies. In 1688 the Glorious Revolution occurred which decreased monarchy power and increased citizenry rights. By 1867 a third of the population had the right to vote. In 1918 some of the women citizenry were given the right to vote. By 1928 women and men over 21 years old could vote.

Great Britain's democracy is a complicated parliamentary form with representation of common people, nobility, religious leadership, and monarchy translated into governing structures. It is an evolved system which is different from American democracy which sprung with immediacy by revolution from British colonial rule.

The Post World War II World

Since the liberating promise of World War II many countries around the globe have attempted to establish and maintain some form of democracy. In adapting to the issues of their own peculiar cultural history, some have been successful and some have not.

Why Democracies Fail

Freedom House is a respected and independent American democratic watchdog agency. It measures the success of nations seeking to establish and maintain democracy and proposes reasons for failure. Its 2019 *Freedom in the World Report* indicates that success in such attempts have been declining over the past thirteen years. A few of the nations in decline are Poland, Turkey, Nicaragua, Ecuador, Venezuela, Thailand,

Bahrain, Israel, India, and the Philippines.

Unfortunately, American democracy is listed as in measurable decline, particularly since the George W. Bush administration, through the Obama administration, and rapidly during the Trump administration.

Following are some of the reasons offered by Freedom House for democratic decline in these countries.

Populism

Populism is a view of politics that the white hats are at war against the black hats. This polarity has been stated in multiple ways:

- The virtuous against the vile.

- The pure against the corrupt.

- The exploited against the exploiters.

- The marginalized against the empowered.

- The oppressed against the oppressors.

The black hats are those in power who are making the decisions and who seem unconcerned about the outcome except for their own well-being. They are the establishment. They have no interest in change except that which is to their profit. What is ethical is who they are and what they do. They have the guns and the white hats are usually unarmed.

The white hats normally view themselves as the disenfranchised. They believe they are victims and that their cause should prevail over all other concerns. Populists see themselves as the real voice of the people.

For the white hats, there are no legitimate rules that govern accomplishing their goals:

- They are divisive.

- They demand simple answers to complex problems.

- They are generally anti-establishment.

- They assume their issues can only be resolved through conflict.

This attitude of being an underdog easily legitimizes behavior that

13

would normally be viewed as inappropriate or wrong.

The danger of populism is that it easily empowers negative dissent without offering positive solution. Destruction without creation is often the end result. Moreover, its focus is usually on symptoms rather than causes. Income disparity is an example.

Populism can be conservative or liberal. But whatever its orientation, it assumes the will of the virtuous people must prevail with immediacy over vile leadership. In this regard, populism is normally the enemy of established representational democracy which requires deliberation, due process, and the honoring of guiding rules. Populism is revolutionary in spirit and behavior.

Populism is easily aroused and intensified if the virtuous feel frustrated when their concerns are not corrected with immediacy and when there is an inspiring leadership that enflames this frustration.

Populism also conveniently converts into despotism once its leadership gains government power. When this happens despotic goals that benefit the dictator take the place of virtuous goals that benefit the people. However, this twisted result may be viewed positively by the virtuous if it is tied to the overthrow of vile leadership and the superficial fulfillment of their demands.

Nationalism

Nationalism is the elevation of the interests of one's own nation, culture, and concerns, above that of all other nations. During the Russo-Turkish War of 1877-78, Great Britain displayed a hostile foreign policy toward Russia. This hostility was captured in a popular song that used the word jingo in its lyrics. Since then the word jingoism has come to stand for an over aggressive nationalism in foreign policy and is often used to imply attitudes that lack regard for the rights of other nations.

Nationalism is jingoistic patriotism. Its intention is to boil the blood of resentment and call for heated confrontation. Its attitude defies collaboration among nations in favor of using them as means to private ends. It fosters undemocratic relationships and war. Its spirit of superiority toward other nations prohibits the expression of democratic principles within its own national populous.

Nationalism is anti-democratic. However, it may be engaged anyway because it is a rallying point for the superficially patriotic and those who feel disenfranchised.

Nativism

Nativism is the practice of protecting the interests of native born citizens against the presence and concerns of immigrants.

- It is anti-multicultural and pro status quo.
- It is anti-immigration and pro isolation.

It is anti-democratic since democracy is embracing of multiculturalism, politically progressive, open to immigration, and pro engagement.

The problem is that nativism rarely roots in the concerns of original natives but springs with immediacy from the exclusive concerns of the presently empowered natives. But this illogic and blindness of origin may be inconsequential since racism gives it specific focus and provides the glue for a unifying negative identity.

Despotism

Despotism is individual or small group rule over the larger community. Despotisms are often disguised as democracies. But there is one social expression that cannot be hidden. It is a free media. It is the media that reports on the status of democracy and those issues that threaten its survival. It is media that braves identifying democracy's enemies and suggesting remedial courses of action. A critical measure of democratic vitality is the visible extent to which freedom of an independent press is affirmed and protected. In nations with a failing attempt to institute democracy there is usually the parallel attempt by a despotic government to:

- Control the media.
- Determine its content.
- Discredit its reporting.
- Destroy it.

When the media is under attack for its revelations then democracy is in danger of being hijacked by despotism. But if this hijacking supports the goals of the disenfranchised it may be overlooked in favor of the possibilities of political empowerment.

Conclusion

Populism, nationalism, nativism, and despotism are visible measures of failure in attempts to institute and sustain a democracy. However, they are only symptoms of more subtle and profound causes that lie underneath the failure of democracies. These more profound causes are about how humans connect which are dictated by views of reality. The reason is because democracy is, at its heart, a way of citizenry relating.

OF, BY, AND FOR

Democracy cannot succeed without some form of governing that allows for a free and informed populous to express itself with such benefit that it remains true to this government.
It must be of, by, and for the people.

2

A DEMOCRATIC PRINCIPLE MODEL

There are some stable principles that seem inherent in trying to establish a democracy. The following suggests a model based on these principles. They are grounded in the notion that a true democracy can only be instituted and sustained by commitment to the equal worth of all citizens. This grounding means two things:

- If equality of worth is the lens of perception it will permeate the total vision. If any human is born worthy, then all humans are born worthy.

- Every issue that confronts a democratic society can find a proper resolution by seeing through this lens. It is only when this lens is lost that democracy is lost.

These two perceptions are the ground of all democracies.

The Three Intents of Democracy

This vision suggests a threefold definition of a version of democracy where the citizens elect representatives of their views to govern the nation. Such a democracy is a way of governing grounded in a spirit, a conscience, and a rule:

- **Its spirit** is the equal worth of the citizenry.

- **Its conscience** is the common good of the citizenry.

- **Its rule** is the vote of the citizenry.

This spirit affirms that citizenry worth is innate. This conscience acknowledges the citizenry's collective worth. This rule is the citizenry asserting its worth. These are the three governing intentions of democracy. These three characteristics are an integrated trilogy and an inseparable trinity. They are the prerequisite of democracy. If they exist democracy can exist. If they do not exist democracy cannot exist.

The term democracy is generic, representing this spirit, conscience, and rule in a nation's existence. It cannot be contained by minimizing party affiliations such as Republican, Democrat, or Independent. It transcends ethnicity, gender, religion, and class, embracing the citizenry in fullness. It is not the social label but the intent posture that defines the true democrat. Here is this definition of intent:

> *Democracy is a way of governing compelled by the citizenry's*
> *worth equalty, devoted to the citizenry's common good,*
> *and ruled by the citizenry's vote.*

In an actualized democracy, every aspect of government will yield to these intentions. Domestic and foreign policy will model these intentions and armed force will only be used to uphold their necessities. The ethics demanded by equality of worth will instruct all relationships, decision making, economics, and justice designs. The common good will be the goal of every branch of government and their attendant agents. The citizenry will keep these intentions inviolate through their voice and vote.

Governing Principles of Democracy

With this definition of democratic intent in mind there are seven governing principles that instruct the fulfillment of an institutionalized democracy. When these principles are being evidenced democracy is being evidenced. When these principles are being violated democracy is being violated. All violations are invitations to despotism—whatever its form or name.

The Grounding Principle

The grounding principle of democracy is:

> *All relating, organizing, decision-making, and envisioning*
> *will affirm and sustain the equal worth of every citizen.*

18

Any violation of this principle is a violation of the foundation upon which all governing structures are built. These structures are as secure as this foundation. That which undermines any aspect of democracy begins with weakening this principle. All attitudes and behaviors of both citizenry and leadership that violate this grounding are anti-democratic and destructive of its possibilities—inviting of despotism.

The Evidentiary Principle

This principle is rooted in the grounding principle and is visible evidence that democracy is being instituted:

The common good is the first good and all other goods are subservient.

Every branch of government and their agents serve this principle or find themselves in anti-democratic violation of common good conscience. This principle is the primary allegiance of every citizen, whatever role they might play in the democratic drama. There are no exceptions.

When the people's common good is sustained, so is its equality of worth and its rule of vote. All policies, laws, and actions will be supportive. Pursuing the common good is the primary evidence of democratic fulfillment. Allowing any private good to supersede the common good is anti-democratic and inviting of despotism.

The Voting Principle

If democracy is to be representational every citizen, regardless of gender, ethnicity, religion, or class, must be guaranteed the vote. Here is the principle:

The government must guarantee the right of every citizen to vote and must administer severe penalties for any attempt to infringe upon this right.

For any political party, group, or person to reduce this right in any manner is to violate the democratic stewardship instructed by election, appointment, and citizenship. It is to reveal a character commitment to anti-democratic attitude and action. It is to give an inviting nod to despotism.

19

The Investment Principle

The vitality and health of democracy is determined by the citizenry. Here is the principle:

> *The degree of the citizenry's investment in the intentions and functions of democracy will reflect its health and potential.*

Of, by, and for means that it is not the structures of governance but the involvement of the citizenry in energizing these structures that determine democracy's well-being and potential to raise the quality of the nation's existence. All *laisse faire* citizen attitudes of indifference are anti-democratic. All failures to vote are anti-democratic. All voting for spoof names rather than actual candidates are anti-democratic. Since these attitudes and failures relinquish the right of citizenry responsibility they also relinquish the right of criticism. And they invite despotic rule.

The Economic Principle

The singular purpose of whatever monetary system a democracy uses is to enhance its citizen's well-being. Capitalism is an example. The singular purpose of capitalism in a democracy is to facilitate the common good. Here is the stratagem by which it exists:

> *Economics is a means not an end.*

When capitalism becomes anything else besides a means to facilitate the end of the common good, it becomes an anti-democratic violation. The inevitable outcome of sustained violation is the rise of some form of economic imperialism. Economic imperialism places profit making before the common good and reverses governing roles which makes democracy a tool of capitalism. Such affirms both democratic failure and the rise of despotism.

Whatever the economic means used to support a democracy, when it becomes an end to itself rather than a means, it will contend for allegiance above democracy. It will become a foe of democracy and invite despotism.

The Taxation Principle

The primary means by which the common good is funded in a democracy is equalized taxation. Taxation is the instrument by which all who benefit from democracy contribute their fair share of this funding. Here is the principle:

Every citizen and every business enterprise will pay their fair share of taxes based on real income profit.

When taxable entities become exempt from this principle in any way an anti-democratic violation of shared responsibility toward the common good has been instituted. Any attempt by an individual or business to avoid real income profit taxation is an attempt to gain from democracy without fair return. And any attempt by government to favor any class or business over another is a violation of democratic fairness. What are birthed of these violations are anti-democratic parasites that feed off the taxation commitment of the general citizenry. Such announces that democracy has become a profit-making-utility for economic despotism.

The Reciprocity Principle

The officials of every branch of government, being bound by these foregoing sustaining principles, are consequently bound by the principle of reciprocity:

Whatever the rewards of public service, they must be returned in like kind to the citizenry who are also the servants of democracy.

If these elected and appointed officials are provided fair wages, business expenses, affordable health care, safe working conditions, paid vacations, and a livable retirement by the citizenry, then they are obliged to reciprocate by law so that every citizen can access the same possibilities. Otherwise, they rule by anti-democratic hypocrisy without the guidance of democratic fair play for those they represent. The reciprocity dictum of democracy remains, as it has always been: What is good for the governing is good for the governed. All other attitudes traffic on the inequalities of despotism.

Measuring Extent

The extent to which a nation practices the spirit, conscience, and rule of democracy as evidenced by these guiding principles is the extent to which a representational democracy actually prevails. And that extent has to do with devotion to citizenry equality, their common good, and their voting rule.

An acclaimed democracy can be such to lesser or greater extent. All other ways of measuring democratic success are false – including economics, religion, party loyalty, cultural devotion, and notions of conservative, moderate, liberal, and independent. Extent has to do with actual practice and nothing else.

Conclusion

If it avows mutual worth, affirms the common good, and is ruled by the citizenry, it is of, by, and for the people. If it is democratic – it is E Pluribus Unum—out of many, one. This people focus and unity is expressed community.

A Community Event

Whatever else a democracy might be about it is first of all and primarily a community event – of, by, and for the people. While individuals make it up it remains community generated and focused. This is democracy's paradox: The individual is always birthed of and sustained by the community while simultaneously making successful community possible. It is only an individual event in that every citizen is responsible for honoring the community's democratic intents. Yet, it is the individual that profits most by commitment to the intents of the democratic community.

A Community Collaboration

The American Declaration of Independence suggests that among the rights government should champion are life, liberty, and the pursuit of happiness. Whatever they meant by this it was emphatically brought about by government—by community collaboration. They were rebelling to make such possible because it could not happen under the British despotic rule of economic imperialism. This was not simply a blood-letting so individuals could romp in private play and capitalistic money-making ventures. It was the explicit institution of rules and structures that bound the community in covenant so that the common good could be achieved. When this good is achieved then such makes possible the desired liberties for every citizen. That is why they called it a democracy. It was about the total community.

A Community Empowerment

There can be no actualized democracy until the citizenry's primary focus is beyond the individual and embracing of its entire self. It is the empowered and multiplied benefits of this wholeness that causes democracy to glow. It is the lack of such that causes the nation to be diminished with democratic dimness. Above all else democracy is a community event that visibly reveals itself for what it is or is not.

A Community Organization

A functioning democracy is its intents translated into organization. This is how a democracy becomes a reality. The face of a democracy is a reflection of this constant translation. This means democracy and organization are inseparable. Organization makes democracy real by giving it focus for citizenry vision and energy commitment. Organization is the bones of democracy's body. It is citizenry's common good given concrete focus.

OF, BY, AND FOR

Democracy is of, by, and for the people and the people is community—the whole of the citizenry. Therefore, democracy is of by and for community.

3

THE AMERICAN MODEL

The Declaration of Independence, which led to the nation's constitution, begins with a statement about the evident truth of human equality:

WE hold these truths to be self-evident, that all Men are created equal…

Whatever the founder's individual understanding of its source, they believed equality of the white male citizen to be the ground of the democracy they were creating. It would take over one hundred and forty years for the black population and women to be included but the nation ultimately embraced the whole of its citizenry in its original affirmation of mutual equality.

It is this notion of inherent equality, irrespective of its source, which is the necessity of democracy. All other aspects of democratic intention spring from this ground.

This declaration ends with a vow that:

"…we mutually pledge to each other our Lives,
our Fortunes and our sacred Honor."

There could be no stronger affirmation of commitment to a government devoted to the citizenry's equality than the community's dedication of life, fortune, and honor. It is the commitment of total community being.

The Common Good

The first paragraph of the constitution clearly indicates that the government of this new nation was to be devoted to the common good of the whole citizenry:

24

We the People of the United States, in Order to form a more perfect Union, establish Justice, insure domestic Tranquility, provide for the common defense, promote the general Welfare, and secure the Blessings of Liberty to ourselves and our Posterity, do ordain and establish this Constitution for the United States of America

The purpose of the constitution was to both protect and facilitate the citizenry's well- being as a holistic community. The common good has a singular bias—it recognizes only that which affirms citizenry equality. Common good is equality of good. This is the American guide. Daniel Webster, American senator and Secretary of State during the mid-nineteenth century avowed:

We may be tossed upon an ocean where we can see no land—nor, perhaps, the sun or stars. But there is a chart and a compass for us to study, consult, and to obey. That chart is the Constitution.

This is the map that guides America over the often tumultuous ocean of governance.

The Right to Vote

Curiously, there was no explicit statement in the constitution about the right of citizens to vote. It took almost two hundred years for this right to be granted the total citizenry. But eventually, through various constitutional amendments, the entire citizenry has been embraced legally. Here is the sequence of constitutional amendments that moved toward this embrace.

- Amendment XV – The right to vote despite color, race, or prior servitude (1870)

- Amendment XIX – The right to vote, despite gender (1920)

- Amendment XXIII – Citizens of the District of Columbia granted the right to vote for the President and Vice-President (1961)

25

- Amendment XXIV – It is illegal to use forms of taxation to prohibit the right to vote (1964)
- Amendment XXVI – Anyone eighteen years of age or older is entitled to vote (1971)

Although this legal embrace set the stage for a greater acknowledgement of voter rights, it has not necessarily accorded with actual reality in many areas of the nation's life—including this moment in history.

Gaining the Right to Vote

The difficulty in securing such a right with immediacy for all citizens was varied. The black population at this time was generally viewed as inferior to white people in all respects and was not accepted as citizens. Women were generally viewed as inferior to men in respect to decision-making and bringing about civilizing necessities, thus, insufficiently informed and endowed to vote. And some men saw women as property without rights.

Another reason was that it was believed non property owners did not have a sufficiently vested interest in the community and therefore should not vote. Property owners were almost exclusively white males in the post-revolutionary period.

Yet, another reason was that a large segment of the populous was devoted to economic imperialism over democracy and wished to continue exploiting slavery and other forms of cheap labor for personal profit. As well as slaves, these forms included women, children, the poor, and indentured servants. The influence of economic imperialism in suppressing the right to vote of all citizens except white males has been long term and pervasive in western and American history. While this imperialism has finally lost the legal voting battle it still retains strong influence in voter suppression where it remains politically powerful through the devotions of racial and gender prejudice.

Despite such anti-democratic biases, disenfranchised voters eventually won the legal right to vote as an affirmation of democratic intent.

Steps Further

If America was assertively committed to the citizenry's right to vote it would go much further than it has in the past to secure this right and encourage citizen engagement. There would be stringent laws that protected the people's right to vote irrespective of ethnicity, gender, or class.

Beyond the privilege of mail-in ballots there would be National Voter Responsibility Days when workers have paid holidays to pursue their obligation to vote, to voluntarily assist others to do the same, and where government provides both encouragement and transportation for those who needed such in order to vote. There would be organized voter celebration and assistance rallies. The nation would be organized for maximum voter education and turn-out.

During these days profit-making entertainment venues would be voluntarily closed for business as further encouragement to use the holiday as intended. Through all manner of education and motivation it would be a day of various events upholding the right and responsibility of the citizenry to determine their political future. Holiday would assume its prior meaning of holy day – holy because it affirms mutual worth and sustains the common good which is the heart of democracy.

Historical Context and Adaptation

The American model of government is a unique blend of influences innate to both the founding fathers European history and the encountered culture of Native Americans.

Native Americans

Native American Indians had been long time residents of what we now know as America before the arrival of Europeans. Europeans were invaders. And they were required to either vanquish these original inhabitants or figure out a manner of peaceful co-existence. In attempting the latter, especially in the northern colonies, they confronted an Indian environment of democratic living.

There were five northern and western tribes that were bound together by the Iroquois confederacy's constitution: *The Great Law of Peace.* This was primarily an oral tradition intimately known and subscribed to by all these tribes. Its essentials were grounded in what was considered natural laws that touted freedom of speech, egalitarianism, racial and gender equality, appreciation for diversity, mutual respect, courteous and fair treatment, people empowerment, and personal responsibility. Its governing structures provided primal leadership, a council of sages, divisions of responsibility, and customs that precluded the need for punishments and incarceration. A peaceful mutual existence that benefited the common good was its goal. As an example of this sentiment, there is a Haudenosaunee treaty of 1520 that begins with these words:

We, the people, to form a union, to establish peace, equity, and order...

This phrase should sound familiar since the opening words of America's Constitution have a similar ring. Many colonial leaders had interactions with the people of these tribes and were acquainted with this oral document and consistent tribal behavior. Scholars and philosophers who wrote about democratizing European nations such as Locke and Rousseau were influenced by this constitution. Benjamin Franklin and Thomas Jefferson and others of the Constitutional Convention were acquainted with the Indian confederacy's leadership, constitution, and resultant style of living. Both its philosophy and structure stands behind our nation's grounding document in support of the intents of democracy.

In 1988 a resolution was passed by the United States House and Senate (H.Con.Res.331) regarding American Indian treaties that read in its introduction:

...to acknowledge the contribution of the Iroquois Confederacy of nations to the development of the United States Constitution...

It is only a white European style of educational propaganda that has kept American citizens ignorant of this background to its own constitution and democracy. But it is difficult to acknowledge that the people a nation demonized as godless savages who needed to be exterminated were actually models of the democracy their Founding Fathers sought to establish. Such acknowledgment requires the humility of an honest and accurate civic education. But this style of education has been a primary lack throughout America's history.

Great Britain

The other model used by our founding fathers was the government of Great Britain. The philosophy and structures behind this model was what the founders also understood with intimacy. It had three primary branches. There was the king who served in some executive fashion and was an inherited position. There was the House of Commons which membership was an elected position. There was the House of Lords which membership was an appointed position. There were versions of checks and balances between these various branches.

The founding fathers adapted this structure into its three branches of the Presidency, the House of Representatives and The Senate, and the Judiciary. The primary difference was the president and representatives were elected by the people. The Senators were originally appointed by their state legislatures but through the constitutional amendment XVII of 1913 were also elected by a state's popular vote. Specific powers and checks and balances were assigned to each branch. Currently, the population of each state determines how many Representatives in the House are permitted for that state, while the Senate provides states with equal representation irrespective of population size.

This senate adaptation was due to less populated states fearing that they would always be out-voted by the states with larger populations. It also satisfied the deep seated need for legislative independence exemplified by thirteen colonies with separate social, religious, ethnic, and political backgrounds. So, from the beginning, the smaller states did not favor a direct representational democracy. In order to lure them into the union, the founding fathers created the Senate, with special powers, to equalize representation for each state with two votes. This provincial representation in the Senate balanced the democratic representation in the House. So the House represented the population that made up the nation while the Senate represented the independent states that made up the nation. It is a structural means by which the citizenry as a whole population and the geographic entities of individual states supposedly govern in a balanced manner.

It must also be noted that the Senate, which was provincially equal in representation of the states, holds extraordinary power—such as confirming cabinet members, Supreme Court and federal judges, ambassadors, treaties with other nations, and yea or nay on impeachment of the president. In brief, it is the least representative of the country's population while being the most powerful in consulting and approving power. In terms of our national congress, we have a hybrid government with the House representing a democracy of citizenry equality rule while the Senate represents a democracy of state equality rule.

The Electoral College

The Electoral College was created by the founding fathers for a variety of reasons—fear of a centralized government, lack of adequate communication systems, issues of gentleman civility about campaigning, fear of political parties, and concern about the general ignorance of the population. It remains a complicated system with each state assigned a certain number of delegates which will make the final selection of a president despite the popular vote. Supposedly, these pre-selected delegates will be fully informed of the political profile of all the candidates and be able to correct any unwise choice made by the general citizenry. There are 538 electoral votes with 270 votes needed to win an election. However, instead of correction for the sake of wise leadership for the nation it has served as correction for political party empowerment.

This awkward construction has resulted in the popular vote being overruled by the Electoral College on five different occasions in American history. The most recent two of these was the election of George W. Bush over Al Gore (2000) and the election of Donald Trump over Hillary Clinton (2016). The creation of the Electoral College was a case of the founding fathers trying to address the issues and fears they confronted about both government and fair representation. Their concerns have no particular relevance to modern circumstance. The primal issue of our current moment in history is how voter suppression and gerrymandering deny and corrupt the citizenry vote. It is about the states controlling elections over the popular voice of the total citizenry. As with the composition of the Senate, it is about state empowerment over populace empowerment.

Moreover, the communication revolution of the Twenty First century has revealed a major weakness in the entire election process which the Electoral College cannot correct and may even make worse. This revolution has enabled pro-imperial and anti-democratic forces within the nation to reach directly into the minds of those who feel disenfranchised for any reason and to capture their allegiance through deception. It has created a fake media upon which segments of the citizenry totally rely for their information and perspectives. Essentially, the communication revolution propagates ignorance and falsehood as well as valid information. And, thus far, there have been no proposed remedies for its regulation that would favor a factually informed citizenry. Confronted with this issue, the state and federal governments remain mute.

When the founding fathers built the Electoral College into the election process they thought they were protecting its integrity. They could not have perceived that it might result in the opposite outcome, namely, the election of unqualified presidents without majority endorsement—actual voter disenfranchisement through party politicization.

Cobbled Compromise

America, as a government, was cobbled together through the art of compromise with the goal being the largest measure of democratic rule possible. This was done without perfection but with what the founders perceived to be maximum citizenry protection. They could not have envisioned this present moment in history.

Slave Anomaly

An anomaly is something which is abnormal, deviant, and strange. Here is a historical anomaly. Even though non-citizens, three out of every five slaves were counted as ballot votes—which the slave owners controlled. Slaves were deliberately kept ignorant for the purpose of owner exploitation. Essentially, this counting fraud was a means by which white economic imperialists land owners voting capacity was enlarged while their tax base was decreased since they paid no taxes for two out of five slaves. This was a further enticement for southern states to be a part of the union.

31

Our Founders and Slavery

We may tend to perceive our founder's slave ownership as a hypocrisy that conflicted with their proclaimed notion of human equality. But the perspective of inherent human worth transcends these shortcomings. It seems obvious that they knew the meaning of the words "*all men are created equal*", despite some of their contradictory attitudes and behavior regarding slavery. Another perception may have been behind this statement for some of the founders – that slaves were not actual persons.

However, many of them spoke out publically declaring slavery an evil and some gave their slaves freedom as an expression of this understanding. Moreover, a number of them were the political leaders who led their states to abolish slavery once independence was achieved. These leaders were able to do so because the promoter of slavery, Great Britain, was no longer dictating and enforcing the laws of the land. But whatever their inner moral turmoil or inconsistencies, the words that open the Declaration of Independence stand in memorial to the intention of the majority of the founders. It remains the grounding principle of American governance.

Nothing exemplified the true meaning of this democratic intention more than the abolition of slavery. President Abraham Lincoln's Emancipation Proclamation of 1863 officially added this purpose to the Civil War's aim of preserving the union. And the Thirteenth Amendment which prohibited slavery, ratified in 1865, made this a concrete legal reality in American culture. From that moment, the notion of male citizenry equality, despite African ethnicity, became a constitutional staple of American democratic perspective.

The Trinity of Democracy

Having a popular vote is often misconstrued as the essence of being a democracy. However, merely having a popular vote does not fulfill democratic criteria. To have an actualized democracy, this vote and its outcome must be explicitly dedicated to the citizenry's worth equality and their common good. This threefold intent is intrinsic, inseparable, and mutually sustaining. The right to vote does not stand alone. It stands for the right to affirm citizenry worth and its common good. Voting is the political sacrament by which the citizenry expresses its support of the relational ground of democracy. It is the means by which the ideal becomes the real.

The Guiding Documents

All valid attempts by any government agency to interpret the meaning of American democracy's guiding documents must be predicated on citizenry equality, the citizenry's common good, and citizenry rule —which are all expressions of community—the entire populous. The intentions of these grounding documents, including the Bill of Rights, are summarized in their opening paragraphs. All other criteria for gauging interpretation are secondary and must be supportive to be valid. As examples, consider:

The blessings of liberty: Which are often interpreted as individual freedoms, are really about benefits for the total community that are made possible by established legal and social boundaries.

The right to bear arms: Which is normally viewed as an individual right, was instituted explicitly for the community's protection by its own members, before the establishment of larger protective local and national bodies.

Free Speech: Which is usually understood to allow any private view to be expressed, was intended to preserve the right of dialogue within the community for the sake of democratic process in the community's decision-making and rule.

None of these can be legitimately divorced from why the constitution was created—to sustain the union, to maintain justice, to ensure domestic tranquility, to provide for common defense, and to promote the general welfare. These are all community goals. Thus, all legitimate interpretations of documents or laws will focus on community well-being—the common good.

Community First

All individual rights become illegitimate the moment they transgress any of these constitutional community purposes. The rights of the community take precedent over individual rights. Any decree or judgment by any governing or judicial body that violates this principle is in violation of democratic intent and the constitution upon which it is grounded. All valid interpretations will begin and end with the community and not the individual. However, given our individual views of reality, we are prone to take information and twist it to fit our perspective. Objectivity is in the eye of the beholder and not in the object being viewed. Individualism distorts reality into community violation.

A Living Document

In The Declaration of Independence the citizenry was given the responsibility to add to or change the constitution in order to safeguard the community and democratic intent as the guiding principles of national living. In brief, while imperative in terms of guidance, the constitution was intended to be a living document that could be changed to accommodate the growth of community understanding and demanding circumstance. This is the purpose of constitutional amendments.

Rights Protection

Inherent in these statements is this notion: There need be no concern about the upholding of legitimate democratic individual rights when legitimate democratic community rights are being upheld. The first is inherent in the second. Protecting community rights protects individual rights. The reverse is not necessarily true.

The American Dream

The American Dream is a vision of individual citizens gaining an economic status that reflects a comfortable lifestyle. This dream and democracy are only synonymous in one respect: An actualized democracy must exist before it can be a reality for all the citizenry. The citizenry must be treated with equal worth, the common good must the goal, and the citizenry must vote in allegiance to these ideals. The capacity of all the people to achieve such a lifestyle is dependent on the nation's devotion to these three intents of democracy as reflected in governance.

What makes the American Dream both legitimate and possible is the fulfillment of the intents of democracy—the creation of a community of support in dream pursuit. The necessity of these intents in dream fulfillment means that it is not simply an individual or economic transaction. It is a community and democratic achievement. As such it is pervasive of all classes. If it is not pervasive of all classes it is not a democratic fulfillment. The fulfillment of the dream does not preclude the necessity of individual initiative or gain. However, individual initiative and gain must support the common good if it is a democratic action. Thus, democratic intent and dream fulfillment cannot be separated.

Since the nation's inception, only the wealthy have consistently accomplished a comfortable economic lifestyle. And only since the end of World War II have members of the middle class been consistently rewarded—a reward which largely evaporated with the 2008 economic meltdown. The lower class has always struggled and only through unyielding persistence, luck, and quirks of fate has a sparsity of its membership grasped the economic comfortability implied in this vision. For the poor the American Dream has mostly been a nightmare.

Up to this point in time, it appears that the only guarantee of achieving a comfortable economic lifestyle in America is to be birthed into its lap. This portrait of inequitable possibility and achievement is one painted by an unrealized democracy. Without an actualized democracy, fulfilling the American Dream has more to do with fateful context and less to do with individual initiative.

Citizens are born into gross circumstances of inequity. These inequities have to do with a multitude of factors such as ethnicity, gender, genes, religion, class, time, economics, geography, parentage, health, and culture. These factors favor some and disfavor others. There is only one social context that deliberately attempts to equalize privilege and opportunity within this inherited system of inequities—that of democratic living and governance.

It is only when the entire public is treated with worth equality and the common good is paramount in all the nation's transactions that the American Dream will become available in some measure to the entire citizenry. Worth equality does not mean economic equality but it does mean relational equality, treatment equality, opportunity equality, and reward equality. And such is always the true goal of an actualized democracy.

The so-called American Dream can only become a reality for all the citizens when the dream of equality is fulfilled.

Conclusion

There were fifty six men who initiated the American Revolutionary War by signing the Declaration of Independence. They were mostly merchants, jurists, farmers, and plantation owners—the educated leaders of their communities. They vehemently debated the pros and cons of this signing for they were aware of the extraordinary risk they were taking in doing so. And the risk they feared turned into the reality of profound sacrifice.

Some of these men were captured by the British and tortured and killed. A sizable group fought and died from wounds and hardships. Others lost sons to death or capture. A number had family members jailed. Many had their homes ransacked and burned and a few died from the consequent destitution.

They paid a heavy price that we might engage the democracy they could only envision. We owe our allegiance to this democracy—an allegiance that demands we rise above our self-centered goals and petty alliances and stand tall in devotion as they stood tall in sacrifice—an allegiance that compels us to fulfill the dream that inspired their self-offering. We owe this to both ourselves and the generations to come.

Critical to this owing is an adamant refusal to allow the democracy they created to be captured by the very kind of despotism their revolution sought to overthrow. Such would be the ultimate desecration of their sacrifice. Indeed, in their Declaration of Independence they affirmed that it was the right of the people to alter or to abolish any government that did not match their expectations of democratic intention. It is the rights of the citizenry that is sacred and not the government established to secure these rights. In brief, we citizens must be in a constant state of political correction and must, if necessary, revolt again and again until the democratic goal is achieved. This is our ultimate obligation as citizens.

OF, BY, AND FOR

The American model is unique in world history. It seeks to embody the essential principles of the democratic model. Yet, it is its intents that energize and sustain the model. And it is the citizenry who will determine the extent and quality of this energization because it is of, by, and for the people.

4

AMERICAN PATRIOTISM

The intentions of democracy are to affirm the citizenry's equality of worth, achieve their common good, and facilitate their governing rule. Patriotism is loyalty to these intentions and their implied values in the nation's life both at home and abroad. This means that support of national leaders, investment in political parties, administration goals, initiated wars, the intelligence industry, capitalism, the military, or racial and national superiority may not have anything to do with patriotism. It is only patriotism if it fits the criteria of the relational outcomes of democratic intent – the people's equality of worth, the people's common good, and the people's rule by vote.

Patriotism: Tarnishing the Term

Simply calling an endeavor patriotic does not make it patriotic. Simply calling people patriots does not make them patriots. Such willy-nilly naming is not only false it can be misleading and detrimental to any real sense of patriotic meaning. It sentimentalizes and politicizes patriotism and dissipates the power of its definition. It dishonors its true nature.

Being unpatriotic is to deliberately fuse the notion of being patriotic with support of goals that are anti-democratic. An example is using individuals or nations as economic pawns. If citizens are making substandard wages and can ill afford appropriate health care or a retirement account they are being used as economic pawns for business benefit. This is unpatriotic. If another nation's independence is being suppressed by our nation for economic reasons they are being used as a pawn for our nation's benefit. This is unpatriotic.

If the citizenry is to refuse being hoodwinked by devious definitions of patriotism it must remain keenly aware of the difference between democratic goals and despotic goals. This requires wearing the mantle of democratic intent in an assertive fashion and asking the right questions before making assessments of patriotism. Here are the assessing questions, which harken to the three intents of democracy:

- Does it affirm citizenry worth?

- Does it support the citizenry's common good?

- Does it demand citizenry rule?

If these questions are not answered positively, it is not patriotic. It may even be a despotic deception in patriotism's name. This assessment applies whether it is of internal relationships within America or of America's international relationships.

Patriotism: The Pledge, and the Flag

The American flag is a symbol of American democracy and the pledge of allegiance is commitment to this democracy. They intend to honor the democratic rebellion that birthed the nation and the continued sacrifice which has kept it free from despotism. These intents are their only ground of symbolic pride. All other motivations degrade these intents.

The Pledge

In 1892, a Baptist and Christian Socialist minister, Francis Bellamy was concerned about the low level of devotion to American ideals. So he wrote a pledge he hoped would be used in the public school system to instill such in the minds of students. Here is the original version:

I pledge allegiance to my Flag and the Republic for which it stands, one nation, indivisible, with liberty and justice for all.

In 1923, because of concerns that immigrants might be confused as to the focus of their pledging, the phrase *my flag* was changed to *the flag of the United States of America*. And in 1954, as a way of identifying the pledge as American rather than that of the perceived atheism of communism, the phrase *under God* was added. The end result of these changes was:

> *I pledge allegiance to the flag of the United State of America, and to the Republic for which it stands, one nation under God, indivisible, with liberty and justice for all.*

The purpose of the pledge, whatever its additions, is intended to express patriotic commitment to the democratic nature of the American nation.

The National Anthem

The same is true of the national anthem. It was composed in the midst of a primary battle of the War of 1812 with Great Britain. That war was a complicated bundle of causes that had to do with British trade restrictions, impressment of American seamen into the service of the British fleet, and the attempt by Britain to retard America's northwest territorial expansion. After the capture and burning of Washington, DC, the British were attempting to capture the port of Baltimore. But they needed to move past Fort McHenry which helped guard the port. A several day siege of the fort was undertaken by a British naval and land bombardment that failed to subdue the fort.

On the morning of September 14, 1814, its old tattered flag was lowered and a new flag of 15 stars and 15 stripes was raised to signal that the fort was intact despite the severe bombardment. This inspired Francis Scott Keys, an observer of the battle, to write a four stanza poem which became known as the Star Spangled Banner. It was set to the music of a British drinking song and became popular as praise for the endurance and commitment of American patriotism. In competition with other songs such as *Hail Columbia, My Country Tis of Thee*, and *America The Beautiful*, it was adopted as America's national anthem on March 1931 by congressional resolution. Generally, only the first verse of this poem is sung. But this verse captured the spirit of this event. And its singing is intended to be in praise of that American independent democratic allegiance that defies despotism. Lesser motivations in its singing degrade this intent.

And this raises the question as to what it is about sporting events that warrants the stating of the pledge of allegiance to the flag and the singing of the country's national anthem? Does such over-usage at competitive events trivialize its meaning and open it to political exploitation?

It seems that the original reason for introducing sports into America's educational system was to promote the ideals of team work and fair play. But such a motivation has long since been corrupted by economic motivations. Sports have become a primary means of profit making for higher education institutions. And on the professional level it has become a multi-billion dollar corporate industry. This has made it possible for a few minorities to enter this up-scale business of profit-making. While this may be socially beneficial is not necessarily the result of democratic relating. And while the business of sports may build pride in provincial identities this is not necessarily a benefit to democracy. Indeed, a great deal of unsportsmanlike conduct occurs during professional games. In brief, the corporate sports business has nothing to do with democracy other than underscoring that the citizenry is free to pursue economic interests. But that is the case for all businesses and most do not begin the workday with employees quoting the pledge of allegiance and singing the national anthem. The marriage of sports and patriotism suggests the marriage of culture and democracy.

Patriotism vs. Love of Culture

What must be guarded against is confusing patriotism and love of American culture. The face of a democratic culture will mirror democratic intent. However, aspects of the cultural face and democratic intent may be antagonistic. This is true of present American culture. Its face is only a minor mirror of democratic intent. Largely, it is a reflection of minimally constrained capitalistic prowess; a citizenry lifestyle of utilitarianism; an image of irresponsible individual freedoms; and a large expression of citizenry racial and regional prejudices. It is a design of gross self-interest and a social scale of unequal worth. If current America is a picture of patriotism it is a distortion made to fit anti-democratic posturing.

It is possible that the average American, having been born and raised in this skewed atmosphere, labeled as democracy, will simply accept such as the being of democracy. Moreover, this illusion may perpetuate itself from generation to generation as democratic reality.

Patriotism is profound commitment to the intents of democracy. A euphemism for profound commitment is heart belief. It is not simply supporting the various structures put in place to process this heart belief such as elections, the branches of government, political parties, and the military. As John Ralston Saul, award winning Canadian novelist, essayist, and political philosopher, suggests:

But if the heart of belief is only in structures, then the whole body will gradually lose its sense of direction and then its ability to function.

False patriotism is invested in democratic structures that can be manipulated for private ends. True patriotism is invested in the democratic intents which the structures were intended to facilitate.

It is both a misunderstanding and a distortion to confuse the culture with democracy fulfilled. Before equating American culture and democracy, the trilogy of democratic intent must be used to measure the validity of culture's correspondence: To what extent does it affirm the citizenry's equality of worth, contribute to the common good, and encourage the citizenry's vote. For example, what is the democratic reflection when congress votes tax benefits for the wealthy and tax burdens for the poor? What is the democratic reflection when immigrants are denied entry simply because of their skin color and educational or economic status? What is the democratic reflection when political parties deliberately depress voting rights and gerrymander election results in order to achieve political power?

Any facet of democracy can be wrapped in false patriotic labels by economic imperialists or disguised despots. Labeling is not synonymous with being. A culture with democracy's label can actually be anti-democratic. An example is the label Democratic People's Republic of Korea (North), which is a brutal authoritarian political regime. Real patriotism in a democracy is always an embodiment of its intents. Present American culture and the intents of democracy may have many questionable alignments that should not be confused as synonymous.

Patriotism and Gerrymandering

It is possible for anti-democratic practice to become accepted as both legal and legitimate politics. Here is an example. The American constitution mandates that a population census shall be taken every ten years. Based on this census, district boundaries within each state are required to be redrawn in order to create a fair political representation of voters.

However, this process has become a clever ploy to undermine democratic outcome rather than facilitate it. Gerrymandering, which draws these boundaries so that a particular political party or candidate is given a distinctive advantage in the electoral process, illustrates this point. It is to use the structures of democracy to create an undemocratic outcome. While a legal and acceptable practice it has become politically and democratically corrupt. Further, it is difficult to prove abuse of the practice although some federal courts are beginning to do so.

The term gerrymander was first used in 1812 to describe a Massachusetts governor's attempt to politically influence the state's senate election by redrawing district lines in a manner that would favor this outcome. The word, itself, was a combination of the governor's last name, Gerry, and the distorted image produced by redrawing district lines - mander. It gradually came into vogue as a description of this practice as a way of undemocratically swaying the outcome of elections.

Here are four ways districts can be gerrymandered to create a political party's advantage during an election:

Packing: To redraw district lines so that there is a high concentration of one party's voters.

Cracking: To redraw district lines so that there is less concentration of one party's voters.

Kidnapping: To redraw district lines so a political incumbent's home address is in a different district and creates the appearance of that person being an outsider.

Hijacking: To redraw district lines so two districts are pitted against one another and one of the candidates is eliminated.

All of these are corruptions of democratic intent.

Undemocratic Outcomes

Gerrymandering is generally an accepted practice by both the Democratic and Republican political parties. However, it not only skews the outcome of the citizenry's votes it cancels their vote and encourages the assessment that one's vote does not count. It is an example of how undemocratic maneuvering becomes acceptable political behavior. Such denies all democratic intent.

It can be rigged so as to put into office a majority of one party even though the opposing party wins the popular vote. Moreover, its outcome can be designed in a manner that makes it almost impossible to change, particularly if the designer's interest is political empowerment over democratic outcome. Unfortunately, this perspective is growing among both politicians and political parties. It is a primary way of rigging elections with the blessings of legality. Politicians use this practice to manipulate elections while, hypocritically, claiming that their opponent has used the ballot box for this purpose.

Gerrymandering is a practice used by those who wish to corrupt voter outcome because they, themselves, are corrupt. In the 2018 midterm election outcomes this became glaringly obvious in many state elections. It is one of the most unpatriotic maneuverings in American politics.

The Solution

There seems to be only one way to overcome the threat of gerrymandering and restore the goal of safe-guarding fair elections. This means has already been instituted by a number of states with positive outcome. The solution is to place re-districting in the hands of a non-partisan judicial commission. To aid such a commission, algorithm technology has been invented that enables a fair outcome based on the current census.

But even more protective of citizenry rights and fairness in the political process would be for the federal government to require such an approach as mandatory in every state. It is obvious that many states have become too politically corrupt for fairness to happen any other way. Political parties and politicians who oppose such regulating reveal their own corrupt anti-democratic character.

Other Corruptions

Gerrymandering is only one device that corrupt politicians are using to skew elections in favor of their self-interest empowerment. Voter suppression laws are another means. And yet another is to maneuver the election of judges who will rule in favor of devious gerrymandering and voter suppression schemes. If there are to be fair elections in the nation it appears that the federal government must intervene and enact laws that protect voter rights. Otherwise, corrupt politicians will use their party machinery to process personal prejudices and agendas at the expense of democratic intent. Such deviousness will continue until voters elect politicians to both state and national congresses who, themselves, are uncorrupted.

Patriotism and Dissent

Patriotic loyalty is invested in doing whatever is necessary to keep America on track with its democratic intents. It is easy to lose sight of these intents in the midst of political skullduggery and social turmoil. And it is even easier to become intimidated by those who would use the structures of democracy to become demagogues.

During the early 1950s Senator Joseph McCarthy of Wisconsin used his position and power as chair of the Senate's Government Committee on Operations to foster an anti-democratic witch hunt for Americans who did not fit his personal profile of a loyal American. His victims were labeled as communists. Most of America, including the congressional and executive branches of government, was intimidated by and succumbed to his demagogic bullying. As a result, the lives of many devoted Americans were ruined.

The premier radio and television broadcaster of that era was Edward R. Murrow who had set the standard of courage, honesty, and integrity for broadcast journalism following World War II. Unintimidated by McCarthy he, along with a small number of others, exposed McCarthy for the anti-democratic and corrupt bully he was and helped bring his campaign into disrepute. Murrow was not afraid to dissent from the nation's timid posture when such posed a threat to its democratic intents. He commented:

We must not confuse dissent with disloyalty.

There is nothing more American and patriotic than to voice dissent in the midst of what one perceives to be democratic violation. In this respect, dissent and patriotism are often synonymous.

Dissent is grounded in citizenry ownership. It springs from an affirmation that the United States belongs to the people irrespective of how unevenly it has placed into practice its devotion to democracy. It is our responsibility to remain committed to giving our energy to it becoming a model of legitimate pride in this practice. One of the true hallmarks of patriotic citizenship is the determination to name what obstructs democracy's actualization and to offer corrective advice. James Baldwin was one of America's premier black novelists, playwrights, and political activists of the 20th century. He speaks to this commitment with clarity:

I love America more than any other country in the world, and, exactly for this reason, I insist on the right to criticize her perpetually.

It is the obligation of the citizenry to both offer criticism and correction and seek to live the correction.

Conclusion

Unfortunately, patriotism has come to mean whatever affirms our individual view of politics and supports our private economic well-being. John Brockenbrough, in a letter to John Randolph concerning the Embargo Act of 1808, saw this at work in his own time when he observed:

Patriotism is a mighty precious thing when it costs nothing, but the mass of mankind consider it a foolish thing when it curtails their self-indulgence.

46

Until patriotism becomes loyalty to the three intents of democracy, confusion will prevail in the culture as to what actually bonds us in national unity. It may require us to see what we do not wish to see and to do what we do not wish to do. Perhaps Anonymous was pointing in this direction when making this tongue in cheek observation:

*A real patriot is one who gets a parking ticket
and rejoices that the system works.*

OF, BY, AND FOR

*A real patriot will yield one's personal goals and desires to the goals
and desires of democratic intent because if democracy actually exists
with its life-giving community benefits it will be
of, by, and for the people.*

PART II

INTERNAL NECESSITY AND THREATS

5

RELATIONAL SUBVERSION

The first and greatest human freedom is the privilege of relating through equality of worth. Equality of worth means that every citizen is viewed as of equal worth to every other citizen irrespective of ethnicity, religion, gender, class, social position, or any other consideration. This is the heart and ground of democracy. It is both the architect of a democracy's ends and means and the soul of a democracy's attitudes and actions. When it thrives democratic possibility thrives. When it languishes democratic possibility languishes. It is democracy's *sine qua non*—that without which it does not and cannot exist.

If democracy were a matter of measure then the extent to which the citizenry relates in equality of worth is the extent to which democracy exists. The opposite is equally true. The extent to which any person or thing is given worth above that of the community of individual citizens is the extent to which some form of despotism rules, irrespective of its label. This being the case, American democracy is woefully incomplete. This may be why Al Smith, four time mayor of New York City during the early 20th century, once suggested:

> *All the ills of democracy can be*
> *cured by more democracy.*

Democracy is not simply a government label. It is the inherent meaning of that label actualized. To become actualized is to be fulfilled or to be filled full. It is to make real. It is to become fact.

Secondary Freedoms

This singular freedom to relate through equality relegates all oth-

51

er freedoms to a secondary and subservient status. It is this freedom, alone, that determines the necessity, the quality, and the usefulness of other freedoms. Thus, when there is a declaration that democracy is about freedom, unless the freedom proclaimed affirms and supports this grounding freedom of worth equality its declaration is a perversion of democracy.

For example, the notion that democracy is simply about the freedom to pursue individual economic interests, under the guise of achieving The American Dream, is a perversion. The freedom to pursue economic well-being is explicitly tied to honoring the common good as that which sustains the individual good. In a democracy the two are inseparable. Any freedom that violates this grounding principle of equality of worth is a violation of democratic intent.

The same is true of capitalism. Capitalism invites an unrestrained freedom to pursue economic interests. However, the intents of democracy impose clear restraining boundaries on capitalism that protect citizenry worth and the common good. When these boundaries are violated, democracy is violated. As a tool, capitalism can be either an asset or a liability to democracy. This is determined by whether or not the users of capitalism honor democracy's restraining boundaries by honoring democracy's intents. Capitalism has never been an enemy of democracy. The enemies of democracy are those capitalists who violate democratic intent.

Ample freedom exists for all citizens, endeavors, and institutions when this first freedom is held as inviolable because it is the root of all righteous freedom. When any freedom is divorced from this grounding freedom it becomes both false and misleading in a manner that threatens democracy. All true democratic freedoms are supportive of citizenry equality, common good, and citizenry rule. All other freedoms are adversaries of democracy.

This means that the notion of freedom and the notion of democracy do not automatically equate. Freedom only equates to democracy when it embraces this sine qua non. Freedom is a responsibility as well as a liberty. It is this responsibility toward mutual worth which maintains its continuous possibility.

The Threat

American democracy is in danger of committing suicide. John Adams, second president of the nation, predicted this happening. From the perspective of his moment in history, he concluded:

Remember, democracy never lasts long. It soon wastes, exhausts, and murders itself. There never was a democracy yet that did not commit suicide.

Adams had far less history of attempts by nations to establish democracy to look at than we do today. We have had all the intervening years since the beginning of American democracy. Despite this historical deficit, he saw the issues that democracy faced with a pessimistic outcome. His observation prompts the question: What causes a democracy to self-destruct? The answer for those of us in this current moment of history is:

The lifestyle of the citizenry.

Abraham Lincoln, president during the Civil War and issuer of the Emancipation Proclamation, summarized this citizen responsibility when he suggested that democracy is of, by, and for the people. It is the people who create it, sustain it, and determine its destiny. Aside from foreign conquest and economic failure, whether it lives and flourishes or languishes and dies is in the hands of the citizenry. They can nourish it and grow it or starve it and kill it. They, alone, are responsible.

It seems doubtful that a citizenry would deliberately sabotage a form of government as promising of blessing as a democracy. This is especially true in light of the available knowledge about the deficits and destructions of all forms of despotism. This suggests that a democracy's descent into suicide is enticed by subtleties—by citizenry investment in attractions toward political death which they do not recognize. Such attractions are disguised as beliefs and freedoms which seduce citizenry commitment. Otherwise, why would a citizenry invest in democratic suicide except unwittingly?

The Relational Heart of Democracy

Given the intentions of democracy as a community event it is, above all else, relational. What makes it political are the structures of government designed to carry out its relational goals – that of citizenry worth, citizenry good, and citizenry rule. Therefore, all its structures must accommodate to these relational intentions before they are democratic. This means that all political, policy, justice, military, and economic expressions are means to relational ends and not ends unto themselves. Thus, any attitude of despotic superiority reduces the ability to practice democracy.

This is why democracy is the most difficult of all governments to institute and sustain. For example, the history of America reveals it to be one of defiant citizenry resistance to the relational heart of democratic intent. Every possible attempt has been made to subvert democracy into varied forms of despotism while cleverly labeling such subversions as the outcome of democratic freedom. To subvert is to sabotage, convert, or undermine a purpose.

The following examples illustrate.

The Civil War: Ensued from the attempt to subvert national sovereignty into state sovereignty and democratic intent into the despotic white male racial capitalistic profit-making of slavery. Attempts to enforce constitutional law and the Civil Rights Movement continue this battle against democratic sabotage.

Women's Rights: Although the fight for equal rights between women and men started long ago it officially began in America with the Women's Suffrage Movement of the eighteen hundreds. This movement endeavored to end the subversion of despotic white male gender dominion by granting women the right to vote. This battle was continued in the Women's Liberation Movement of the mid-twentieth century and lives on today through modern-day feminism and the fight for equal recognition and equal pay in the workplace.

The Alternative Sexual Lifestyle Movement (LGBTQIA+): Ensues from the attempt to subvert democratic intent into despotic sexual lifestyle suppression. This subversion is an attempt to defame as perverted all who would engage in sexual behavior that is not typically and visibly birthed male-female oriented. Although progress has been made the battle for complete liberation continues.

Voting Barriers: Ensue from the attempt to subvert democratic intent into despotic political party rule and white racism. The electoral and legal process in America is fraught with the attempt to keep non-white ethnic groups from participating in democracy. Despite protective laws, these attempts remain an openly defiant subversion.

Freedom from Obligation: The legislations enacted by politicians designed to free their corporate sponsors from taxation and other common good obligations to the nation's citizenry ensues from the attempt to subvert democratic intent into a despotic predatory capitalism. Elected and appointed officials and large segments of the electorate continue to bow in servitude to this subversion.

Ethnic Servitude: The unethical and political devious game-play employed to keep the non-white citizenry in economic servitude to the white citizenry ensues from the attempt to subvert democratic intent into a despotic white male racial superiority. While the forces of history and immigration are diminishing the social impact of this democratic violation, it remains a dominant influence in party politics and citizenry relationships.

How Did We Get Here?

Given the obvious intents of democracy, why has America's history of implementation been so subverted from its original purpose? Why have many past attempts in history failed?

The simple answer is that, aside from economic crisis or external conquest, the citizenry has given permission to democracy's internal and avowed enemies to sabotage its intentions and distort them into a disguise for the rule of despotism.

Conclusion

The democracy of America is in the process of fulfilling John Adams prediction of suicide. And it is doing so through commitment to two subtle underlying causes that remain disguised as the American way of life but, in combination, guarantee a suicidal grave for democracy.

OF, BY, AND FOR

If democracy is in the process of committing suicide then it is of and by the people for whose benefit it was created. Whatever the reasons for the suicidal journey, it roots in the attitudes and behavior of the citizenry.

6

EXTERNALIZED WORTH

The first avowed enemy of democracy is the externalization of human worth. In most all cultures, humans are viewed as being born without innate worth. Worth is viewed as a commodity that must be imported from outside of one's self. It must be earned to fill this internal personal void. This means people are unequal in their social worth. Everybody is at a different place on the culture's hierarchy of worth. Such a worth scale violates democracy's spirit of citizenry equality in absolute fashion. This violation prohibits the possibility of an actualized democracy and invites its suicide.

The Hunger

The desire to be viewed as worthy is an all-encompassing and driving force of history. It is the natural hunger to be connected to other humans in an accepting and affirming manner. Gloria Steinem, 20th century American feminist, political activist, journalist, and founder of MS magazine, puts it this way:

Self-esteem isn't everything; it's just that there's nothing without it.

In human relating, the compulsion for worth affirmation becomes an addiction which drives attitudes and actions. All human behavior kneels in service to this need. It is this hunger for worth affirmed connection that motivates the possibility of democracy as relational equality. But it also motivates the desire for despotism because every form of suppression and slavery glorifies the worth of the owner above the owned. It is obvious that worth affirmation can be both positive and negative with resultant reflecting governance. The positive and negative political expressions are democracy and despotism. Thus, the desire for worth affirmation unleashes all that is both noble and ignoble in human possibility.

The Jonestown Example

In 1955 James Warren Jones founded a movement that eventually was known as the Peoples Temple. Supposedly, it was about creating a community where everyone's worth was equal and social justice was, therefore, a non-issue. Suggesting that American culture was too oppressive to attain this goal, he invited a thousand women, men, and children to move to a jungle setting in Guyana, South America to establish this utopia which he called Jonestown.

But things turned ugly when people began to realize that Jones' personal behavior betrayed him as non-egalitarian and even despotic. Opposition rose and some tried to escape with disastrous results. Seeking an end to contention, Jones persuaded about nine hundred of the group, including children, to drink cool-aid laced with poison so they could enter a paradise beyond death that affirmed their absolute worth. While such idealistic suicidal behavior might seem extreme, it illustrates how endemic and integral the desire to be viewed as worthy is in history and the extreme ends to which we humans will go for its affirmation.

Being viewed as worthy is so critical to our human sense of well-being that we will believe anything and do anything for its affirmation—no matter how absurd or destructive such might be—as evidenced by the Jonestown massacre. There seem to be no primal motivations that are not ultimately rooted in this passion. It is the baseline for all views of reality whatever their source or goal.

We affirm the worth of others by expressing respect for their being. This does not require that I like them or agree with them. What it requires is that I afford them the same rights and privileges which I demand for myself to engage fullness of living. This is not the same as love which is relating on a different dimension – one that transforms into a bond of mutuality. What democracy demands is the minimal embrace of mutual respect – the affirmation of a birthed worth that levels the playing field of all endeavors. It is the extent of this embrace by the citizenry which will determine the extent of democracy.

The Con

A con is the attempt to persuade by deception or trickery. It is a flim- flam or a hoodwinking which is to derive profit from the transaction at the expense of someone else. The externalizing of human worth into a commodity of purchase is the biggest con in human history. The reason is that it intends to divest humans of their innate worth, shape it into a product, and sell it back for allegiance or profit. This con shapes the life and destiny of all major cultures. It is the ultimate peer pressure.

The root of the con is obscure. It simply seems to parallel human history. It may root in the competitive nature of the animal world of which humans are the most creative. We know that individuals in our species have always sought as high an elevation as possible in community stature and it may have grown out of this desire. It is also possible that it roots in a culture's desire to claim and maintain citizenry allegiance and being the dispenser of worth enables this. But how it began is irrelevant to the fact that it is a masterful con that became inbred in the human system of culture building. Whatever its source, it is the primary obstacle to fulfilled human relating and to the advancement of peaceful civilization.

It is this con that is the essential instrument of democratic suicide. The reason is that the pursuit of the common good and the devotion to citizenry rule are firmly rooted in the equality of human worth. It is this sense of common worth that motivates the electorate to build and maintain institutions that sustain democracy as common good government. However, the con justifies the most ignoble of human behavior by replacing collaboration with competition and reducing mutual good to individual good.

How the Con Works

Here is how the con works. At birth humans are divested of their inherent worth which is externalized into a commodity of purchase. The primary means for acquiring worth are through achieving the status of position and wealth. Every strata of society offers importing opportunities. Citizens import increments of social worth through the investment of their time, skills, and devotions. The more they accumulate the greater their perceived social worth. The greater their accumulated worth the higher is the probability of the endowment of cultural rewards such as participating in exclusive experience and exemption from social penalties.

Worth Scale

Most people spend their entire existence kneeling before this con in anticipation of its rewards and in fear of its loss. The reason is that they are born into it as reality. Their life is spent processing concerns about where they stand on the social worth-o-meter scale. This scale is built into the culture's structures, media of recognition, and fashions. It is systemic and sustains the culture's drama of soap opera angst. The dominance of a cultural worth-o-meter scale is the most obvious symptom of the con's triumph. And there are no major cultures without an obvious identifiable scale.

Wealth Worth

Wealth worth has to do with amassed economic value and how it is made visible by accumulated things and the ability to buy exclusive social experience, apply social leverage, and avoid social penalties. Examples of such wealth holders are Wall Street CEOs, corporate executives, business dynasty inheritors, aggressive entrepreneurs, and people who live a grand economic lifestyle.

However, achieving wealth does not automatically make one anti-democratic. It is assigning wealth possession as a gauge of social worth which is the con that undermines the possibility of democracy. An economic class structure is an example of a created scale of social worth.

Position Worth

Position worth has to do with the nature and extent of the social influence which any particular position offers and its ability to provide exclusive experience, social leverage, financial gain, and avoidance of social penalties. Examples of such positions are presidents, governors,

CEOs, politicians, media stars, city council members, and managers.

However, holding a social position is an activity of social responsibility. It is not holding the position but making its occupancy a gauge of personal worth which is the con that undermines the possibility of democracy. That there can be a perceived hierarchy of worth in any size group makes this expression of the con as pervasive as class worth.

The Con's Instability

A cultural worth-o-meter scale is inherently unstable because it is an external valuation, which means it can materialize and vanish quickly. One's social worth status can range from zero to an unlimited number. It can be generated by multiple means including luck, inheritance, legitimate work, special skills, chicanery, crime, and the will to sell one's soul to the company store. It is an unstable quantity that depends on maintenance and constant generation. Processing worth as a commodity is much like investing in the stock market. It holds forth the possibility of both exhilarating success and demoralizing failure. It is an unstable market value.

The Grand Inconsistency

The founding fathers deliberately grounded their act of revolution and its government in the inherent worth of every citizen. This worth was a birthright and was understood to instruct the democratic means of governing.

The grand inconsistency of our national existence is that, at the moment of our birth, we shifted the focus of governance from inherent worth to the imported worth of the great cultural con and scaled it to the so-called American Dream. This shift sustains the sabotage of democracy that will eventuate in its suicide. It does so by changing the focus of citizenry behavior from collaboration to competition and the ground of good from the community to the individual. This guarantees that citizenry energy will be spent fighting against its own best interests. What equality gives, inequality takes away.

Derrick A. Bell's life spanned most of the 20th century into the first part of the 21st century. He was a black law professor and civil rights activist who took socially costly courageous stands and fought for the equal rights of all citizens, irrespective of race or gender. In his book, Ethical Ambition (Living A Life of Meaning and Worth) he names this inconsistency:

We live in a system that espouses merit, equality, and a level playing field, but exalts those with wealth, power, celebrity, however gained.

Bell's observation underscores the conversion of innate worth into a socially imported commodity in American culture. We claim mutual equality yet affirm that some are more equal than others. It is the blending of perspectives that are mortal enemies—of birthed worth and imported worth.

America has an obsessed devotion to worth as an imported commodity which is the opposite of democracy's intent of avowing and practicing the inherent worth of every citizen. We have set up democracy's failure by making it a contention about worth that cancels itself.

Worth and Social Contribution

It is important to underscore that cultural standards of success and failure stand apart from democracy's embrace of the citizenry's inherent worth. While all citizens are of equal worth, all may not contribute equally to social goals or receive equal compensation or recognition for success. In a true democracy, personal worth is not involved in those measurements that are used to determine the rewards of individual economic achievement or social contribution. The extent of a citizen's contribution to the nation's expressed goals or its gross national product has no bearing on their worth status. This acknowledged separation is imperative to democracy's existence. And its ground is that citizenry worth is inherent and not imported.

It is natural and important that social contribution to the nation's success be recognized and celebrated. However, it is a destructive perversion of democratic intent to make it synonymous with personal worth status. Social honoring is important but should be done without attaching personal social worth to this recognition.

Visible Social Expressions

The social triumph of an externalized worth-o-meter scale is the ultimate sign of democracy's failure. This scale is a study in graduated degrees of worth that parallels graduated degrees of despotism. Whoever is above on the scale is always more worthy and assumed more powerful. Whoever is at the bottom is least worthy and least powerful. A great deal of the human drama is created by how humans react to where they find themselves on such a scale.

The most extreme reaction to a sense of profound worth deficit is the attempt to artificially elevate one's own worth by negating the worth of others. This converts democracy into a ruthless quagmire of competition for a greater worth acquisition that betrays and destroys its very ground of worth innateness. It invites callous and devious competition to guide relationships. It designs hierarchies of social power.

A childhood example of this attempted transaction of artificial elevation is the playground bully who believes physical domination can make this transfer of worth happen. An adult example is the working place boss who believes the worth of subordinates can be transferred by claiming their success as one's own.

A Military Example

While serving in the military it became obvious to me that this was one of the primary means by which leadership sabotaged its own effectiveness. It is called Rank Has Its Privilege (RHIP) and is one of the first things taught to all new enlistees, whatever their rank. Essentially, it was the justification for assuming the responsibility and merit for all the good work done by those in lower rank. While it was supposedly an incentive to gain higher rank it was often used to exploit those of lower rank for this purpose.

This perversion of democratic intent was justified by claiming that the military is, of necessity, a despotism and not a democracy. However, the issue is the nature of leadership and not the purpose of the organizational structure. Most all social organizations are despotic in structure but this does not justify despotic relating or forms of leadership.

Two things often happened in this transaction of RHIP. One was that those who did the actual work were divested of its recognition and reward. The other was that it educated members of the service to be exploiters of their troops rather than their leaders. In this transaction, the art of leadership is sabotaged of one of its most effective instruments—that of building trust by recognizing the merit of those who empowered leadership with follow-ship. Thus, many ranking members of units are only followed because of the penalty imposed for not following. Those in higher ranks are often devoid of any real leadership power except that of rank coercion. The necessity of obedience to the command of rank in the military is vital to success, especially in combat. However, the effectiveness of leadership because of trust is far superior to that of rank coercion. It is the difference between relational leadership and structural leadership. That the function of the military in America is to safeguard democracy only makes its modeling more demanding and apparent.

Such subversion of leadership is as common in corporate business life as it is in the military. The only difference is the prideful recognition given to it as a privilege of rank in the military. But, wherever it is used it is a gross violation of democratic intent as well as a self-sabotage of leadership empowerment. Nothing builds leadership trust as profoundly as does an actual relationship grounded in democratic intent.

White Male Superiority

The most obvious and persistent expression of such artificial elevating in American history is that of white male superiority. This is the claim that white males should be honored above all other humans and are the rightful recipients of the culture's common good. This view and claim has driven America's democratic experiment in varied forms since its birth. The attempt to liberate social groups from its dominion has been a major aspect of those forces creating the nation's dramatically contentious history. This is prominent in the current suppression of the African American population, Hispanics and women of all ethnicities.

The Native American population is a sustained historical example.

After almost two hundred and fifty years of seeking to overcome this male despotism it still prevails in the culture. With the election of Donald Trump to the presidency in 2016 it became aggressively emboldened both socially and politically. Two primary underlying issues characterized his beginning term in office. One was constant negative aspersions about having had a black man, Barrack Obama, attain the office of the presidency. The other was the attempted character assassination of a woman, Hilary Clinton, for nearly becoming president instead of himself. In so doing he not only modeled but invited citizenry participation in this racial and gender bigotry that has boldly defied the actualization of American democracy.

Nothing could be a greater affront to white male racial superiority than the actual elevation of a black citizen to the presidency and the near elevation of a woman citizen who won the popular vote while losing the Electoral College vote.

Hate Groups

Because it is believed by many that displaying superior power over others expresses superior worth, forms of anti-democratic extremism often beget social and physical violence. The National Socialist Movement, Ku Klux Klan, White Supremacists, Neo-Nazis, Skinheads, White Nationalists, Neo-Confederates, Alt-right, NRX, The Proud Boys, Identitarians, Traditional Workers Party, and Christian Identity are examples of such socially destructive anti-democratic groups prone to violence in their expressions of superiority.

Religions

Throughout western history religion has also often postured itself as anti-democratic through its own expressions of superiority. The fundamentalist white right wing of Christianity is an example. It is a group which elevates the white male to a position of superiority in every area of living. What it proposes is a theocracy rather than a democracy—the rule of a white male Christian god over the nation and the white male as head of the household and all other positions of social power. This means that its bible has priority over the constitution as the guide to both personal and national living and males have priority over females and children. Since this is a form of traditional despotism these radicals inevitably give support to whatever political candidates come closest to espousing white male despotic values. This brand of Christianity is inherently anti-democratic while justifying its belief as a democratic right. This is also the case of other religious fundamentalisms in the world—fundamentalisms that outsource human worth.

The Primal Paradox

A paradox is what appears to be contradictory but is true. The primal paradox of democracy is that it allows anti-democratic attitudes and behaviors to be freely expressed. This is an obvious contradiction necessitated by its very nature. The hopeful assumption behind this freedom is that the democratically unredeemed will become democratically redeemed through social exposure and dialogue. It is an assumption that believes history is on the side of modeled democratic enlightenment. However, for such to happen would require that democratic enlightenment be both apparent and empowered by an actual model. Nothing is transformed except by that which is transforming.

The Attraction

The citizenry that is most attracted to forms of despotism are those who believe in the importation of an externalized worth. It is the amassing of artificial worth that defines despotism and motivates its cruel manners of institution and sustainment. Those who feel the necessity to artificially confirm their worth are usually those who feel a desperate need of its affirmation. People who know they are innately worthy need no such external confirmations. It is they who are most likely to believe in and invest in the merits of democracy for they understand the blessings of devotion to birthed equality.

A Story Metaphor

The television series Downton Abbey, a fictional British period drama, is a metaphor for life lived under the dominion of the con of externalized worth and the social worth-o-meter scale the con produces.

Downton Abbey is a manor in the English countryside and the action commences during the first half of the twentieth century. The metaphor itself is exemplified in the radical divergence of separate lifestyles of those who live upstairs and downstairs in the manor—the wealthy owners and their servants. Those who labor on the manor's grounds play minor subservient roles in the drama. These same class structures are duplicated in the town community outside the confines of Downton Abbey.

Those living in the manor reflect clear social delineations of worth both between and within those to the manor born and those to the manor's service born. The drama between and within these states of worth are the basis of the social value contentions of the story line. It is the source of the psychological tensions within the various characters that have to do with issues of social conformity and self-liberation.

The world of Downton Abbey is the world created by the externalization of human worth. It is the clarity of this scale of worth, the relationship dramas it creates, the occasional victory of acknowledged innate worth, and the effect on human living that is the appeal of the series.

The difference between Downton Abbey as a metaphor and the real world of the big con is that in Downton Abbey the wealthy oligarchy are much more likely to acknowledge a measure of worth of their servants or the grounds laborer and be far less exploitative and contemptuous of the general population. Some reasons are their mutual proximity, recognized dependency, and legacy of moral responsibility. The opposite is the usual reality in human history. The absence of proximity and moral legacy lowers a sense of moral responsibility and elevates the tendency to exploit. Thus, the gulf of perceived worth is usually grandiose between the haves and have nots, along with equally measured exploitation. This is the case whatever the form of governance.

The worldwide popularity of this television series reveals the cultural pervasiveness of the externalized worth con and the drama of its contentions and deprivations. Media is its cultivating and reporting agent and, in America, Madison Avenue its persistent advocate.

The Antidote

All death-inducing conflict, both psychologically and physically, is brewed in the caldron of worth inequality – all arrogance, all contempt, all prejudice, all envy, all greed, all humiliation, all ruthlessness, all exploitation, all revenge, all torture, all brutality, all murder, all war, all. The basic ingredient of this brew is a belief in an imported externalized worth and its assumed superiority. All social institutions that advocate this notion are the distillers and distributers of this brew of defeat and death.

There is only one antidote—a birth brew that affirms the essential equality of all humans irrespective of their life circumstance. Social institutions that advocate the innate worth of all humans are the champions of this life-giving brew. Social worth conflicts will only cease to exist and democracy will only prevail to the extent that the citizenry drinks of this birth brew antidote.

The Key

The key to the administration of this antidote is education in every area of the nation's life. It must begin in the home and continue in the public arena of schools. A focal song in Roger's and Hammerstein's musical South Pacific is: You've Got to Be Carefully Taught. The message of the song is that hate and prejudice must be carefully taught in a child's early years—the learning years of susceptible mind molding.

However, this message applies to all human beliefs and values. It is particularly applicable to the notion of inherent self-worth. Little can be done to guarantee that inherent equality of worth will be taught and modeled in the privacy of the sacred and protected spheres of home and religion. But the public school system is under the authority of the local and national community. Equality of worth must be the very heart of the nation's school curriculum beginning in the social drama of kindergarten and remaining focal through every subsequent grade including college and graduate levels. There can be no exemptions if democracy is to be actualized and sustained. Education is the key because education is what creates the eye through which life is given meaning and purpose.

Administrators, teachers and other employees must model inherent worth in their relationships and teach students in every grade level. They must relate inherent worth to the success of democracy. They must distinguish between inherent worth and personal social achievements, acquired social positions, and amassed wealth. Only a school system devoted to teaching the inherent worth of every person can overcome the influence of those who hold to worth as an imported commodity. If teaching inherent worth were the heart of the nation's education system it would also become the heart of the nation's democratic process. The two are inextricably bound together. Thus, at the core of educating educators must be how to model and teach the inherent worth of democratic intent.

Abraham Lincoln had his finger on the issue when he suggested it is necessary to:

Teach the children so it will not be necessary to teach the adults.

In present America the issue of inherent worth is a profound adult education issue. The primary sign that democracy actually prevails in America is when it becomes only a children's education issue.

Conclusion

Those who do not believe in their own innate worth are likely to seek its acquisition by robbing others of theirs. This is the root of all forms of despotism. A few social manifestations of this robbery are racism, sexism, classism, prejudice, arrogance, slavery, and elitist despotism. Imported schemes of worth urge democracy toward destruction and suicide. Imported worth is the avowed enemy of democracy.

OF, BY, AND FOR

Democracy was not established of, by, and for those selected as the most worthy in a culture. It was established of, by, and for all the people— which assumes the equal worth of the total citizenry.

7

INDIVIDUALISM

The second avowed enemy of democracy is individualism. An individual is a distinct person who is in charge of their own decision making whereas individualism is the view that everything exists to serve one's personal whim. Individualism makes fulfilling private whim the goal of democracy and violates its conscience of the common good in absolute fashion. This violation prohibits the possibility of democracy and invites its suicide.

Critical Distinctions

Individuals are the reality of human existence. It is me among we. Individualism is a self-centered philosophy of living. It is me before we. While individuality is the base of democracy, individualism is its bane. While individuality acknowledges unique citizenry diversity that contribute to a democracy's conversation, creativity, and progress, individualism is a form of supreme self-interest that contributes to a democracy's dysfunction, impediment, and destruction. Individualism in pursuit of a greater social worth is the root of monumental miseries and misfortunes in the human drama. It is the wellspring of social worth-o-meter scales. It is that which creates, feeds, and sustains despotism. It wields the rods of suppression and destruction to keep itself in power. It is grossly anti-democratic.

Individualism's Expansion

Individualism is empowered by expanding the strength of citizenry devotion. This enables it to seize political entities and transcend social

71

boundaries. It increases itself by capturing larger identities. Its triumph progresses from the individual to the community to the state to the nation and to the world.

When it dominates a person its demand is individual rights over community rights. When it dominates a state its demand is state rights over national rights. When it dominates a nation its demand is national rights over international rights. Integral to this progression of triumph is the loss of the common good to individual whim. This unleashes all the identities it has captured to behave in total self-interest with the resultant miseries and misfortunes.

Individualism simultaneously invites the disempowerment of community and the empowerment of despotism.

A Recipe for Disaster

A Hagar the Horrible cartoon aptly summarizes the ultimate outcome of any group that is devoted to individualism. In a Viking boat, some of the crew is rowing with the paddle end of the oar and some with the handle end. Some are rowing forwards and some are rowing backwards. The boat is going in aimless zig zags and circles despite the energetic commitment of the rowers. Hagar, standing at the helm with his hands cupped as a megaphone around his mouth is shouting: "Will you quit saying different strokes for different folks!"

A democracy dominated by individualism will go nowhere toward its intended purpose because everyone will be moving in different directions in devotion to private whims. This is the ultimate outcome of all individuals, institutions, states, or governments that are dominated by this self-centered philosophy. Individualism is the final recipe for social disaster because it offers no social bonding or community goals except of shared despotic devotions. Tyrannizing individualism deliberately destroys the relational community of democracy for the sake of private goals. And it has been a driving force in American culture since the nation's inception often disguised behind the rhetoric of pursuing the American Dream, the freedom of capitalism, and the sacredness of state's rights.

Community as Antidote

The perversions and destructions of individualism exist by elevating the part over the whole. Democracy is about the whole community. The individual within this community is the part. Although they are inherently compatible they can be purposely opposed. They can be in conflict in a manner that perverts and destroys democratic intent. There is only one antidote—positioning the individual and the community in their natural relational roles.

The key to doing so is an ancient wisdom distilled in the Latin phrase *pars pro toto*—which means the part exists for the sake of the whole. In turn, the whole sustains the life of the part. This is the natural ecology of community. This is a mutually dependent relationship which becomes death-dealing when reversed. Individualism reverses the relationship and initiates the destruction of community.

Democracy is of, by, and for the community. And it can only exist when the individual, the part, gives ultimate devotion to community, the whole. The most immediate material example of this principle of reciprocal interdependency is the relationship of the parts and whole of the human body. Consider what would be the state of the body's health if its parts were in contention over which gets the lion's share of sustenance. Larger examples are all the ecologies that sustain human existence and the necessity of mutual nurturing that sustains their interrelated vitality.

It is only within the scope of this scenario of devotion of the part to the whole that the part, itself, finds its ultimate and most gratifying blessings—its ability to maximize its own possibilities. This is the paradox of the relationship between the individual and the community. Individual blessing is most finely and rewardingly worked out socially and politically in a true democracy. This principle is at the heart of all democratic endeavors. It is what saves democracy from the threat of despotism.

Education

Everything that has been said about the role of education in respect to the teaching of innate worth is equally true of teaching how community protects and nurtures the individual. Such teaching must be central throughout the entire education system. Until the citizenry clearly understands both the nature of democracy's foundation and the nature of the enemies of this foundation, they will remain the captive of that which destroys the democracy to which they aspire and upon which they depend.

Conclusion

What restrains individualism is community—its goals, laws, ethics, customs, rewards, and punishments. Without the boundaries of community there would be no ordered civilization, only individualistic predatory chaos. Individualism urges democracy toward destruction and suicide.

OF, BY, AND FOR

Democracy was not established of, by, and for the individual. It was established of, by, and for the community. The individual's destiny rides in the saddle of the community's destiny.

8

PARTNERSHIP OF DESTRUCTION

Externalized worth and self-centered individualism are mutually attractive, supportive, and inevitably wedded. As devoted partners they mock equality and encourage the basest forms of social depravity. They are attracted to what degrades the worth of other humans for the sake of their own elevation – prejudice, contempt, deceit, robbery, slavery, rape, savagery, murder, war, and suppression.

The Wedding and Nationalism

The colonialism of the European nations of the 18th and 19th centuries is an international example of this wedding of destruction. These nations sought to elevate their own status above other nations by expanding their grasp of new territories and the enslavement of the inhabitants for their own profit. Colonialism was nothing less than the partnership of expanded national individualism wedded to expanded national external worth at the expense of those who they conquered.

Spain, France and England were critical players in this game of colonizing the territory of what we now know as America. They not only aggressively conflicted with each other over dominance but also killed the native inhabitants who refused servanthood for the sake of individual national whim and worth expansion. Eventually, the colonists rebelled against this exploitation and, unwittingly, established their own fragile nation partially grounded in this wedding of imported worth and individualism—despite calling it democracy.

The Wedding and Democracy

The wedded partnership of externalized worth and self-centered individualism in a democracy does the following:

- It denies democratic intent by shifting citizenry commitment from the whole to the part.

- It distorts democratic intent by shifting responsibility from community well-being to individual whim fulfillment.

- It destroys democratic intent by shifting relationship focus from collaboration to contention.

Externalized worth and individualism begin as personal despotisms. When culturally endowed they become social despotisms. They become the wedded enemies of democracy and motivate its suicide by encouraging despotic triumph.

The Wedding and Justice

Democratic justice is grounded in respect for the worth of both the whole citizenry and the individual citizen that makes up the whole. The purpose of democratic justice is redemption of the violating part. It intends to enable the part to restore respect for its own worth so it can respect the worth of the whole. It is a desire for the part to assume its natural role of support within the whole's worthiness. If such a restoration is not possible then incarceration is required to protect the whole from further violation. The whole takes precedence over the part. The function of the part is support of the whole.

Democratic justice has no bias toward gender, ethnicity, class, religion, or wealth. It cares only for the honoring of the common good. Where it reigns there is minimal violation of the common good and maximum honoring. A high degree of honoring of citizenry worth and redemption of violators is one of the hallmarks of an actualized democracy. On the other hand a high level of social injustice corresponds with the degradation of democracy and its slide toward suicide.

It is the partnership of externalized worth and individualism that initiates injustice in the democratic community. Injustice is violation of the common good which is the same as violation of community well-being. This violation is a disregard for citizenry worth in some manner and in some degree for both the individual citizen and the whole citizenry. Justice is a call for the correction of this violation—a life giving re-alignment of purpose.

The innate worth of the citizenry and its common good, demands that such violations be named and corrected. They necessitate redemptive justice for the sake of both the whole and the part. This ground of justice announces the necessity of democracy as community governance. There can be no actual model of justice in a nation that is dominated by externalized worth and individualism.

The False Conflict

That there is a natural conflict between the individual and the community is false. The people are both the part and the whole—the ruled and the ruler. They create and sustain each other. Again, the human body and its parts are an example. They only come into conflict when a part is corrupted of its purpose. To set them in conflict is to destroy their natural unity. This is why individualism's sabotage of democracy is so ironical. Without the community the individual has no social identity or sustenance. And since democracy is one of humankind's most noble forms of community it is one of the individual's most powerful benefactors. Bernardo DeVoto, early 20th century American Pulitzer Prize winning historian, essayist, and conservationist, reminds us:

The trouble with the sacred individual is that he has no significance, except as he can acquire it from others, the social whole.

I take DeVoto's comment to mean that there is neither the good of individuality nor the bad of individualism except as such is made possible by the existence of community. The part is not a part except as it is defined by the whole. Thus, the whole is the source of everything that sustains or fulfills the part—both good and bad.

A true democratic community maximizes individual potential in a manner that mutually benefits both the individual and the community. There is no greater benefit for the individual than a community where the worth of every person is held high, where individual work is enhanced and rewarded by the group, where fulfilling relationships of depth are promoted, and where the resultant culture hums with individual possibility.

Thus, the extent to which the democratic community is made strong is the extent to which the individual is made strong. They mutually enhance and enrich. However, community well-being is always a priority over individual well-being because the individual depends on the community for both its sustenance and its benefits. This means that within a democracy, whenever there is conflict between individual goals and community goals, the latter must prevail.

Conclusion

When the shift of a culture's focus is from the whole to the part, then the citizenry's focus is shifted from the common good of community to the frenzy of individual freedom—which is prelude to the part's corruption and whole's social suicide.

The wedding of externalized worth and individualism will always subvert or destroy the relational goals of democracy. The end result of the triumph of these enemies is the suppression of democracy which invites the rise of some form of despotism. Thus, where individualism and a scale of imported worth characterizes the social order some form of despotism is already controlling life and government.

There is only one way to prevent the slide of democracy into a suicidal grave. The citizenry must choose innate worth over imported worth and community over individualism. Such a choice only underscores the historical fact that the individual is most free and open to potential within a community that affirms the innate worth of its parts and works for their common good. It is the citizenry that determines the destiny of democracy by its choices. Democracy cannot be pulled into its grave without the citizenry allowing it to happen through self-sabotaging decisions.

Aside from subjection to external control, all the enemies of a democracy will be born of citizenry commitment to some form of individualism and imported worth.

OF, BY, AND FOR

Democracy begins committing suicide when of, by, and for the people forgets its purpose of, by, and for the community. Suicide becomes inevitable when the focus is shifted toward of, by, and for the individual.

9

THE THREAT OF IGNORANCE

Ignorance is a lack of insight sustained by a lack of information. There are two primary threats of ignorance that defy the democratic intents of citizenry equality, the common good, and the vote. One is by the government and the other is by the citizens.

Either threat will undermine the possibilities of democracy and contribute to its suicide. Both threats have to do with the failure to instill in the minds of the citizenry the nature and necessities of democracy which is the source of its blessings. It is to leave that page blank in the educational system that informs citizens of their civic contribution to their government's destiny. And, if the blank page is filled in, it is a failure to highlight that page as critical to the nation's destiny.

The Meaning of Civics

In the 1500s of Europe an award was created to present to members of townships who had saved other members from some threat or disaster, particularly in military action. It was a garland of oak leafs to be worn on the head called a civic crown. Its intention was to recognize the merit of community responsibility the act had dramatized. This intention evolved into the notion of citizenship which meaning was captured in the term civic – a reference to the rights and duties of citizens within the function of community government. At the heart of citizenship is commitment to mutual worth and the common good that was symbolized by the civic crown. It is relational in respect to both attitude and action.

Real civics is understood against this historical background that birthed it and gives it meaning. Thus, civics can only be given rightful meaning and have sustained motivation when its primary focus is the responsibility and privilege of honoring citizenry mutual worth and common good through attitude and action with willing sacrifice being its ultimate expression. Implied in this definition is the responsibility of government to not only award the civic crown but to teach the principles that motivate this awarding. This means that the heart of patriotism is citizen civic devotion to and sacrifice for the common good. This also means that political heroism is fulfillment of civic duty above all other goals—primarily, acts that affirm human worth and the common good.

There are two basic thrusts to the evolution of the notion of civics. One is how the government of a community works on its behalf. The other is the role and responsibility of the citizen within this community and government. The two are integrally and inextricably interdependent. Each relies on the other for its fulfillment and health.

Government and Civics Education

If a democratic government expects citizenry commitment and participation it will make certain that civics will be the mandatory and foremost exposure in all public education and national commemorations. America's first president, George Washington, called it the science of government. He said,

> *A primary object should be the education of our youth*
> *in the science of government.*

This is imperative because when the nation's understanding of civics is lost to the citizenry the commitment of the citizenry's behavior is lost to the nation.

Civics should be a primary mandatory subject of every grade level throughout the nation's educational offerings. Irrespective of class or ethnicity, students should be exposed to the basics of why the nation exists, how it is run, and their role in its success.

A Personal Example

My personal early education was during the Great Depression. Historically, it was a prejudiced version of the Texas story that glorified white male heroes and villainized Mexicans. Civic responsibility was about a prideful swagger that honored this provincial tale. It reflected an isolated view of the world before World War II altered the nation's history and pulled it into the global community.

It was not until I attended college at the end of the war that I was exposed to information that positioned Texas as a part of the United States and positioned the United States as part of a global community. And it was not until I found myself in the middle of the Vietnam War that I realized how arrogant the teaching of American history remained with respect to other nations. With this insight my country ceased being the center of the universe and became one among many. This did not decrease its importance on the world stage for me but did give it a civic responsibility beyond its own well-being.

But that was my personal evolution that required involvement in a questionable war for its enlightenment. My experience tells me that current generations have not been provided the same humbling historical perspective. They have not been taught the difference between civic pride and civic arrogance. And civics remains blindly provincial and nationally self-centered.

A National Example

On July 4, 2017, as it had done for twenty-nine prior years, National Public Radio used media to expose those who accessed it to the American Declaration of Independence. Some of the people who tuned in to the program after it had already begun found the words to this document disconcerting. Some of the interpretations were that NPR was spewing liberal propaganda, that it was condoning violence, that it was defaming the president, or that it was calling for a revolution. At the least, some thought it had been hacked or was spreading spam.

Irrespective of why a citizen might draw any of these conclusions, their response indicated a lack of familiarity with one of the nation's grounding democratic documents and, primarily, the meaning of this document and the history that provoked its creation. This is underscored by the fact that it was actually July 4th with specific focus on celebrating America's revolutionary birth and the document that announced this birth.

Whatever its extent, this is an example of a general civic ignorance which speaks to larger problems in American democracy and its system of education.

Diverting Citizenry Commitment

Such Civic ignorance opens the citizenry's allegiance to be captured by other interests that are being modeled in national life. For example, if capitalism is being advocated and modeled without a background of civic responsibility then capitalism easily becomes a private investment that stands outside civic responsibility and may even become adverse to democracy's well-being. The corruption of economic imperialism is easily the result.

Several years ago I was listening to a broadcast interview of two of America's wealthiest entrepreneurs by members of a university economics class. A student asked about the role of ethics in the teaching of economics. One of these entrepreneurs suggested that ethics was something taught in the privacy of the home and not in the open forum of an economics classroom. Essentially, what the entrepreneur was saying was that ethics and economics are unrelated except by accident. That might be a correct answer if the context were not the teaching of economics within a democratic society. This answer revealed that the entrepreneur either had little understanding of democracy or had separated economics from democracy – he had divorced capitalism from democracy.

Democracy is aggressively ethical in its call for everything that sustains the worth of every citizen and their common good. Democracy is boldly ethical in its call for noble human relating and action. An economics course that even hints at democratic values requires a strong grounding in fair play ethics that affirms human worth, looks to the common good, and abhors despotic attitudes. Ethics is the heart of democratic civics. Thus, ethics is the heart of teaching economics in a democracy. Nothing in a democracy can be separated from the ethics implied in democracy's three intents.

Franklin D. Roosevelt, four term president, leader out of the nation's Great Depression, and consolidator of the nation to engage World War II, reminds us moderns what is necessary to avoid the ignorance that kills democracy:

> *Democracy cannot succeed unless those who express their choice are prepared to choose wisely. The real safeguard of democracy, therefore, is education.*

When civic responsibility is no longer the primary focus of community education the erosion of democratic intent is already in process. Evidence of this erosion is when the main focus of education is a shift from civic responsibility to individual vocational goals and, particularly, to fulfilling the vocational needs of capitalist corporations. The vitality of a nation's citizenry commitment will be a reflection of how important civics is in its education endeavors – on every level.

This general exposure type of education at one time was called liberal arts. It was the attempt to inform students of a broad spectrum of ideas and knowledge that empowered the student with an expansive view of citizenship which included civics. If civic commitment is the result of education, then such seems to be only an option among many or simply in the background of today's education system.

Education and Taxation

A primary indicator of the citizenry's commitment to civics is its willingness to pay, through taxation, for a quality and rounded education of the community's youth. Unfortunately, such commitment seems to be on the wane in America with expenditure for education seen as secondary to private goals and selfish economics. Initiatives supportive of quality education that require an annual increase of just a few tax dollars per household are often defeated. Teachers, the shapers of young minds, are grossly underpaid and necessary materials for teaching are often in short supply. In many states, less is presently spent on education than during the Great Depression. This is the result of a growing un-civic-mindedness that diverts the devotion of the people to other pursuits. Such ignorance feeds investment in individualism and imported worth, the enemies of democracy.

The shift from a community focus to a private focus initiates the suicide of the nation's democratic governance because it is the endorsement of individual freedom above the commitment to the community's mutual worth and common good.

Citizenry and Civic Ignorance

The second threat of ignorance belongs to the citizenry. When our founding fathers spearheaded the American democratic revolution, they were fearful that the people would express a level of individual ignorance that would betray the necessities of democracy. They understood these necessities to be grounded in the shared information of education, whatever its source.

Education as Enlightenment

Education is about learned enlightenment that expands vision and possibility. Education, whether formal or informal, occurs when bodies of knowledge collide and sparks of insight enlighten the mind. Ignorance is lack of exposure to insight. It is unenlightened vision. It may even be resistance to the collision of disagreeing bodies of knowledge. The foremost fear of those who established our nation was not disagreement of opinion but an unenlightened dialogue. As Thomas Jefferson, author of the American Declaration of Independence, so aptly expressed:

> *If a nation expects to be ignorant and free, in a state of civilization, it expects what never was and never will be.*

The founding fathers of America were among the most highly educated in the British colonies. This education was not necessarily all formal. It was grounded in deliberate self-teaching and a devotion to reading. They knew how critical knowledge was to the wise selection of those who would represent them in democratic governance.

85

Education as Total Schooling

The teaching of civics is not just the obligation of those who are responsible for courses in government and American history. It is the obligation of every person associated with a school—from the principle to the janitor. It is the responsibility of the total faculty, the administration, and all support staff. The school is every person associated with its existence. There should be annual training workshops for the entirety of those who come into contact with students in any way to teach the intents of democracy. The mission of a school, whatever its level or focus, is to be a model of community democracy. If America is to become a model of democracy for the nations its citizens must be schooled in the model as primary to their educational experience.

The Payback of Ignorance

Our founding fathers understood education to be so imperative to the success of a sustained democracy that many of them promoted the establishment of formal educational institutions for the population's enlightenment. They were fearful of a democracy that only depended on the wits of the average citizen. They believed that the ignorance of the typical citizen left government open to manipulation and bad decision-making.

Thomas Jefferson is an example. He was a strong advocate of education as the foundation of sustaining a workable democratic republic. He advocated public education provided by the people at all levels. He worked to establish the University of Virginia as a means of higher end education. Here is his advocacy comment:

No nation is permitted to live in ignorance with impunity.

He believed ignorance had a negative social payback. It appears Jefferson's concerns were not unfounded. In present America, a large segment of the citizenry seems resentful of the kind of education and learning that ignited the fire of the American Revolution and created the documents that founded the nation. They seem sincerely prideful of that educational ignorance which invites despotism and leads to democracy's suicide.

The fear of our founding fathers was justified. They were placing their lives on the line by defying their British masters. Why do so if the populace they were seeking to liberate would betray the democracy they intended with their ignorance? They understood something that twentieth century civil rights leader Martin Luther King, Jr. would express so keenly:

Nothing in all the world is more dangerous than sincere ignorance and conscientious stupidity.

Sincere ignorance results from lack of enlightenment and conscientious stupidity results from sincere ignorance. The consequence is a citizenry that lacks the knowledge to process the obligations of citizenship with insight. It was this ignorance the founding fathers feared would raise its head to blight the democracy they founded. It was this ignorance that led to the Civil War. It was this ignorance that has suppressed the rights of minorities and women throughout the nation's history. It is this ignorance that causes elected representatives to vote against the best interests of those who elect them. It is this ignorance that fails to distinguish between democracy and economic imperialism. It is this ignorance that continues to undermine even a minimal understanding of the necessity for the citizenry's equality, their goal of common good, and their vote so critical to an actualized democracy.

Political Blindness

One of the greatest threats to American democracy has always been and remains that ignorance and resultant stupidity of the citizenry that undermines democratic intentions. It does so with all manner of both purposeful and unintended subversions which root in individual goals above common good goals that affirm citizenry worth. Some of this ignorance comes from the people's unwillingness to assure that every citizen receives a quality education. And some is maintained by deliberate isolation from information flow by those who wish no disturbance of their view of reality.

But whatever its source, here are some primary vision deficits that result from such ignorance and which supports decision-making that undermines democracy:

- The inability to distinguish between the demonstrating of democracy and the dismantling of democracy.
- The inability to distinguish between democratic leadership and despotic leadership.
- The inability to distinguish between personal goals and the common good.
- The inability to distinguish between capitalism and democracy.
- The inability to distinguish between government purpose and government size.
- The inability to distinguish between politicians devoted to self-service and those devoted to public service.
- The inability to understand that affirming citizenry equality of worth is primal to everything democratic.

The stronger these deficiencies of insight become the stronger is the nation's enticement toward democratic suicide. Moreover, it is citizenry ignorance that invites the government's betrayal of a failed civic education. These betrayals not only predict democracy's suicide they guarantee it.

Sight without Vision

Democracy abhors any social ideology that promotes worth bias. It has only one concern: Affirming the equal worth of every citizen and the consequent common good activated by citizenry rule. For a democratic nation, all liberating knowledge and all democratic guidance are birthed in the womb of civic and educated enlightenment.

Helen Keller was a deaf and blind woman of the nineteenth and twentieth century who overcame her handicaps and became a highly educated and inspiring world civic leader and political activist. She once commented:

The only thing worse than being blind is having sight but no vision.

It is the collective ignorance and stupidity of the citizenry that creates a sighted nation without democratic vision. Thomas Carlyle, 19th century Scottish historian and sociologist, summarizes his rejection of this blindness:

I do not believe in the collective wisdom of individual ignorance.

It is this collective ignorance which caused Winston Churchill to make this comment:

The best argument against democracy is a five-minute conversation with the average voter.

Conclusion

That which should terrify America's citizenry is to know that the teaching of civics, which is the very heart of democracy's sustenance and future, is either being made secondary to other teachings or ignored. The end result of this minimal approach to civic education will always be a shift of allegiance of the citizenry to private interests that take precedence over democratic interests. Such failure becomes the maintenance of civic ignorance. It signals a shift in the purpose of education from general enlightenment to limited self-interest. Again Thomas Jefferson says it clearly:

An educated citizenry is a vital requisite for our survival as a free people.

In this statement he was speaking of far more than simply acquiring a vocational degree. He was speaking of the broad exposure to knowledge that always encourages democratic intent. The bottom line is that schools are where a nation grows its future. If it grows ignorance—that will be its future.

OF, BY, AND FOR

If democratic intent is to be fulfilled then it must be instituted and energized by a high level commitment by the people to civic enlightenment—however it is gained. All such education is instituted and sustained of, by, and for the people.

PART III

A DESPOTIC MODEL

10

ECONOMIC IMPERIALISM

Economic imperialism is the use of power to subdue for the purpose of profit making. There are no moral restraints in the pursuit of this goal. It has been the primary posture of resource exploiters, nationally and internationally, throughout history whether these have been individuals, businesses, or nations. Colonialism is an international expression by nations. Libertarianism is a national expression by individuals.

Despotism can be a deceptive governing process. It will mask its intentions and expressions with remarkable cleverness. This cleverness will seek to clothe itself in the ideals of the governance it seeks to subvert. In American culture, economic imperialism masks itself as that free enterprise which sustains democracy. It facilitates this masking by its appeal to the self-interest goals of individualism and climbing the social ladder of imported worth. In this appeal it hides behind the idealistic face of democratic freedom and the pursuit of the American Dream.

The clue to recognizing its real face is that it will profit the capitalist at the expense of the citizens. Economic imperialism equals citizenry exploitation. Its reality is seen by pulling away its masks and observing its real face which is libertine capitalism. Here is its real tyrannical reflection in American democracy:

- Governing: Government becomes a subsidiary of big business to promote unrestrained enterprise.

- Politics: Democracy becomes a utility for profit making rather than a means of achieving the common good.

- Class: Large business exploits the citizenry and the division between the haves and the have nots grows aggressively.

- Environment: The environment is of no consequence except as a site for exploiting monetary gain.

- Economics: The gross national product becomes the monetary measure of democratic success, replacing the relational gauges of democratic intent.

- Civics: Freedom and capitalism are made synonymous with democracy as a means of hiding the self-interest of individualism and the pursuit of greater social worth.

Role Reversal

Economic imperialism reverses the roles of democracy and capitalism but this remains masked. The focus is a free capitalism irrespective of the effect on the citizenry's well-being. Capitalists become the hidden despots.

There is nothing wrong with capitalism as a servant of democracy. But there is everything wrong with democracy as a servant of capitalism. It is the wrong of economic despotism and democratic suicide.

Euphemisms, Concealments, and Lies

Libertine capitalists are always inventing new ways to disguise the blatant face of economic imperialism. They generously use euphemisms, concealments, and lies for this purpose.

Euphemisms

A euphemism is an agreeable substitute for a term that is disagreeable. It is linguistic masking. Two examples are referring to economic imperialism as economic nationalism and state-directed capitalism. Although less offensive terms, they still share the same character, the same goals, and the same consequences as economic imperialism. But the favorite euphemism is free enterprise—enterprise meaning business and free meaning no constraints. Whatever name might be given economic imperialism will not change its character or goals. It remains economic despotism.

Another less flattering euphemism for economic imperialism is crony capitalism. Crony refers to a pal who is inclined toward dishonesty for the sake of friendship. The limitation of this euphemism is that it describes a social connection but fails to describe the reason for the connection. The connection is how economic imperialists may relate in support of one another. The reason for the connection is why a capitalist actually becomes an economic imperialist. Aiding a crony is different from why one becomes a crony. It is the difference between mutual support and life commitment. An economic imperialist will befriend anyone who will enable the pursuit of greater wealth.

Whatever the label, economic imperialists all share a common reason for being and a common character.

Concealment

Concealing economic imperialism behind a verbal disguise is another major way of deceiving the public. One form of concealment is to falsely portray economic imperialism as a democratic benefit. A prime example of this is the phrase: *Trickle-Down Economics.* Supposedly, if those at the top of the economic ladder increase their wealth it will trickle downward until it showers those at the bottom of the economic ladder. This phrase is used to justify all manner of tax breaks and economic benefits bestowed on capitalists by a government captured by economic imperialists – supposedly so the un-rich can be blessed with a shower of the rich's left-over dollars.

This is not a new approach by economic imperialists to deceive the citizenry of their real motives. It is a perspective that pre-dates the twentieth century in a cruder form called The Horse and Sparrow Theory: If you feed the horse enough oats, some will pass through to the road for the sparrow. This cruder form was also expressed in more picturesque language by those at the bottom of the economic ladder. But, whatever its manner of expression, ways of stating this theory see the middle and lower classes as being sustained by the leftovers from the upper class table. It is the same vision as the historical relationship between royalty and peasantry in European history. It is demeaning of the citizenry, degrading of democracy, and in praise of economic despotism.

On the surface such explanations may sound reasonable but they find no verification in history. They are only ethical masks for the wealthy to wear while they exploit the lower classes. They continue to be used in varied forms because they obviously work as social deceits. That is, whatever the century, a large component of the public will fall for such deceits and, in doing so, continue to empower those who leave them only the horse's leftovers for sustenance.

The Four Major Lies

When economic imperialists seek control of a democratic government which claims to honor capitalism they will perpetuate four major lies to hide their real goals.

Capitalism is Self-Correcting

The first lie is that capitalism is self-correcting. This lie is made apparent by the governmental necessity of creating programs and laws to bail out businesses that have abused their power and created economic crises. If self-correction were a reality of capitalism, there would have been no Great Depression in the 1930s, no Savings and Loan Scandal in the 1990s, and no economic meltdown in 2008. Capitalism would have corrected itself before any of these events could happen. And if capitalism were self-correcting there would be no need for Chapter 11 bankruptcy laws to save capitalists from their own bad decision-making. If capitalism were self-correcting there would be no need for government subsidies to prop up risky businesses such as farming because capitalism would have already provided the corrections necessary to prevent failure.

The reason capitalism is not self-correcting is because it is a tool. Tools, like hammers and saws, are not self-correcting. Only humans are self-correcting and doing so requires deliberate desire and action in tool usage that implies moral consciousness. Economic imperialism has no moral conscience. Self-correction is not a term in capitalism's vocabulary. It is only a deceitful term in the vocabulary of economic imperialists. It is a lie.

Capitalism Equals Democracy

The second lie is that capitalism equates to democracy. This lie is made apparent by understanding that democracy is a style of governing while capitalism is an economic framework for processing productivity and wealth. Democracy is a relationship while capitalism is a facility. A relationship and a facility are not the same. Democracy is an end while capitalism is a means. Ends and means are not the same. As a facilitating means capitalism can be used by any style of government to accomplish its ends including despotisms. If capitalism and democracy are synonymous so are capitalism and despotism.

Capitalism can find compatibility with an actualized democracy when it is subservient to democratic intent. However, that it is synonymous with democracy is a lie.

Capitalism Equals Freedom

The third lie is that capitalism equates to freedom. Freedom is a state of unrestraint. This lie is made apparent by recognizing that unrestrained capitalism inevitably converts into economic disaster such as the Great Depression, the Savings and Loan Scandal, the Financial Meltdown, Chapter 11 bankruptcies, and corporate bailouts. Capitalism, without restraint, is a recipe for economic catastrophe, a creator of economic slavery, and a tool of economic imperialism. Unrestrained capitalism has a strong affinity with tyranny which is why most successful despotic governments use it. Freedom is an act of will. Capitalism is a tool and tools do not possess a will. The equation with freedom is a lie.

Social Programing Is Anti-Democratic

The fourth lie is that social programming is anti-democratic. This lie is made apparent by counting the number and cost of social program subsidies necessary to both sustain capitalism and save it from its abuses. On the other hand, social programs are the absolute requirement of a democracy's existence. Eliminate social programming in America and democracy would cease to exist because such programs are the primary implements by which the common good is achieved. Democracy and social programs are synonymous. The assertion that they are opposed to one another is a lie.

What's the Motivation?

The purpose of all of these lies is to hide the real despotic nature of economic imperialism behind a democratic façade. It is to instill fear in the citizenry that common good programs are the enemy of democracy so that despotic capitalists can convert them into a means of business profit taking. The motivation for this conversion is a dominating economic greed that surmounts all other considerations. This is why it is called economic imperialism.

The Imperial Goal

Domestically, when economic imperialism takes control, its essential goal is to privatize every social program devoted to the common good into a profit making enterprise for its own sake. This is one way it seeks to convert the meaning of civics from devotion to the common good to devotion to free enterprise. By free enterprise, economic imperialists refer to business ventures devoid of all government constraint. It makes no difference what the constraint may be. The economic imperialist labels any constraint on profit taking as anti-democratic because it deceitfully equates unconstrained freedom with democracy.

Nor does it make any difference what the program might be or how beneficial it is toward the common good. The proponents of economic imperialism have no use for any program that does not primarily benefit their own profit making. This covers the entire democratic landscape. Social Security, Medicare, Medicaid, national health care, and public education are a few examples. They will either seek to get rid of them because they offer no economic profit to the capitalist or they will seek to capitalize them so they will.

Such intent also covers any law, policy, or agent designed to protect the environment from exploitation. The only concern the economic imperialist has for the environment is profit. As John Muir, 20th century American naturalist and conservationist, commented when speaking about the drive of economic imperialists to profit from exploiting the environment:

Nothing dollarable is safe, however guarded.

This is why all concerns for the sustainability of the environment, such as global warming, will either be denied or minimized if their acceptance might diminish profit taking. The only vision of the future the economic imperialist is willing to accept is seen through the eye of the dollar $ign.

But economic imperialists will go beyond the outright rejection of apparent truth in pursuing profit. They will create lies in order to convert every component of the democratic system into a servant of capitalistic profit making schemes. Its political advocates are constantly enacting policies and introducing legislation that will fulfill this goal.

Since the goal of economic imperialists is to make a maximum profit void of the restraints of democratic ethical guidance, such conversions will inevitably compound the cost of the programs and increase the national budget. This means that the citizenry ends up subsidizing corporate profit through its own tax dollars. Privatization of common good programs intends to economically bilk the citizenry rather than benefit the citizenry.

A Democratic Reality

One reality of a democracy is that many common good programs cannot be geared to profitability because their design is social benefit that may not equate to economic profit. Democracy is beyond economics. It is about the common good while economics is a tool that can be used for any purpose irrespective of goal or morality. One example of such a program is public education. Its common good benefit cannot be measured by its economic costs. This benefit is the creation of a citizenship base upon which democracy is built and sustained.

A Long Term Vision Example

Economic imperialists have had a long term vision of transforming public education into a private enterprise. They have been working to institute this vision for years. The primary means that presently characterizes this attempt is to convert public education into an economic voucher system paid for by citizenry tax dollars. Vouchers would enable citizens to choose a private school of their liking for their children's education. This vision remains despite the fact that all evidence indicates that such private schools, by whatever name, are neither cheaper than public education nor improves its quality. But this is of no concern for economic imperialists.

Carol Burris is Executive Director of the Network for Public Education and Jeff Bryant is director of the Education Opportunity Network. According to an April 2019 co-authored article in Common Dreams, they reported that upwards of over one billion dollars of taxpayer money was squandered in the current federal budget on the government's Charter Schools Program. These schools either never opened or opened only for a brief period before closing. The wasted money was due to mismanagement, poor performance, lack of enrollment, and fraud. Past history raises concerns about how the charter school project actually fits any democratic educational purpose.

Consider the following potential education suppressing outcomes of a voucher based public school system.

- **Worth Equality:** Parents will select schools that reinforce racial, ethnic, religious, gender, and class prejudices that undermine the citizenry's equality of worth.

- **Intentional Lies:** Curriculum will be written or selected that distorts history into lies that equate capitalism and freedom, and subverts and distorts democratic intent.

- **Quality Reduction:** The national education system will be divested of uniform national standards and the quality of national education will be radically diversified and diminished.

- **Ideals Diminishment:** Family and regional prejudices will

100

increase and the embracing of democratic ideals
will diminish.

- **Religion Encroachment:** The separation of church and
state will be breached with the general citizenry supporting religious beliefs with which they might radically dis-
agree.

- **Reversing Purpose:** Public education will be converted
into a tool for growing economic imperialists rather than
growing democrats.

- **Narrowing Perspectives:** Limited curriculum exposure will
ensure the narrowing of perspectives rather than the en-
larging of perspectives.

- **Individualism Triumph:** Permission will be given for institutionalized individualism to triumph over the community common good goals of democratic intent.

- **Perversion of Civics:** The concept of civics will be
reduced to the support of provincial perspectives, regional goals, and economic imperialism.

In this conversion there is concern that education will become an
indoctrination which will selectively perpetuate the prejudice and ignorance of parents, guardians, and geographic regions. This is in opposition to the ideal public education goal of broadening perspective so
that citizens are equipped and encouraged to bridge differences through
mutual respect, interaction, and dialogue and see themselves as part of
a larger nation. In brief, economic imperialists wish to rewrite history to
favor their goals of profit making. They are not concerned about social
effect.

Benjamin Barber, 20th century American author and political theorist, concludes in assessing America's growing disregard of public education:

*America as a commercial society of individual consumers may survive the destruc-
tion of public schooling. America as a democratic republic cannot.*

However, economic imperialism cares nothing about the quality or democratic purpose of education. It cares only for the billions of dollars that exploiting a voucher system will garner for its bank account.

The Bottom Line

The bottom line is a phrase that intends to state that which is the imperative truth. Here is the bottom line goal of economic imperialism for all public programs: If it hints of profit-making it is ripe for exploitation. An observation by Ambrose Bierce, American journalist, author, and satirist of the nineteenth and twentieth century, sums up, with tongue in cheek, what he understands as politics:

Politics: A strife of interests masquerading as a contest of principles. The conduct of public affairs for private advantage.

However tongue in cheek this statement might be, the comment describes politics as captured by economic imperialism.

There are programs upon which the entire citizenry relies that cannot be privatized nor made economically profitable without detriment to the common good. They must be paid for out of the public coffer because their intention is the common good rather than financial profit.

This underscores that the common good is what determines how an effective democracy must be structured and funded and that capitalism, while being compatible if geared to democratic intent, is only one possible tool for facilitating this goal.

Conclusion

The failure of the citizenry to recognize the disguises economic imperialism uses to pass itself off as democratic good results in the corruption of democratic rule and the enthronement of libertine capitalists. Suzy Kassem is an American poet, philosopher and advocate of world citizenship. She points out:

*When a plutocracy is disguised as a democracy,
the system is beyond corrupt.,*

A plutocracy is government rule by the wealthy. Economic imperialism's goal is a plutocracy. It models the destruction of democracy and the elevation of despotism. Economic imperialists are the corrupting facilitators of democracy's suicide and advocates of enslaving despotism.

Our founders could not possibly have envisioned what economic imperialism has done to degrade what they had in mind when they created the American Revolution. However, they did understand the dangers posed by those who would usurp democracy for their own benefit since they lived under the rule of British economic imperialism. Founding father and second president of the United States John Adams, speaking of democracy, said it pointedly:

Government is instituted for the common good: for the protection, safety, prosperity, and happiness of the people: and not for the profit, honor, or private interest of any one man, family, or class of men.

American economic imperialism is the same in character as the British economic imperialism from which the colonists revolted. The only significant difference is the constraints America's attempt at democracy has placed on the economic imperialist's endeavors to use government as a profit making tool. A democracy without strong constraints on capitalism signals its potential suicide and easy conversion into the despotism of economic imperialism.

OF, BY, AND FOR

Democracy was not established of, by, and for the benefit of the capitalist. It was established for the common good of the people.

11

FREEDOM FRENZIED

The Statue of Liberty, a national historical monument, stands on Liberty Island in the New York City harbor. She greets all who enter the area. Created by France, she was a gift to America in commemoration of the nation's one hundredth birthday. The statue was dedicated in 1886. Her height is that of a twenty-two story building. The crown on her head has seven rays representing seven seas and seven continents that symbolically convey global embrace.

The Statue as Message

The statue's official title is: Liberty Enlightening the World. This is how the French sculptor, Auguste Bartholdi, who created the statue envisioned America. The vision implies that America represents a standard of democratic embrace for the world community. At her base is an inscription on a bronze plate from the poem The New colossus by Emma Lazarus, eighteenth century American author and poet:

Give me your tired, your poor, your huddled masses yearning to be free...

The message is that an actualized democracy is a community free from tyranny and oppression and open to all comers—especially the oppressed. There are broken shackles at the lady's feet that re-enforce the message. This suggests a carefully guarded liberty that facilitates the common good benefits of a democracy. Such liberty is not unlimited just because it stands against tyranny and oppression. It will also oppose all actions and attitudes of freedom that normalize the despotic tragedy of economic imperialism. And most of those immigrating to America have been fleeing the oppression of an economic imperialist state.

The liberty the lady represents is a demanding one that asserts worth equality and mutual devotion toward the common good. Her countenance represents an enormous human sigh. This is more than a sigh of relief for having escaped the destitution of bondage. It is that sigh which believes the restitution of liberty can now be engaged with all of its rewarding social benefits.

Perhaps this is why the lady's face is not the countenance of a happy welcome. There is a different visage expressed by her eyes. It is the burdened eyes of one who must provide healing and sustenance for those who have been deeply broken. It is the obligated eyes of one holding high a torch of enlightenment for those who have been severely oppressed. It is the concerned eyes of one who understands the enormity of her own task. It is the eyes of profound, guarded, and serious liberty.

The message is of an embrace for all those who wish for a community of liberating but responsible freedom.

The Statue as Metaphor

The painstaking process of creating and putting the statue together is a metaphor for democracy building. First there was the vision of its shape followed by an evolving series of models until the desired size was attained. Then there was the molding of its 300 separate pieces that would replicate the model. This was followed by the construction of an inner framework that held all these various molded pieces together with firm flexibility. And, finally, there was the making of a durability base upon which to stand her. This is just as the people must do if a democracy is to exist.

And beyond that there is, at various times, the erection of scaffolding around her in order to repair her of the ravages of elements and people—a repair that intends to restore her original visage and maintain her democratic message. And this is just as the people also must do to maintain their own ravaged democracy.

The Statue as Ideal

The Statue of Liberty is an idealization to which Americans aspire but find difficult to attain. The reason is that freedom invites its own enlargement and beckons toward excess and conversion into forms of individual tyranny and social oppression. Restraining this excess has been one of the battles of the nation's historical drama that has ravaged the American model's countenance.

Freedom and Liberty

The words liberty and freedom have been used historically with different shades of meaning. Liberty has generally referred to the external freedoms granted to citizens by governments. It is social. Freedom has generally referred to the innate personal ability of citizens to make decisions without government control. It is personal. These two meanings can be compatible or in conflict—depending on the nature of government.

The Compatibility of Liberty and Freedom

In an actualized democracy liberty and freedom will find compatibility and mutual support. Indeed, for democracy to exist they must merge into a unity sustained by the acknowledgement of mutual citizenry worth and a devotion to citizenry common good. This means that they find agreement as to permission and limits when democracy exists in reality. In brief, while human inner freedom cannot be contained because it is innate to birth, human social liberty must be contained because it is necessary to civilized community. When these are in agreement, democracy can be created and sustained.

During World War II, Victor Frankel, a Jewish psychiatrist, was imprisoned in Nazi concentration camps. While studying both his own response and that of others to the dehumanizing brutalities of these environments he concluded that all freedoms can be taken from humans except one: The freedom to determine one's own response to any life circumstance. He was speaking of the inviolate inner freedom granted to every human by virtue of birth. Nothing can take it away. It is a major part of what it means to be human. Like self-worth, it is a birthright.

On the other hand, liberty, which is a construction of social freedoms by government, has distinct boundaries that are deliberately designed to facilitate the purpose of that government. The liberties of government will reflect why it exists. A despotic government will reduce liberty while a democratic government will expand liberty. However, there can be no government without boundaries imposed on liberty. They are the social safeguards of the governance, whatever its style.

For example, in a despotic government, citizens will be denied the liberty of free speech and criticizing the government. Doing so is likely to be severely punished. But in a democratic government the citizenry will be given the liberty to freely express anti-democratic attitudes and behaviors. As previously indicated, this is the ultimate oxymoron of democratic perspective which empowers a freedom of expression which is central to a democracy's health.

The issue in a democracy is to what extent anti-democratic expression can be allowed and not become harmful to its health. The answer is that liberty must be curtailed when it becomes harmful to total citizenry worth, the common good, and citizenry rule. When the part threatens the well-being of the whole, the actions of the part must be restrained. Liberty beyond the common good invites the anarchy of individualism and is the prelude to despotism. Thus, liberty is vital to a democracy but is not sacrosanct. Its limitation is imperative to a democracy's health and survival. The boundaries of liberty are the protectors of both individual freedom and community civilized living.

The Problem of Meaning

The problem with addressing the issue of freedom and liberty is that their meanings are so often used interchangeably. This is true in American culture. Liberty and freedom are usually merged in the public mind. Speak of one and the other is implied. This is the land of the free. This is the culture that asserts: Give me liberty or give me death. However, the term freedom is favored because of the over-stress on individualism and personal rights. The issue is: What constraints on freedom will protect it from becoming either chaos or a despotism?

Given this meaning problem the following discussion will not attempt to distinguish between social liberty and individual freedom. Its purpose is not to maintain these distinctions but to explain the confusions between unrestrained social liberty, the intents of democracy, and the consequences of these confusions.

Personal Freedom Focus

While democracy is about the individual's obligations toward community good, individualism converts democracy into a drama about personal freedom. While freedom is vital to democratic relationships, community obligation always places a restraint on any freedom that violates or diminishes the empowerment of community benefit. Thus, to equate unrestrained individual freedom with democracy is to equate democratic dysfunction with social health. It is to reveal a distorted understanding of both democracy and freedom.

Where individualism is paramount, the pursuit of unrestrained freedom becomes one of democracy's most undermining perversions. Otto Kahn, late 19th century and early 20th century American investment banker and philanthropist, implied this when he noted:

The deadliest foe of democracy is not autocracy but liberty frenzied.

Kahn is suggesting that the threat of a dictatorship in a democracy is less than the threat of citizenry freedom run amok. Freedom run amok is individualism in pursuit of a greater social worth devoid of ethical and moral restraint. Individualism converts democracy into an arena of personal freedom devoid of social obligation. Such freedom becomes license, libertinism, opportunism, combat, and chaos – all without any concern for the welfare of the community of others. This is the deadly foe of a democracy which is always community centered good. It is the soil in which despotism thrives.

When corporations are legalized as individuals, as the Supreme Court did in 2010 in its Citizens United vs. Federal Election Commission decision, they are encouraged to embody all the perversions of autocratic individualism and to convert democracy into institutional despotism. Unlimited personal freedom always invites a larger despotism whether it is of an individual, institution, or nation.

Despotic Invitation

When personal freedom becomes the main battle cry in the democratic political drama, the soul of democracy has already been lost to the marriage of externalized worth and unrestrained individualism. The end result is that relationships cease being democratic and become endowed with the morality of dog-eat-dog and the ethic of the end justifies the means – all for the purpose of purchasing a greater social worth irrespective of the cost to the common good.

Such freedom invites the entire cultural drama to become an arena without any ethical or moral boundaries.

The national manifestation of democracy gone awry through individualism is the conversion of the political process into some form of tyranny created by those who have achieved the greatest social worth accumulation. Plato was an Athenian philosopher during the 300-400 BC Era. It was a time when thinkers were considering the possibilities of democracy and its effect on the human enterprise. Here is one of his observations,

Dictatorship naturally arises out of democracy, and the most aggravated form of tyranny and slavery out of the most extreme liberty.

Freedom frenzied, which is extreme citizenry liberty, is an invitation for despotic rule – whatever its form or name and however it might be disguised. And such despotism roams the democratic landscape of America in the guise of giant corporations – corporations that would pull the strings of government in a manner favoring their exploitation for profit of both the citizenry and the environment.

As examples, consider the two Wall Street financial giants Enron and World Com. Enron was an energy, commodities, and service company that filed for bankruptcy in 2001 due to accounting fraud that violated freedom's boundaries. It employed 4500 people. World Com was a communications giant that filed for bankruptcy in 2002 due to the same kind of accounting fraud. It employed 60,000 people. A major reason for the failure of these corporations was lack of restraint on their freedom to do as they wished. One end result of these bankruptcies was that these employees lost jobs and pension plans. But the economic consequence was much broader. We citizens have ended up paying for their lack of responsibility. According to Brookings Institute, in a 2002 report, the estimated financial impact on the nation of these two bankruptcies would be around 35 billion dollars, or, almost a third of the national domestic product. But this estimate was only for the first year following the bankruptcies. The nation would continue to pay in many unseen ways. Both are prime examples of companies led by economic imperialists who only see democracy as a utility for profit making and push the boundaries of restraint and responsibility until they are breached. Uninhibited free enterprise can be quite costly to the citizenry. Freedom requires boundaries or it ceases to be freedom and becomes license.

Democratic Freedom

All freedoms are neither equal nor beneficial. The freedom to exploit one's neighbor is not on par with the freedom to benefit one's neighbor. One is despotic while the other is democratic. True democratic freedom only exists to the extent that citizenry equality exists. All other freedoms are grounded in the false and fragile dispensations of externalized social worth and the whims of individualism. Democracy is not about freedom. It is about equality and the common good. Responsible freedom is not a democratic goal. It is a symptom of democratic engagement. It is what happens when the people join in commitment to their mutual worth and common good.

Democracy is about the good of the total community. And the total community is all the people. Democracy is a level playing field of worth acceptance and common good devotion. Since this is its devotion it motivates the most noble forms of human relating because it maximizes community benefit and elevates individual potential to its highest possibility.

Frenzy refers to something that is madly intense and wildly out of control. Unfortunately, in America the constant call is for liberty frenzied which is a self-serving style of freedom that elevates the individual above the community and, therefore, above democratic intent. Liberty frenzied is the child of the pursuit of external worth and individual whim. And it is a primary symptom of impending democratic suicide.

110

The Economic Edge

Libertine capitalism is the economic edge of freedom frenzied. It is profit making for the sake of the user without concern for community effect. Libertine capitalism elevates profit above people. It is contemptuous of democratic intent. Libertine capitalism is a form of anti-democratic tyranny. It sees democratic ideals as human weakness. Libertine capitalism is the avowed enemy of democracy.

Freedom frenzied is the primary characteristic of American culture. Such inevitably leads to libertine capitalism and democracy's conversion into economic class despotism. Will Durant is a 20th century American philosopher historian known for his definitive works on the story of western civilization. Here is one of his conclusions,

When liberty becomes license, dictatorship is near.

Dictatorship is not only near in America; it is enthroned in the unrestrained libertine capitalism of a wealthy elite. This is economic imperialism—the pursuit of profit without concern for the common good. In a democracy, economic imperialism easily happens when unrestrained individual freedom is substituted for the common good. However, the very meaning of freedom is desecrated when it is made a servant of capitalism. Freedom frenzied is the hallmark of the triumph of individualism which is the death knell of democracy.

The Test of True Democracy

As previously suggested, only in an actualized democracy will the citizenry be given the freedom to speak and behave in an anti-democratic manner. The issue of this oxymoron is the extent to which the government or the citizenry will allow such expressions before declaring them as traitorous. Those who hide behind such freedoms will push them to their limits to see how far they can behave anti-democratically without penalty.

Thus, an actualized democracy must walk a fine line between keeping freedom open for democracy's facilitation and denying those free-

111

doms that undermine democratic intent. The only measure of where this line is drawn is the intents of democracy: the equal worth of all citizens, the achievement of the citizenry's common good, and the freedom and obligation to control government through citizenry rule. This is the line that must be drawn to protect democracy from its self-destruction. Here is this measure summarized:

Any freedom that benefits the whole should be encouraged while any freedom that diminishes such benefit should be restrained.

There is a valid purpose for stop signs, speed limits, and other laws that constrain excessive human behavior. That purpose is to protect the common good which is the same as safe and civilized living.

Conclusion

Why are unrestrained freedom and democracy so easily confused and viewed as synonymous? There is a web of reasons. One is the false equation of democracy and individualism. Another is the false equation of capitalism and freedom. And a third is the false equation of democracy and capitalism. Given these confusions it is easy to falsely equate unrestrained freedom with democracy.

However, this confusion is clarified when the following is understood:

- Individualism is an enemy of democracy because democracy is about the common good.

- Capitalism is a tool and can be used by any form of governance including despotism but is constrained in democracy as a servant of the common good.

- Freedom is a servant of democracy and is limited by any negative impact on the common good.

What sustains the common good in a democracy is commitment to the people's inherent worth. The greater is the community's commitment to citizenry inherent worth the greater is the freedom of the individual to pursue personal interests within the community.

112

Every issue confronting democracy can be settled by beginning with an acknowledgement of the equal worth of every citizen and ending with an acknowledgement of the common good as its goal. As long as the people are unable to close this loop they will continue to equate democracy and capitalism with unlimited freedom and liberty frenzied will continue to reign.

Liberty frenzied gives birth to personal and public despotisms. Despotism enthrones those with the greatest liberty to act with the greatest self-interest. This induces democracy's suicide because it places personal whim above common good.

OF, BY, AND FOR

Democracy was not established of, by, and for individual freedom. It was established for the common good of the people so that the rewards of freedom are shared by the entire community.

12

BIG GOVERNMENT SCAPEGOAT

The phrase Big Government is a figure of speech the economic imperialist uses for government that inhibits an unrestrained capitalism in any manner. In America, the scapegoat economic imperialism most often uses to hide its real agenda is the claim that all the country's ills are due to Big Government. Here are two ways it plays this deceit card:

- **Removal of Constraints:** All constraints on free enterprise's ability to make money are viewed as Big Government interference of citizenry rights. Big government is the scapegoat economic imperialism uses to justify the removal of all legal constraints on private enterprise's ability to bilk the public or rape the environment for profit. With corporations declared to be persons, they claim the same right as the individual citizen to be free of all government regulatory constraint in pursuing wealth. Controlling government for profit-making is the economic imperialist's version of achieving The American Dream. And this is made possible because the economic goal of the dream and the intents of democracy have been essentially separated in the citizenry's mind and the wall of separation is the term freedom.

- **Government Handouts:** Any benefits, like social services and welfare programs, that are not rewards for capitalists are declared to be Big Government doling handouts to lazy citizens unwilling to work for a living. Lacking finances is viewed as social irresponsibility. Corporations, declared to be persons, view themselves as the only legitimate recipients of government handouts. The hypocrisy is that corporations, not individual citizens, are the recipients of the largest government handouts. The size of government doles to a single corporation is staggering compared to the welfare an entire generation of citizens might receive during an entire life-time. However, whatever the comparison, if government welfare does not facilitate capitalistic profit-making Big Government becomes the villainous scapegoat.

In actuality, the mismanagement and deliberate abuse of so-called Big Government that the economic imperialist decries is essentially the product of its own deceitful manipulations so it can make excessive profit through inflated contracts, cost overruns, and constant subsidies. My own research of cost over-runs in government contracting concludes that this is the norm rather than the unusual. I find there to be three major reasons for such over-runs:

- **Deliberate low-balling original costs:** In order to secure a contract the bidder deliberately bids low knowing that it can later inflate the costs to whatever is desired for maximum profit.

- **No consequences:** There are no real consequences for claiming and getting cost over-runs – particularly in dealing with the defense industry—it's the expected game-plan.

- **Political Ambition:** For politicians who wish to secure their place in government, getting high-end contracts that profit and gratify their constituent's businesses is one means of doing so at no cost to themselves.

The bottom line is that there is deliberate corruption and mismanagement without any disciplined oversight in government contracting. It is economic imperialism controlling the entire system for maximum profit without concern for the citizenry. And it reflects gross congressional failure.

The term Big Government is an obfuscation used to hide these profit making schemes and to reduce all profit making constraints. It is a mask to conceal government being controlled by big business. It hides the face of the military-industrial complex expanded into the economic imperialism-industrial complex. It is deliberate fraud with congressional approval.

Corporate Hypocrisy

There are no institutions in America that are more hypocritical about government than large corporations. Many corporations exist by government contracts. And many receive countless billions of dollars in government subsidies and tax breaks, most hidden from the public, while railing against the evils of Big Government.

Many of America's corporations would fail without government subsidies and enormous tax breaks. That capitalism sustains itself is a gross deceit. This does not mean that capitalism is bad. It only means that it is generally not survivable in a democracy without the support of various forms of government welfare and constraints against abuse. And that is because capitalism is a tool. Tools are neutral and their use and abuse reflect the goals of their wielders. It is the unprincipled capitalist that abuses the system. It is such capitalists, using the corporation as a tool, who must be constrained from economic double-dealing that threatens the financial well-being of democracy.

There are corporations that make grossly obscene profits and conceal them in national and international hidey-holes and continue to be subsidized by government as if they were living on the edge of bankruptcy. The fossil-fuel industry is an example. Read most any report on government subsidies and it becomes clear that through loans, price controls, below market resource assistance, research and development, tax provisions, etc., this industry is subsidized between 20 and 30 billion dollars annually by tax payers. This does not include the price of environmental destruction. Moreover, when this cost is expanded to the global market place it rises excessively. Yet, this industry corporation will portray Big Government as a villain that stays the hand of the industry from making a fair profit.

Hypocrisy is a typical posture of unethical schemers. Corporate leaders will often denounce government welfare for poor families, who depend on it to stay financially afloat, while claiming the right to receive millions for them-selves. Here is one example. Good Jobs First is an economic development watchdog group. In a March 2015 report entitled Subsidizing the Corporate One Percent, it listed the top five companies receiving government subsidies of 100 billion dollars or more.

116

These subsidies included loans, loan guarantees, and bailout assistance. They are: Bank of America, Citigroup, Morgan Stanley, J.D. Morgan Chase, and Goldman Sachs.

Here is another example. The Cheat Sheet is a pop media company. According to a June 20, 2017 article, some of the corporations receiving top dollar government subsidies are: Boeing, Alcoa, Intel, General Motors, Ford, Fiat Chrysler, Royal Dutch Shell Oil, Nike, and Flatirons Construction. These are all companies that make enormous profits, many in the billions, without government subsidies. The subsidies are bonuses out of the tax payer's pocket.

State Hypocrisy

States will often play the same hypocritical role as corporations in relation to the federal government. They will behave as if they were economically independent while relying heavily on federal funds to exist with any degree of fiscal health. Individual American states reliance on federal money to stay afloat financially ranges from 17.5 % to 41.9 % of their annual budgets according to an April 19, 2018 report from the non-profit organization Center on Budget and Policy Priorities. These dependencies include housing supplements, education, public welfare, Medicaid, entitlements, roads, conservation, etc. The politicians of these states will often complain of the heavy handedness of the federal government with one hand while receiving hefty benefits with the other.

Texas is an example. Glenn Hegar, the state's Comptroller of Public Accounts, in his May 2019 Fiscal Notes reminds people that between 1953 and 2018 Texas made 206 requests to the federal government for disaster relief with positive response. According to The Texas General Land Office, Texas has received over 1.4 billion dollars from the Federal Emergency Management Agency just for relief from the 2017 hurricane Harvey. And according to a House Urban Development report of February 25, 2019 it has approved 5.7 billion to Texas for the same hurricane relief. Do the math and consider how much government relief assistance Texas has received over the past 65 years. It would be comparable to a rich uncle bailing out a poor relative for staggering medical emergency costs for the same number of years. And they are on the verge of requesting more due to a recent flooding disaster.

In an article entitled TEXAS MILITARY INSTALLATIONS (Economic Impact 2017) Bruce Wright quotes Glenn Hegar about his assessment of the financial impact on the Texas economy of the existence of 15 major military installations in Texas. The article reads:

The comptroller study found that the 15 major military installations located in Texas generate more than $136.6 billion in economic activity here each year, and add $81.4 billion to our gross state product. They also generate $48.1 billion in annual personal income and support, directly and indirectly, nearly 806,000 Texas jobs.

Actually, as of this writing, there are 28 military installations in Texas. Consider a Fiscal Notes article, November 2017, by Kevin McPherson and Bruce Wright, entitled: Federal Funding in Texas. It states that according to the Office of Management and Budget, the federal government provided more than one third of the Texas net revenue.

Given the financial impact of the presence of the military, the monies received from disaster relief over the years, and the monies provided by the federal government in assistance to the Texas state budget, one wonders if all of this federal support disappeared what would be the financial status of Texas? How well could it do without the federal government's assistance? If Texas were an individual it would be viewed as existing on government welfare assistance.

States wish for federal maintenance of national parks and monuments, for the funding of dams and water projects, for financial institutions to be backed up by federal guarantees, for farmers to be subsidized with federal money. They wish to be bailed out of the cost of natural disasters such as drought, floods, hurricanes, etc. which in recent years has reached billions of dollars. The list is long and the dependency is high. Good citizenship behooves its citizens to investigate their state's actual dependency on the federal government. This means looking beyond the propaganda of their elected politicians.

When it comes to federal money, states normally insist on the federal government behaving as a wealthy parent toward dependent children – with grand generosity. Yet, they will constantly criticize that same government for over-spending and over-regulating—for being too big and too heavy handed. Their hypocrisy is as grand as the financial benefits they receive.

A False Issue

The entire notion of big government versus small government is a false issue of deliberate design to shift public focus away from economic imperialism's goals and methods. There is only one criterion for judging democratic government and it has nothing to do with size. It has everything to do with the strength with which government facilitates the democratic intents of the citizenry's worth, common good, and rule – whatever the agency or program.

So beware of the notion that any issue of import in American democracy is due to so called Big Government. When this accusation is leveled it is usually a ploy of economic imperialism to hide its real agenda of profit taking at the expense of the citizenry. When the words Big Government are used negatively, it usually reveals a corrupt capitalist that sees democracy primarily as a utility for profit-taking, hidden monetary handouts, and tax exemptions—a disguised source of unlimited profit which is the same as the people's bank account because we finally pay the bill.

What Do They Want?

What economic imperialists wish to do is take over government and dismantle all agencies that have been created to protect the citizenry from business exploitation. Economic imperialists wish total license to pursue profit taking in any manner they desire. Controlling the government and all its components is the primary means of accomplishing this goal. If one is an economic imperialist, with an unlimited bank account, there is only one obstacle to becoming a controlling national despot—strong democratic government.

In a democracy, the easiest way to overcome this obstacle is to purchase politicians and elected officials who will vote away the obstacle. And economic imperialists readily find self-interested persons to be their advocates and voice in this voting. Being elected to congress or high office is the means by which many politicians enter the profitable vocation of corporate lackey. This lackey-ship is a quid pro quo means of securing both a present and future economic security. It is also a betrayal of the citizenry that elected them. And congress comfortably becomes a national economic imperialist lackey-dom. The reason for submitting to this demeaning status is a constant flow of money that invites it to become a lifestyle.

When economic imperialists speak of Big Government they mean strong government devoted to the common good. They are opposed to it because it is strong government that stands between democracy and economic oligarchy. A weak government is impotent to regulate the skullduggery of economic imperialists and, thus, desirable.

Edmund Burke was an 18ᵗʰ century Anglo-Irish statesman and philosopher and member of Great Britain's House of Commons. He is often referred to as the father of modern political conservatism. Here is one of his observations:

Nothing turns out to be so oppressive and unjust as a feeble government.

Economic imperialists wish for and work for a feeble government for precisely this reason.

Here is the contradiction. When economic imperialists take over a government, they will stop using the term Big Government as a negative term. The reason is that they will now wish for a strong government to pursue their goal of converting it into a profit making agent. Since it is no longer advocating for democracy but for big business it can now be legitimately strong (or big).

Imagining the Possibilities

Whether you believe the means or outcome to be morally good or bad, consider just a few possible scenarios that might exist without the leadership of strong government in American history:

- **Geography:** Without all the westward expansion made possible by federal government subsidy, land purchase, war, and genocide, America would be one third its geographic size.

- **Slavery:** Without the federal government's engagement and funding of the Civil War and its consequent constitutional changes, legalized slavery would still exist as a primary utility for capitalistic profit making.

- **Poisoning and Disease:** Without the federal programs that protect the environment from poisoning and the health measures instituted by similar programs, many citizens alive today would not exist because their ancestors would have died from pollution poisoning or uncontrolled disease.

- **Power:** Without the dams and electrical projects of the federal government, those of us today would be living with minimal electricity and water that government provides through power production and water control.

- **Expansion:** Without the federal government's permission, subsidies, and regulations there would be a limited railroad system to connect the geographic boundaries of the nation.

- **Recreation:** Without the vision of the leadership of the federal government there would be no national or state parks or monuments for the public benefit.

- **Roads:** Without federal government planning and funding there would be no local, county, state, and national highway systems.

- **Feudal System:** Without federal government regulations, modern Robber Barons would have total control of a national economic feudal system.

- **Colony:** Without a powerful and invested federal government, America and its allies would have lost World War II and the United States would be a divided colony of Germany and Japan.

Without all of these foregoing benefits provided by a strong federal government, Canada would have built a wall to keep Americans from illegally migrating into its safe and civilized culture.

Strong Government and Being Civilized

A historical metaphor for an America without the constraints of strong government is the chaos, mayhem, and lawlessness of the nation's original westward expansion. It was a time when safety was minimal and life was cheap because there was little civil ruling strength to embrace life value and enforce safe-living. Without the moral constraints of strong democratic government, human evil tends to capture the structures of social existence.

This scenario has been memorialized in the nation's fascination with mythic law enforcement heroes who gathered those constraints into a single person's action to create and protect civilized living. They were the marshals, sheriffs, and constables of towns and territories. Think of the mythologies of the Lone Ranger, Wyatt Earp, and Gene Autry along with the western stereotypes played by movie actors who instituted law and order for towns or counties to become civilized.

Being civilized means abiding by those legal restraints and social customs which make safe and comfortable living possible for all the people. At the heart of the civilizing process in the old west was the prohibition of gun toting within the town limits. What early law enforcement knew was that many citizens lacked restraint in taking the law into their own hands in a manner that violated the possibility of safe and comfortable living for others.

Law enforcement was the triumph of communityism over individualism. And comunityism was the triumph of citizenry innate worth over imported worth. In these triumphs the common good of the whole became the focus over the personal whim of the part. Being civilized is about community good as the first good.

Taming of the West

The so-called taming of the west was created by strong local government that made civilized community living possible. As civilization advanced it was the community, itself, that assumed the role of law enforcement – by teaching, modeling, and insisting on the necessity of fair-play rules. Individuals played a key role in this process but it was for the sake of and at the behest of the community. It was the community that suffered and persevered until it overcame the self-centered individualism that fought against it. Rugged individualism may have played an important role in initial exploration of the west but it soon became counter-productive in terms of civilized living.

As communities grew it became apparent that law enforcement needed to be a specialized institution for the sake of itself. When this institutionalizing was successful there was little need for individual citizens to possess guns. In an actualized democracy, which is the practice of noble civilized living, only trained law enforcement agents need weaponry to protect the civilized from the uncivilized.

Game Hunting and Despotic Fantasies

I grew up in a hunting culture. I possessed two guns – a shotgun for fowl and a rifle for animals. These two weapons were all I needed. We hunted for food not trophies. The attitude was that if you required more than two shots to kill a deer then you needed to go back to the practice range before you went hunting again. An assault rifle is nothing less than a hand carried machine gun. No respectable hunter would ever need such a weapon since it is for combat and animals don't shoot back.

Moreover, a real hunter only needed a low cartridge capacity rifle and, even then, it was not very sporting for the prey. My father used to say that if you really wanted to be sporting then hunt with a bow and arrow. Otherwise, understand that you are hunting for meat on the table which justified the excessive fire power of a five round cartridge. Obviously, the need to own assault weapons is about fulfilling ego fantasies that have nothing to do with game hunting and its minimal requirements. Only a strong government can protect the people from those individuals who harbor personal fantasies that require social destruction for fulfillment.

Safety and Hate Groups

The issue of gun ownership is not about private citizen safety. As a commentator in Michael Moore's documentary *Bowling for Columbine* suggested: If guns made people safer, America would be the safest country in the world. The reason for this conclusion is that there are more guns in our nation than there are people. Here is what is important about this statistic: Half of these guns are owned by around 3% of the population who are almost exclusively white males. Why these people have amassed so many guns has nothing to do with safe living.

The National Socialist Movement is an umbrella organization that promotes white supremacy and violence against non-whites and all who embrace non-whites. Their goal is a violent overthrow of the American government and the conversion of the nation into the new Nazi Germany. They would need a huge arsenal to accomplish this purpose. And they are stockpiling weaponry. They are a magnet for other hate groups, who are also mostly white males, who espouse violence as a means of accomplishing their goals. If you want to overthrow the government you need massive amounts of weaponry and you become an advocate for freedom of purchase.

It is such hate groups from which the people need government protection—those who promote violence as the answer to their personal self-worth issues. Only strong government is capable of providing such a shield of safety from those who have rejected democracy in favor of despotic destruction.

Civilized Regression

The cultural demand for the citizenry to maintain private arsenals is indicative of regression to an uncivilized past. At the least it evidences the existence of a remnant of the population which fantasizes enjoying the fruits of civilization while remaining uncivilized. It is a fantasy world in which gun-totters visualize themselves as the lost remnant of true individualists ready to defend themselves against the rest of the citizenry who have capitulated to the community-first style of democratic living.

A Measurement of Community Health

The lack of need for individual citizens to carry weapons is a hallmark of civilized living because the focus is on equality of worth and the common good of community. This hallmark insists on a living environment free from the intimidation of gun totters whose lives are driven by private fantasies spawned by the perversions of individualism.

Crime Rate Drop

In the early twenty-first century crime in America dropped significantly. According to an Atlantic Magazine article of April 15, 2016, the crime rate had dramatically plummeted over the past twenty five years as much as 42%. Other publications give higher percentages of crime rate drop. But whatever the percentage it is high enough for the conclusion that we live in one of the least violent periods of our history despite the continued mass shootings that are so morally disturbing. There are multiple reasons for this drop but it seems primarily due to the community's investment in both its presence and programs that deny the opportunity of crime. Again, this underscores the lack of need of gun arsenals when the civilized community upholds its own sense of innate worth and makes the common good its goal.

Community First

With around 327 million people in 2018, America had almost 40,000 gun related deaths. According to a Business Insider February 18, 2018 article, Japan has a population of around 127 million people but seldom has more than 10 shooting deaths per year. The immediate reason is extraordinary strict gun control laws that demand good mental health and good reason for owning a gun. But there is a more pertinent reason that is native to the Japanese culture – a stress on community and the common good and a trust of leadership that keeps this national focus.

It is this latter factor that informs the strict gun regulation. This affirms that in a democracy where the citizenry is viewed as innately worthy and the community's common good is the goal of living there is a civilizing character that precludes the need for private gun ownership other than for limited hunting rights. This underscores the need of America to complete its transition from individualism to communityism. Democracy can only become actualized when this transition is completed. The old west must finally die if the new America is to finally live.

The Second Amendment

The states of the new nation America were very guarded about their rights. Fresh from a revolution against British despotism, there was lingering fear about a federal government exerting repressive powers over state and individual rights. In response to a call for further clarification about these issues, the Bill of Rights was devised – the first ten amendments to the constitution in 1791.

Amendment II had to do with clarifying the right to bear arms. Its text reads:

A well regulated Militia, being necessary to the security of a free state, the right of the people to keep and bear arms, shall not be infringed.

Militias were the military groups that the individual states called forth to protect themselves from perceived threat. It was militias that formed the early armed rebellion against the British. And, although the new federal government had the constitutional right to raise an army, the state's militias were the most likely source for this to happen.

The word construction of the amendment makes it obvious that the right of the citizenry to bear arms was based on the necessity of having well-regulated state militias. In addition, there were animal threats, the need for hunting to provide meat for households, and relationships with some Native Americans were not peacefully secure. Other than cities, the nation was still a primitive environment. There was ample reason for possessing a weapon. Other than for hunting, none of these issues exist in modern America. Thus, the interpretation of the amendment to justify acquiring arsenals with enormous killing capacity is without justification. Such clearly reveals other more devious motivations for this outdated interpretation.

Conclusion

The reality of American history is that strong government has made it possible for the nation to create the blessings of a civilized democracy which is the same as the blessings of a rewarding community. It is the only factor that has kept economic imperialism at bay in its attempt to totally control America for its exclusive benefit.

In any attempt to counter that which threatens democracy it is imperative to name the real enemy. To name a false enemy subverts citizenry focus and the real enemy becomes even freer to pursue its goals. Government is not the enemy. The enemy is that force which would use government for economic benefit at the expense of the common good, namely, economic imperialism which is the same as unrestrained predatory libertine capitalism.

OF, BY, AND FOR

Democracy was created of, by, and for the civilized living of the people and not for the uncivilized subterfuges of economic imperialists.

13

CLASS AND HUMAN NATURE

One basic question that faces a democracy is whether such a way of governing can exist and still be socially structured with unequal economic classes. Actually, the question is far deeper: Can any large and growing human society exist without class structures? The philosophy of communism asserts the necessity of a classless society but has never been able to move any of its national experiments beyond acts of sustained brutal despotism. And while democracy has been able to raise the level of equal opportunity and relationship it has never been able to do anything beyond maintaining the class structure.

Is Class Division Natural?

George Orwell was a respected 20th century British journalist, novelist, and critic who championed social justice and opposed totalitarianism. His study of history brought him to this conclusion:

> *Throughout recorded time...there have been three kinds of people in the world,*
> *the High, the Middle, and the Low...even after enormous upheavals and*
> *seemingly irrevocable changes, the same pattern has always reasserted itself,*
> *just as a gyroscope will always return to equilibrium, however far*
> *it is pushed one way or the other. The aims of these three groups*
> *are entirely irreconcilable.*

Irrespective of the style of governance employed, economic classes of varied privilege seem to emerge and maintain themselves. And there are normally three—the upper, middle, and lower. Where there seem to be only two they are upper and lower. But some class structure will exist.

These classes have been defined in various ways metaphorically. At the end of the 19ᵗʰ century Lawrence Sutton won a contest offered by a British newspaper for the best definition of the middle class. He wrote:

Wearing overalls on weekends, painting somebody else's house to earn money? You're working class. Wearing overalls on weekends, painting your own house to save money? You're middle class.

Sutton's metaphor could be rounded out this way:

Never wearing overalls because you don't need money and somebody else is painting your house? You're upper class.

Economic classes seem to be a natural expression of social living where economic bartering is the method for exchanging goods and services. But whatever the reason for their existence, they will find expression in both despotisms and democracies. And this expression will be dramatically different. In a despotism classes can rarely be bridged. In a democracy classes can be bridged. And this incapacity or capacity to bridge will indicate the strength of the government. If this is true of history then the issue about class is the nature of its relating rather than the fact of its existence. It will be how class is addressed rather than how to make class disappear.

The Nature of Classes

In a despotism, the nature of class will be about the suppression of human rights and possibilities. It will be about the elevation of the rights and possibilities of the few over the rights and possibilities of the many. It will be about empowering the few to live off of the sacrifice of the many. It will be about maximizing the freedom of the few by minimizing the freedom of the many. It will be about ennobling the few by dehumanizing the many. It will be about destroying the bridges that exist between classes.

In a democracy, the nature of class will be a commitment to engender the quality of life of all the citizenry by a commitment to the primary intents of common worth, common good, and common rulership. It will be about elevating the rights and possibilities of the whole. It will be about empowering the whole through mutual sacrifice. It will be about creating and sustaining those freedoms that ennobles the life of the whole. It will be about equality of humanity. It will be about strengthening every bridge that causes the classes to relate in equality of worth and opportunity in commitment to the common good.

In an actualized democracy, classes may exist but they will not be barriers to relating or opportunity. They will be a reflection of the rewards of economic achievement and endowment but will not be as extreme as between prosperity and poverty. There will be struggles over the relationship between worth and achievement because despotism will always seek the defeat of democracy and the false division and elevation of artificial worth is one of its primary tools of destruction. Democracy will always be a work in progress to actualize its intents because despotism will always be a work in progress to achieve its intents.

Economic Imperialism and Class

Economic Imperialism is a despotism that will seek to maintain rigid class structures. The people will be maintained in grades of class worth, depending on their economic benefit to big business. Distributions of power, privilege, and pay will be distributions of assigned worth status. The less is the worth status the greater is the utility status. Thus, when economic imperialism controls government, the middle and lower classes are always the utility servants of the upper class.

These grades of worth are exemplified in how the classes are treated in the midst of national economic crisis. If the metaphor of treatment were a rescue at sea, the upper class would immediately be pulled into the lifeboat and given full care; the middle class would be promised a life preserver when available; and the lower class would get a shout: "We hope you know how to swim!"

Eugene V. Debs was an eighteenth and nineteenth century American socialist, unionist, and political activist. He once pointed out:

The class which has the power to rob upon a large scale has also the power to control government and legalize their robbery.

Consider the history of class relationships in the late eighteen and early nineteen hundreds in America. It was a time when a small group of wealthy and powerful members of the upper class ruled the nation. And it was a study in the suppression of the lower class into various forms of economic and social slavery for corporate profit taking. It was a time when these so-called Robber Barons controlled both law enforcement and the military and used them as their private soldiers. They had minimal concern for the well-fare of either of the lower classes. Their only concern was maximizing profit. And they wanted no government interference in this pursuit although they were willing to use government agencies to facilitate this purpose.

As the 18th and 19th century British essayist and journalist G.K. Chesterton observed:

The poor have sometimes objected to being governed badly; the rich have always objected to being governed at all.

One reason economic imperialists eschew the common good is because it requires tax dollars to sustain. And economic imperialism is loath to pay tax dollars for any reason except its own potential profit because it views itself as the highest good. Moreover, the common good is an ethic of democracy and economic imperialism has no concern for either ethics or democracy. Its only concern is for the maximum profit afforded by non-restraint, irrespective of negative outcome to the lower classes.

Deceit and Code Language

The goal of the economic imperialist is to achieve a sufficient bank account in order to become part of a superior and privileged upper class. To minimize the negative face of this ambition, economic imperialists have grown shrewder about how they present their agenda to the public, such as imaging themselves as advocates of public good. They spend inordinate sums on advertising to create this false face. Energy companies are prime examples. They position themselves as champions of public benefit that are heavily invested in alternative sources of

131

energy. While they are doing so they are working diligently to get rid of all government agencies that would hinder their destruction of the environment in finding and exploiting sources of fossil fuel for the sake of a greater profit. This contradiction is an act of deliberate deceit.

The economic imperialist uses code language to normalize unethical behavior. Lying is called having misspoken, a discordant note, a disconnect, or being misunderstood. Corruption is called mistaken behavior. Expressed hypocrisy can be undone by "walking back" the revealing statement or simply denying its obvious original interpretation.

There was a time when economic imperialists were openly contemptuous of the other classes of the citizenry and arrogantly honest about this posture. They unabashedly enlisted the help of law enforcement and the military in violently putting down any attempt by the working class to improve its economic lot. They did not care what the other classes thought of their behavior.

In the late nineteenth century, a reporter of the Chicago Daily News interviewed William K. Vanderbilt of the New York Central Railroad. The reporter asked if Vanderbilt ran his trains for the benefit of the public. The reply was: "The public be damned!" Further remarks from Vanderbilt indicated that the railroad was run for the sake of corporate interests and if the public benefited it was a residual effect. This captures the intent of economic imperialism, irrespective of the century of its existence. Its paramount self-interest remains both static and pervasive.

The economic imperialist sees America's middle and lower classes, whatever the domain, as subservient to business interests. They are cheap labor to be utilized for profit.

Class and Politics

Humans have inevitably divided classes according to economic status. The upper class is viewed as the wealthy class. The middle class is viewed as fairly well off economically. And the lower class is generally viewed as in destitute economic condition. People move between classes based on these perceptions.

It is both a mistake and an injustice to assume that the entire upper class is an enemy of the other two classes. Certainly there is a large portion of the upper class which is devoted to economic imperialism. But there are also a large number who are committed to the intents of democracy. In the same manner, there are large portions of the middle and lower classes that hold conservative political views and vote accordingly. The classes are a mixture of political views.

This means that political views cannot be assigned to people based on their class without engaging in false stereotypes.

OF, BY, AND FOR

Democracy was not created to benefit any specific class of society. It was created to benefit all the citizens irrespective of class because it is of, by, and for the people.

14

DEMOCRACY AND SOCIALIZATION

In 1776, congress tasked Thomas Jefferson, John Adams, and Benjamin Franklin with designing a national motto and seal. While the image of the seal was plagued with differences of opinion and took several different committees and years to reach agreement it was eventually adopted: An American Eagle with one talon clutching 13 arrows and the other clutching an olive branch. Its original meaning was a complex of ideas reflecting the values of the founding fathers. A simple meaning is that of thirteen united states with the stability of peaceful interaction.

Diversity in Unity

However, the motto enjoyed instant agreement and adoption: *E Pluribus Unum*—which is Latin for from many, one. This was a strong declaration of unity despite all diversity—a unity that transcended the individual sovereignty of separate states—the strength of commonality—the United States of America.

The United States of America is a radical diversity of geography and corresponding lifestyles, contentious racial perspectives, varied sexualities, differing religions, and opposing views of reality. How is *E Pluribus Unum* possible given such conflicting differences? What empowers diversity to become unity?

The Answer

The answer to that question is a way of seeing that transcends difference. It is the gathering of these differences into a common eye—the democratic vision. The lens of this eye affirms the citizenry's equality, intends the citizenry's common good, and requires the citizenry's voice and vote.

It is this way of seeing that is the covenant that creates, nurtures, and sustains democracy. It is this way of seeing which heats differences in the social pot and melts them into unity. It is this way of seeing which demands *E Pluribus Unum*.

It is the failure to see through this eye that empowers the destruction of unity.

The Common Good

There is another Latin phrase which denotes the democratic intent of the common good: *Unus pro omnibus, Omness pro uno*. The translation is: One for all, all for one. It was made famous in 1844 by Alexandre Dumas's historical novel *The Three Musketeers*. In this tale the phrase was often repeated as the motto to which a group of French musketeers swore allegiance. It was the source of their strength and ability to overcome opposition. Through its dedication they radically compounded their capacities and confounded their enemies.

It is this phrase that captures the conscience of democracy—a common devotion to a common well-being—the common good. While *E Pluribus Unum* captures the vision of democracy which is a unity that transcends state rights, *Unus pro omnibus, Omness pro uno* captures the motivation of democracy which is the synergized empowerment of devotion to common purpose.

Democracy is never actualized in any significant measure without devotion to the common good—which is the same as devotion to *Unus pro omnibus, Omness pro uno*. When there is a unified aura flowing from the capitals of the states and the nation that radiates this devotion, an actualized democracy will exist.

The Ownership

What denotes the citizen's ownership of government is its right to voice its opinion, debate its differences, and vote its directions. These directions make the democratic vision a reality in fact beyond its written documents. This means that all voices get heard and considered as part of the public forum—even though they might be in opposition to the very vision that legitimizes their opinion. It is this ownership that em-

135

powers the people with the courage to both think differently and speak differently and, thus, provoke the nation's evolution toward a more fulfilled democracy. This is the citizenry expressing its common worth in pursuit of its common good with a common vision.

Social Is Plural

The common good is always about what is best for the whole beyond the part. It is, literally, of, by, and for the people. People is plural. It is the entire citizenry. Thus, it is profoundly socialistic in character in its governing because democracy is essentially a community enterprise. This is so whether the government is local, state or federal or the uniting of all three geographic units into the United States of America.

The problem is that the people find it difficult to grasp the notion that a democratic society is totally dependent on social programs that are mutually supportive and blend in unity for common good purpose. The reason is that grasping such a notion requires admitting the essential falseness of individualism which has been an adored core of American folklore—the more rugged the better. But historical truth is the opposite. It was not the individual that settled the east or won the west. It was the community. All civilizing is a social enterprise. All human progress is social advancement. The individual, while instrumental, always works within the social whole. Individual stories are single strands woven into the tapestry of the total community story. Social is plural.

The Bogus Claim

Understanding the distinction between political socialism, capitalism, and social programs is imperative to understanding democracy.

- In political socialism the means of production and distribution of goods is owned by government.
- In capitalism the means and distribution of goods is owned by private enterprise.
- The word social simply means groups of two or more people relating together—usually with shared purpose.

136

Social programs, whatever their nature, are those designed to benefit groups of people, whatever their size. When applied to a nation its population is the total social community.

The term bogus originated in the early 1800s. Its reference was to a machine that created counterfeit coins. It quickly became a reference for anything that was fake, phony, or false. To equate social programming designed for the common good with political socialism is bogus. The difference between the two is critical. Social programming is a means of achieving the common good. In socialism the government determines both the nature of the common good and how it will be fulfilled. In a democracy the people, through their representatives, make these determinations. Social programming, like capitalism, is a tool of governing, not a way of governing.

Equating socialism and social programming is another major deceit economic imperialists use to masquerade their own undemocratic despotism. The deceit is intended to identify common good programs with the perceived evils of communism which the economic imperialist falsely equates with political socialism. In his September 24, 2019 speech to the United Nations, this was a false equation Donald Trump made in his attempt to legitimize economic imperialism and downplay democracy in his dismissal of globalism and the glorification of nationalism. Whether this confusion was deliberate or an activity of ignorance is immaterial. It was an act of deception designed to create a false relationship between democratic programming and despotic rule. When common good programs are trashed as political socialism it inevitably comes out of the mouth of an economic imperialist whose only concern is despotic profit making without regard to truth.

Social Programming Examples

A graphic example of social programming in American democracy is the nation's transportation infrastructure. Aside from turnpikes, the moment citizens drive off private property they are almost entirely on government built and maintained roadways (city, county, state, federal). The people's freedom of movement relies on this system. And the nation's private enterprise is totally dependent on it for success. What libertine capitalism seeks to do is convert this system into a profit making venture for entrepreneurs and disguise it as private enterprise when, in reality, it is funded by tax dollars that intend the common good. It is a social program and not socialism. It is funded by the citizenry to benefit themselves.

Another example is airports. Aside from their value to the people they are important to private enterprise. It is from their runways that American business launches its goods toward both domestic and international markets. It is from their runways that corporate jets take entrepreneurs to their destinations. It is a social program and not socialism.

Take away the roadways and airports maintained by government, which means social programming, and capitalism in America would collapse. Imagine driving on any road in America without the presence of delivery trucks—whether for goods or services. Imagine timely transcontinental and international goods delivery without airports.

Social Is Public

One legitimate euphemism for social is the word public—which means the total community of citizens—the larger national social group—the people. Consider this very short list of examples of public programs that are, in reality, social programs designed to enhance the common good:

Public transportation (roadways, airports, buses, light rails, subways, ells, etc.)

Public education (grade one through high school, state universities, subsidies, loans, veterans benefits, etc.)

Public medicine (Medicare, Medicaid, Affordable Care Act, medical research, The National Institute of Health, The Center for Disease Control and Prevention, The Veterans Administration, etc.)

Public retirement (Social Security, all federal employees – including political servants and the military)

Public farming (government subsidy programs)

Public law protection (Homeland Security, Police, Detectives, Sheriffs, Highway Patrol, Federal Bureau of Investigation, Central Intelligence Agency, Bureau of Alcohol Tobacco and Firearms, Marshals, Customs,

Immigration and Naturalization, Army, Navy, Marines, Airforce, National Guard, Coast Guard, etc.)

Public international protection (treaties, trade agreements, military pacts, national alliances, etc.)

Public financial protection (Federal Deposit Insurance Corporation, Federal Reserve Board)

Public water protection and energy (purification, dams, electrification, EPA)

Public Safety Agencies (Occupational Safety and Health Administration, Food and Drug Administration, Federal Aviation Administration, US Department of Agriculture, National Highway Traffic Safety Administration, National Aeronautics and Space Administration, Consumer Product Safety Administration, etc.)

Public equality (race, gender, disability protection)

Public research and programs (science, aerospace, oceanography)

Public international protection (seas, outer space, treaties)

Public currency (a common monetary barter system)

Public welfare (aid for the economically disenfranchised, legal aid services, Children's Health Insurance, etc.)

Public housing (Fanny Mae, Freddie Mac, fair housing laws, subsidized housing)

Public subsidy of cities (transportation, parking, law enforcement, housing, roads, etc.)

Public land (city and state parks, national parks and monuments)

Public justice (common laws, court systems, jails, and prisons)

Public assistance (disaster relief and state subsidies)

Public municipal, state and federal governments (public ownership and maintenance)

This is only a sample listing out of over 450 federal agencies that provide services to the citizenry. For a more complete listing add to these the public service agencies from all 50 states and the cities of the nation. In brief, without public/social programs provided by government there would be no democracy or civilized living in America. And, secondarily, capitalism could not survive or thrive. To refer to such social programs as socialism is either an expression of gross ignorance or gross deception or both. They are owned by the people and designed for their common good benefit.

Self-deception

One irony of a social democracy is that, often, those who benefit most from government programs are those who make the loudest negative noises about the taxation and expenditures required to create and sustain these programs. These are the same people who have been persuaded by economic imperialists to demand least and weak government. Consider what would happen to all the public service programs just listed if they were under the guardianship of weak government.

In its unwitting but obvious commitment to the self-interest of individualism, citizens easily take on the welfare posture that wishes for all the benefits of strong government without having to either pay for them or acknowledge their necessity. Such contradictory posturing could be seen for the self-deception it is if there was a strong national commitment to civics and American history as focal to all levels of the nation's education system. Anyone with a reasonable understanding of democracy could not be deceived by appeals for weak government.

The Common Good

A democracy cannot exist without social programs supportive of the common good. Despite what some capitalists might say, they are totally dependent on such programming for both their own existence and success as well. No corporation is an island.

What economic imperialists are opposed to are expenditures that would serve the larger common good without fundamentally serving the monetary interests of the capitalist. The common good, as a grounding tenet of democracy, is of no interest to economic imperialists except as it benefits their profit making. It makes no difference what the issue

140

or how destructive it might be to either democracy or the environment, the economic imperialist will always make decisions in favor of profit making. What economic imperialists wish for is government by a United Corporations of America. They wish for UCA to replace USA.

Capitalizing the Good

To capitalize is to make subservient to the profit making goal of capitalism. The goal of economic imperialism is to capitalize every government program designed to benefit the common good. And for every common good program that is capitalized, the public will pay a heavy price in both cost and corruption. The end result will always be higher profit for private enterprise and higher taxes for the general citizenry with lower quality and less common good result. When economic imperialism prevails, we no longer have free enterprise. We have government subsidized enterprise. Rather than democracy, we have capitalized socialism.

One example of the gradual capitalization of a normal American social program is the permission given to private enterprise to take over tasks normally performed by the military. While war can hardly be called a common good program, the sustaining of the military to protect the nation can be so classified. And when the nation's existence is threatened the standing military as a common good program is verified.

Since the World Trade Center Twin Towers disaster of 9/11 this has been a creeping process in the unprecedented sustained Iraq/Afghanistan war. It has been enormously costly due to the hiring of private contractors to pursue the war. It is difficult to find concrete confirming data but some estimates for private contracting is at least 2 billion dollars per week. Private contractors greatly outnumber actual combat troops with estimates being over a quarter of a million. The total cost of this privatizing since 9/11 is supposedly over a trillion dollars and rising. Moreover, this private sector is reputed to be undisciplined, unaccountable, often amateurish, and lacking in any overall game-plan supervision by the American government. It is a gigantic and irresponsible economic boondoggle. And congress is responsible for both its funding and lack of oversight.

When there is discussion about withdrawing troops from this war, it is only the tip of the iceberg and has no real meaning unless the private contractors are also withdrawn. But the economic imperialists in America wish to continue this monetary windfall by totally privatizing the war at cost estimates of 5 billion dollars per year. But this could hardly be accurate if that is the present cost for private contracting for only a few weeks. This is a typically low ball estimate which would immediately escalate if the government were to be foolish enough to permit to happen. Economic imperialism seeks to insinuate itself into every aspect of American life through privatization for the sake of profit. And we citizens pay heavily for their every success.

Conclusion

Nothing is more anti-democratic than economic imperialism because it places private economic gain above common good gain and private enterprise above the community. It capitalizes democracy by making both its citizens and its programs economic pawns. American democracy wishes for a strong economy that elevates the common good. It supports a thriving capitalism. However, a strong capitalistic economy that demands a weak democracy is only good for promoting forms of despotism.

Franklin D. Roosevelt, in a speech to Congress in 1938, speaks to what supplants democracy when the people allow it to be usurped by private interests:

The liberty of a democracy is not safe if the people tolerate the growth of a private power to a point which it becomes stronger than their democratic state itself. That, in essence, is fascism—the ownership of government by an individual, by a group, or by any other controlling private power.

In this observation Roosevelt was both reviewing America's immediate past and, unwittingly, foretelling the future plight of American democracy. The only issue is how far a nation need go until it actually conforms to economic fascism which is the same as conforming to despotic leadership—whether apparent or disguised. When the well-being

142

of corporations takes precedence over the common good of the citizenry then fascism has arrived. When the nation's president unabashedly speaks and behaves economic imperialism in a manner derogatory of democracy, then fascism is in the nation's cat-bird seat.

The Danger

In the game of chess, there are pieces called pawns which are means to enable the queen to win the game. In democracy, capitalism is a means pawn of democracy. The danger of capitalism becoming more than a means is pointed out by American President Thomas Kirkman to a Russian diplomate in the television series Designated Survivor:

There is nothing more dangerous than a pawn that thinks it is a queen.

But this is the desire of the economic imperialist—to be the queen with all other pieces on the board its servants.

OF, BY, AND FOR

Democracy was not established of, by, and for a segment of the upper class nor the economic imperialist. It was established of, by, and for all the people of all of the classes which means all the citizenry—the public.

15

RECOGNIZING THE ECONOMIC IMPERIALIST

According to a March 2019 issue of Forbes Magazine there are 607 billionaires in America more than any other country in the world. And, according to a March 2019 report in the New York Post, there are 11.8 million households in America with a net worth of over one million dollars.

Despite this impressive economic array, most of the wealth of America still resides in the bank accounts of a fraction of 1% of the population. And all of these accounts have been amassed through capitalistic ventures.

The Critical Question

Behind this amassing is a critical question: How do we know when a capitalist has turned from democracy to the dark side of economic imperialism? How do we know when a capitalist has ceased serving democracy and uses it as a means of profit making? Here are seventeen hallmark warning flags:

- **Taxation:** They seek to avoid fair taxation by the nation that sustains them and is responsible for both their existence and wealth by resorting to both national and international tax havens to hide their real profits.

- **Bribery:** They expend inordinate amounts of money bribing government officials and elected representatives to pass laws favorable to profit taking irrespective of possible harm to the public good.

- **Bail Outs:** They work to become viewed as so integral to the nation's economy that when they fail financially because of some venture designed to bilk the public of its resources that this very public will bail them out so they can initiate new bilking ventures.

- **Deregulation:** They will try, through any means possible, to have their business deregulated so they can dig deeper into the national and international coffers for unrestrained profit taking.

- **Utility:** They will have no real interest in democracy other than as a utility for profit taking while simultaneously posturing themselves as democratic champions and integral to the public good.

- **Finagling:** They will finagle unneeded government financial subsidies and inflate government contracts while railing against Big Government waste.

- **Privatizing:** They will fight to privatize government common good programs so they can suck deeper from the public teat.

- **Unconcern:** They will create business sites wherever in the world they can find the cheapest means of production and elevated profit with minimal concern for employee quality of life.

- **Employee Detriment:** They will design their business structure and benefit scales to minimize expenses and maximize profit to the detriment of employee well-being.

- **Deception:** They will glibly use fear and lies to convince the citizenry that all they are doing is for the public good rather than private profit.

- **Corruption:** They will boldly corrupt all that is within their reach for the sake of profit-taking and plead innocence when caught because they will see their behavior as for the social good which is their good.

- **Ethics and Morality:** They will ignore ethics and morality, seeking to normalize corruption as a business necessity and as a standard activity that supports good governance.

145

- **Beauty and Health:** They will have no concern for environmental beauty or ecological health except as such might elevate profit making.

- **Patriotism:** They will hail themselves as patriots saving the nation from welfare moochers even though they might be recipients of massive government contracts, financial benefits, and subsidies, which they will cleverly hide.

- **Democratic Subservience:** They will see democracy as the servant of capitalism and seek to lower the taxes of the wealthy while posing this as a benefit to the poor.

- **Secrecy:** They will operate as much as possible in a clandestine manner so as to keep hidden their real agenda, their real tactics, and their real profit.

- **Despots:** They will admire economic despots who excel at economic imperialism while competing to show they are superior.

Economic imperialists are America's modern Robber Barons with the American flag draped over their shoulders. The goal of the economic imperialist is to make government a profit making subsidiary of their business and to pick-pocket the citizenry's social benefits, bank accounts, and retirement plans. They will view public property as a field for private exploitation. In doing so, they will take every possible step to dismantle democracy in favor of a corporate oligarchy while naming this as contributing to American greatness.

The question the citizenry must begin asking is: Which existing capitalists and corporations are really economic imperialists seeking to use democracy to make profit and who have no interest in the people's common good?

Economic Imperialism in Action

When economic imperialism grasps the reins of government securely, it will do seven things as quickly as possible:

- **Business First:** It will assure big business of its welfare and security rather than looking to the pressing issues of democracy which the nation might confront.

- **Business Advocates:** It will seek to fill all consequential government positions with pro-business advocates who will guarantee the fulfillment of an economic imperialism agenda.

- **Business Protection:** It will convert agencies designed to protect the citizenry from corporate corruption and exploitation to protecting corporations from citizenry concerns.

- **Business Benefits:** It will enact tax benefits for the wealthy at the expense of the other classes while disguising their intent as concern for the lower classes.

- **Business Policies:** It will alter national and international policies to favor the profitability of big business.

- **Business Regulation:** It will use its powers and influence to deregulate business to whatever extent possible without any concern for public health or environmental destruction.

- **Business Lackeys:** It will promote the election of congress people and the appointment of federal court judges who will make decisions favorable to big business despite the intents of the constitution or harm to the common good.

Economic imperialist leadership will run the nation as a big business because profit-making is its devotion. The design will be of economic fascism. A model of this style of economic imperialist leadership is the administration of President Donald Trump. These characteristics are reflected in both himself and those whom he appoints as his personal representatives to fill various supportive offices. Rather than a loyalty to democracy and the citizenry, his demand is that all appointees express loyalty to him and his programs—which are those of despotic economic imperialism. His ultimate goal is to dismantle all programs that might inhibit the installation of an economic oligarchy in the seat of America's government.

An Example

A political example of fulfilling this goal has been his appointments to head the Environmental Protection Agency. This agency was created in 1970 with the intent of protecting the nation's environment from capitalistic exploitation and poisoning. Trump's first appointment to head this agency was Scott Pruitt whose record as Oklahoma's Attorney General was of many attempts to end EPA regulations of the fossil fuel industry through lawsuits. He resigned from this appointment amid multiple federal investigations of corruption. Trump's second appointment was Andrew Wheeler a coal industry lobbyist, an advocate of the fossil fuel industry, a proponent of pollution deregulation, and vice president of the Washington Coal Club. These appointments make it obvious that Trump's goal is to use the EPA to deregulate industry and open it to maximum exploitation of the environment. All his appointments convey this goal.

An example of environmental exploitation is Bristol Bay, Alaska. It is one of the pristine prime wild salmon spawning sites in the world. It also sustains a billion and a half dollar a year fishing industry and the lifestyle of a large group of Native Americans. For years Pebble Mine, owned by the Canadian company Northern Dynasty Minerals Limited, has sought to open the area to mine gold, copper, and molybdenum. The primary process for extraction would be open pit mining. Studies show that it would destroy a minimum of 3500 acres of wetlands, lakes, and over 80 miles of salmon streams. It would require hundreds of miles of dams, embankments, pipe lines, roads, and a port that would block waterways and destroy the ecology and watershed. Further, it would release up to 10 billion tons of waste with a catastrophic pollution fallout that would cover the entire area.

In 2014, the Environmental Protection Agency invoked a regulation in the Clean Water Act to stop the project. But, as of August 2019, the Trump administration has rescinded this order and the area has been opened to exploitation by economic imperialists. The reason for his decision is simple: An estimation of over 300 billion dollars' worth of recoverable metals from this mine. Profit will always take priority over environment or the common good for the economic imperialist.

A government of economic imperialism will reflect the character and goals of this kind of political leadership. This means leadership devoted to profit over people and anti-democratic values. Laws that protect democracy have no meaning or useful purpose if they do not fit this economic agenda. For the economic imperialist, when the issue is the environment, there is no concern about destroying the wealth of the present and future if the wealth of the past can be exploited.

The Use of Obfuscation

A primary tool used by economic imperialists to mask their real agenda behind a democratic mask is obfuscation. To obfuscate is to be-fuddle, to dissemble, to perplex, and to mask. It is to deliberately make obscure in order to hide what is otherwise apparent. The tactics of obfuscation are lies, half-truths, misinformation, distraction, deflection, public degrading of the opposition's social worth, character assassination, and frontal attacks. It is the use of smoke and mirrors to make lies appear to be truths and to hide the real agenda of economic imperialism.

The Walk Back

Economic imperialists will use obfuscation to craftily walk back any "miss-speak" that might reveal their true agenda and character. The goal of walk back is to cleverly reverse or undo a statement without admitting it to be a lie. Walk backs are masks to cover falsehoods. Economic imperialists use this tactic because truth for the economic imperialist is a utility to further their money-making agenda and has nothing to do with accepted reality or confirmed data.

This is President Trump's continuous tactic. During a press conference in July 2018 with Vladimir Putin in Helsinki, he indicated that there was no reason to believe Russia had interfered with the American 2016 election. Later he walked back this statement by saying what he meant was that there was no reason the Russians couldn't have interfered in the election. On another occasion, in October of 2017, he indicated that, unlike him-self, other presidents had not contacted the families of Americans killed in action. Later he walked back this assertion by indicating that he meant other presidents had not made such calls often enough. Such walk backs are the norm of his administration required by his incessant lying.

The Purpose

The purpose of obfuscation is to create diversions to hide the real goals of economic imperialist leadership. Those who use obfuscation surround themselves with supporters who also agree to its usage. In defending and perpetuating obfuscation these supporters indict themselves of the unethical and undemocratic character that stands behind its usage. They reveal themselves as either economic imperialists or their willing lackeys.

Economic imperialists have been with us throughout history. They have inhabited every culture. They have exposed themselves no matter the political drama. Whether the background is cold war or hot war; whether the issue is communism or terrorism; whether the focus is nationalism or expansionism; whether the policy is democratic promotion or democratic rights – the economic imperialist will have the same goal and exhibit the same character. Economic imperialists remain true to their nature no matter the circumstance. And by this devotion they are recognized.

The Psychological Goal

An elevated sense of social worth seems critical to the economic imperialist's motivation. And in this pursuit, what elevates profit, winning, or political empowerment will be seen as synonymous with what elevates self-worth. This is consistent with fascist leadership in world history.

This ego elevation need not be tied to the positive or the ethical since these are not important to the economic imperialist. It need only be tied to that ego inflation which the use of superior power enhances. For example, such empowerment is as easily accomplished by destruction as creation. If the economic imperialist fails in the goal of inflated worth through construction then success can be found in the empowerment of worth through destruction.

150

An example of this form of destructive empowerment was President Donald Trump's withdrawal of America from the 2016 Paris Agreement on Climate Change that had required years of negotiation to construct and included almost every nation in the world. For the economic imperialist, power is a self-worth aphrodisiac, no matter the end result of its wielding.

While those committed to the intents of democracy may find such behavior mystifying it is a norm for the economic imperialist. Their only issue of concern is the elevation of the ego which is the same as achieving the self-worth perception of top-dog stature. Whatever the cost, being the top dog will be a major driving force behind the economic imperialist's attitudes and actions. The means of achievement will be secondary to the achievement, itself.

Whether they are friends or enemies, economic imperialists normally admire one another for how they maintain control and gather wealth. They will either work together or combat each other – depending on the expediency of economic and image benefit. In a democracy it is easier to recognize when economic imperialists are being cooperative with a common goal. This is because of a demanding cultural openness and a responsible free press. However, internationally, this will be as hidden as possible because clandestine is their preferred modus operandi.

The styles and skills of economic imperialists might differ. However, their essential character of self-interest and personal glorification and their goals of empowerment and maximum profit at the expense of the citizenry are the same. The people they supposedly serve will only be utilities to flatter their ego and fulfill their economic and empowerment goals.

Image Laundering

Some of the worst economic imperialists in America's past have made their wealth by viciously planting their boots on the neck of labor —the lower class. The late 19th and early 20th century Robber Barons are examples. After becoming enormously wealthy some sought to change their public image from vicious entrepreneur to grand philanthropist by establishing foundations for public good. In doing so they intended to be renowned for the latter and not the former. Philanthropy is investment in some public good. For the economic imperialist it is a form of deliberate public money-laundering.

Andrew Carnegie is one example. He became exceedingly wealthy in the steel business and to achieve this purpose deliberately suppressed his laborers pay and working conditions. Upon retirement he set up the Carnegie Corporation which purpose was making philanthropic donations. He is well known for his contribution of public library buildings. Another example was John D. Rockefeller of Standard Oil. He established his foundation in 1913. He made his money through ruthless practices and creating monopolies that drove out lesser businesses.

In a democracy there are two primary issues that speak to the ethics of capitalistic money-making: How the money is made and how the money is used. The making and the using are an integrated whole and cannot be separated. Money made unscrupulously and spent ethically does not wash the money clean. Both halves of the equation must accord with democratic intent for nobility to actually exist. Otherwise, hypocrisy taints the whole. Showcasing the good half of an apple cannot uncorrupt its bad half—unless the purpose is true redemption. But such redemption by the economic imperialist is difficult to find in history except in fiction.

If entrepreneurs wish to be remembered for democratic nobility, they should make sure that they both make their money and spend their money with democratic intent. Otherwise, history will ultimately reveal them as hypocritical economic imperialists.

Taxation Revelation

According to an April 2019 report by The Center for Public Integrity in partnership with NBC news, the following companies paid no federal taxes in 2018: Amazon, Delta Air Line, Chevron, General Motors, EOG Resources, Occidental Petroleum, Honeywell International, Deere, American Electric Power, Principle Financial, First Energy, Prudential Financial, Xcel Energy, Devon Energy, Halliburton, Netflix, Whirlpool, IBM, Goodyear Tire and Rubber, Penske Automotive Group, Aramark, AECOM Technology, Tech Data, Performance Food

Group, and Arrow Electronics. All of these companies were profitable, earning in the millions or billions.

The ultimate intent of democracy is to promote the common good. Devotion to the common good is the same as contributing to the common good. The primary means devised for making a fair and concrete contribution by the citizenry is the payment of taxes in proportion to income. The same is true for business, whatever its size. If the common good is to be achieved and sustained then every citizen and every business must carry their end of the taxation log.

If paying a fair share of taxes is an expression of commitment to democracy and the common good, how is it possible for corporations to make millions and billions and pay no taxes without revealing themselves as economic imperialists? One answer is that they are taking advantage of legal tax breaks in the same manner that every citizen will in order to decrease tax burdens. But how is it possible that a citizen will pay taxes on an income of thirty thousand dollars while a corporation will pay no taxes with an income in the billions?

Here is one answer. Corporations contribute to the election of politicians who will devise tax laws that allow these corporations to avoid paying taxes through all manner of loopholes and breaks. In turn, these politicians are rewarded by these corporations with financial benefits that empower them to stay in office and look toward a comfortable financial future. It is economic imperialists supporting each other by passing financial benefits back and forth. This is a despotic transaction that thumbs its nose at the intents of democracy and attempts to convert the nation's purpose from the common good to corporate greed. The average citizen does not have the financial capability to buy politicians to distort democratic intent into private profit in the same manner. So, they pay taxes despite a low income.

Another obvious answer is that many corporations have a legal staff that is devoted to finding ways of hiding the company's real profit with the deliberate intent of elevating profit by not paying taxes. This is the means by which a corporation can divest itself of commitment to the democracy that sustains it. It is corporate robbery of the citizenry. It is evidence that a corporation's ultimate devotion is to economic imperialism rather than democracy.

Lack of Wisdom

While not paying corporate taxes does not necessarily make a capitalist an economic imperialist it does make that capitalist critically unwise in demonstrating support of the nation's common good. It implies greed over democratic responsibility. It denotes lack of appreciation for the citizenry whose own taxes make such corporate profits possible —such as creating and maintaining the transportation infrastructure. It shouts that financial profit is more important than fair play. It is a message that corporate profit supersedes the common good. Essentially, it postures one as an economic imperialist whether one wishes that label or not.

Not paying taxes when billions are made in profit may display economic smarts but it does not display democratic commitment. If a corporation makes billions and pays no taxes those with modest income who do pay taxes will see this corporation as without democratic principle or concern about democratic intent—as an economic leech sucking the common good life from the public body. And such a perception would be warranted.

Who Cares?

But what difference does such a citizenry interpretation make? To an economic imperialist conscience it will make no difference and provoke no response. However, to a democratic conscience it will make a profound difference and provoke remedial action. The head of an economic imperialist corporation could care less about democratic ethics and fair play and how it is perceived by the citizenry. It will always pay as little taxes as possible. However, the head of a democratic oriented corporation will care a great deal about democratic ethics and fair play and how the people view their real public image. The democratic capitalist will make sure that its government is supported with a fair share of taxes because its conscience will require it to do so. Actions still speaks louder than words and reveal true character. If a corporation cares about democracy beyond simply being a utility for profit making it will pay its fair share of taxes.

154

Who Is Responsible?

We citizens are responsible for this kind of taxation inequity. We elected the legislators who make it possible. If we don't like it then all we need do is vote out the corporate lackey politicians and vote in those committed to democratic principle and fair play. We are responsible because we are the voters. If we did our job with seriousness then those we elect would represent democracy rather than economic imperialism and all corporations would be paying their fair share of taxes in support of the common good.

Conclusion

It is not difficult to spot the economic imperialist. Their lifestyle is a constant revelation. They are easily known by:

*   Their hallmarks of behavior.

*   Their attempt to convert democracy into business.

*   Their use of obfuscation.

*   Their ego-need displays.

*   Their unethical money-making methods.

*   Their self-imaging as ideal Americans.

*   Their avoidance of fair taxation.

While economic imperialists seek to mask themselves as devoted democrats they are, in reality, despotic capitalists and will behave accordingly.

OF, BY, AND FOR

*Democracy was not established of, by, and for the capitalist.
It was established of, by, and for the people which capitalism
is intended to serve.*

16

THE MINI-MES AND THE MODEL

In the late nineteen nineties and early two thousands, there appeared a series of movies about a super-hero called Austin Powers. In these movies there is a clone of Austin Power's adversary Dr. Evil. This clone is only one-eighth the size of Dr. Evil but often exhibits extraordinary powers. The name of the clone is Mini-Me—referring to a smaller version of the larger evil power.

The politician and the political party are in a position to become the Mini-Mes of corporate economic imperialism – the smaller version enemies of democracy.

The Politician Mini-Me

Given those factors previously discussed that raise the red flag identifying the economic imperialist, it is not difficult to recognize those politicians who make their empowerment possible. Here are some types of support that make such politicians apparent:

- **Diminishment and Destruction:** They support policies and laws that legalize the diminishment of human health and the destruction of the natural environment for the sake of corporate profit making. Examples are permitting polluting enterprises to prevail over public health and safety and advocating for public lands to be converted into private enterprise usage.

- **Avoiding Taxation:** They support policies and laws that legalize businesses to avoid paying their fair share of taxes. Examples are tax breaks, loop-holes, and shelters that both minimize corporate taxes and allow them to be non-existent.

- **Scamming Subsidies:** They support policies and laws that permit business to scam the public through so-called government subsidies. An example is payment of subsidies to large farms and agribusiness that already make unseemly profits.

- **Bogus Contracts:** They support policies and laws that permit business to defraud the public through bogus cost-over-runs in government contracts. Examples are military contracts and cost over-runs that charge outrageous prices for services and items that could be purchased otherwise for a fraction of the cost.

- **Deregulation:** They support policies and laws that remove regulations from financial institutions that were designed to prevent the public from being swindled for profit taking. An example is repealing the Glass-Steagall Act of 1933 and undermining the Dodd-Frank Wall Street Reform and Consumer Protection Act of 2010. These acts sought to impose regulations on business to prevent corrupt practices that adversely affected the financial world and the citizenry. They both were enacted following historic financial crises initiated by business corruption that threatened the nation's well-being.

- **Common Good Capitalization:** They support policies and laws that advocate for the capitalizing of common good programs essential to democratic equalization. Examples are Social Security, Medicare, Medicaid, affordable health care, and the public school system.

- **Voter Suppression:** They enact procedures and laws designed to keep the supporters of the opposition party from either not voting or making their vote meaningless. Examples are stringent voter ID laws that make voting over-difficult or impossible for minorities, make convenient voting sites unavailable, make voting days working days, and support gerrymandering.

- **General Voting:** They support any law or policy that empowers economic imperialists and disempowers the citizenry.

158

This is a posture of willingness to violate their position of trust to the citizenry for the sake of their own economic benefit and secure financial future. Their voting record will mirror the goals of economic imperialism.

Why?

Why will politicians bow in subservience to economic imperialism when it is detrimental to the well-being of the general citizenry that elected them? Why will they withhold adopting a federal budget which punishes public employees as a means of pushing a political agenda? Why will they give tax breaks to the wealthy while the poor languish? Why will they support a health care system that profits corporations while leaving segments of the population unprotected from financial and physical ruin? Why will they bail out a Wall Street that robs the citizenry's retirement accounts and creates disastrous financial crises? Why will they resist enacting laws that support decent living wages for the financially depressed? Why will they remain silent when segments of the population are being ethnically trashed?

The answer to these questions is that they have already enacted laws that protect themselves from the problems and disasters their votes create for the citizens they represent. For example, they have safe-guarded wages, retirement plans, health care, and professional expenses. Thus, while the people suffer from their callous voting they remain insulated in a cocoon of legal self-protection of their own making. This induces further democratic callousness. It becomes a political lifestyle of sustained reward.

The Political Party Mini-Me

What applies to the individual politician applies to the political party. To identify alignment with economic imperialism only requires looking at how a party supports policies and votes on bills that elevate economic business interests over democratic people interests. Simply review the votes of the two major parties since the year 2000 and clear patterns emerge. Following are examples.

- **Suppressing Voting Rights:** One of the three primary intents of democracy is to ensure the right of every citizen to have their voice heard through their vote. In whatever ways a political party, on any geographic level, seeks to divest the citizenry of this right it favors despotism over democracy which is in alignment with economic imperialism.

- **Legalizing Bigotry:** When a party's leadership publicly avows that it will seek to negate any common good legislation or program proposed by a black president it has openly indicated that, along with economic imperialism, democratic intent is secondary to racial bias and political agenda.

- **Disregarding Democratic Intent:** When a party's political goals have little concern for the economic welfare of the lower classes, its disregard for citizenry equality and the common good matches that of economic imperialism.

- **Capitalizing the Citizenry:** When a party consistently fights against regulations that prohibit despotic capitalists from using the citizenry as a field of economic exploitation it has expressly indicated its alignment with economic imperialism's philosophy that profit takes precedence over people.

- **Making Health Care a Pawn:** When a party prefers citizenry health care to be a pawn of profit-making enterprises rather than a democratic common good obligation, it has made democracy a servant of capitalism and finds itself in accord with economic imperialism.

- **Villainizing:** When a party is comfortable with the use of cheap illegal labor to enhance big business profits while simultaneously posing these laborers as social villains it reflects the double-speak hypocrisy of economic imperialism.

- **Denigrating:** When a party's leadership deliberately trashes the worth of segments of the citizenry because of their ethnic background and the party makes no objection, it has already sold its soul to economic imperialism's dismissal of democratic intent.

- **Minimizing Morality:** When a party cuts programs that benefit those who live in poverty in order to provide tax cuts for the wealthy, that party has indicated a moral deficit that mirrors the heartless perspective of economic imperialism.

- **Winning as Paramount:** When a party breaks all historic congressional protocols in order to steal the appointment of a Supreme Court Justice that party has aligned itself with the ethically corrupt perspective of economic imperialists that the only issue of any transaction is winning.

- **Ignoring High Crimes:** When a party ignores and seeks to suppress information about potential high crimes by national leaders in favor of a unified political agenda of empowerment it has aligned itself with the anti-democratic self-interest vision of economic imperialism.

- **Suppressing the Press:** When a party is more concerned about indicting and suppressing a free press for revealing the truth than it is about exposing intrigues that threaten the nation's security and political health, it mirrors the fascist posture of economic imperialism.

- **Supporting Violence:** When a party consistently refuses to address the issues behind public shooting rampages lest they lose the financial support of the gun industry and its devotees, they manifest the same disregard for the common good and human life as economic imperialism.

- **Demeaning Citizenry Worth:** When a party endorses candidates for public office whose words and behavior deliberately demean the worth of other citizens for the sake of party agenda it endorses the lack of democratic perspective characteristic of economic imperialism.

- **Favoring the Wealthy:** When a party flagrantly favors the wealthy over the other classes in its tax proposals it is implementing the utilitarian greed agenda of economic imperialism.

- **Hiding Intent:** When a party seeks to keep hidden the intent and effect of legislation until after it has been passed, it reflects the secrecy that is fundamental to the devious and unethical manipulations of economic imperialism.

- **Corrupting:** When a party is willing to engage in unethical activity, deliberate lies, and disinformation to win elections it shows itself to have the same lack of democratic character as economic imperialism.

- **Making Democracy a Utility:** When a party uses military and intelligence agencies to undermine democratic progress in the international community in favor of facilitating profit for big business it is modeling the goals of economic imperialism.

- **Concealing Goals:** When a party tries to divest the Office of Congressional Ethics of its independence so as to exert control over its coverage, it has aligned itself with economic imperialism's devotion to hidden goals over democratic transparency.

America's politicians and political parties constantly make visible their support of or opposition to economic imperialism. They will mirror one or the other posture in every decision and vote they make. They self-declare.

A Prototype in Practice

A prototype is a standard example or an original model. Nothing in current American history exemplifies economic imperialism in organized practice as does the perspectives and initiatives of the Koch brothers industries and the various organizations they have created to openly reshape democracy into a government that exerts zero control over business.

Fred C. Koch developed a profitable oil refining process and company. After his death, two of his sons, Charles G. and David H., transformed the company into a multi-billion dollar industry that included agriculture, chemicals, finances, and electronics. According to a January 2018 report by Money, the Koch Brothers are among the ten wealthiest people in America. They are a part of that small percent of one percent that controls the wealth of the nation. Their corporation and its goals continue despite David's death in 2019.

The Allure of Libertarianism

Behind the business perspective of these two brothers is a political philosophy called libertarianism. Libertarianism espouses the total freedom of the individual in every area of life as long as nothing is done that is harmful to others. It believes individuals, left to their own devices, will naturally regulate their behavior in deference to the rights of others. Conservative politicians and economic imperialists find this philosophy appealing because politically it translates into minimal restrictions on personal and business behavior sustained by minimal government.

This philosophy may sound harmless but is misleading and deceptive. Here are three reasons why:

1. **Human Nature:** There is a dark side of human nature that totally resists such deferential treatment of others. This side can easily master personal motivation and behavior when left without deliberate social constraint. Humans do not naturally gravitate toward nobility. They gravitate toward where their taught vision points them—which can be noble or ignoble or agnostic. The philosophy of libertarianism is grounded in a false premise. It fails to account for either the appeal of human evil or the shaping of human environment.

2. **Community Boundaries:** There is no historical evidence that such a philosophy can sustain itself without the strong influence and clear boundaries provided by community. This is totally counter to its baseline claim that civilized society needs no such boundaries except those provided by individual whim. It is anti-community while using and depending on community to fulfill its agenda of self-elevation. It is a philosophical contradiction which makes it false.

3. **Historical Model:** There is no actual historical model that displays the validity of either the philosophy's premise or sustainability or any ethical or democratic outcome. The closest social/political model it can mirror is some form of despotism as exemplified in the outcome of economic imperialism.

Libertarianism claims a noble schematic that has shown no historical capacity to overcome the ignoble motivations of the individualism which is its ground. It naturally gravitates toward self-centered libertinism. And the unethical political skullduggery of its adherents underscores this conclusion. The philosophy seems only a justification for self-centered living that ignores all responsibility to community. It is a high sounding guise for the low dealing behavior of economic imperialists and other forms of despotism.

The Agenda

The brothers placed this philosophy at the center of their political activities. In 1980 David ran unsuccessfully on the Libertarian Party ticket as its Vice-Presidential candidate. On the other side of this failure the brothers decided to approach their politics from a different standpoint, namely, to use their resources to get politicians and officials elected who share their views. The larger end game was purchase control of local, state, and federal government with their vast resources.

To accomplish this goal they have created an array of organizations such as foundations and think tanks that promote radical conservative causes and Super PACS that hide their donor base. A mothership of these organizations is Americans for Prosperity which is devoted to the election of extreme right wing politicians under the guise of working for a free society. They are also supportive of groups like the American Legislative Exchange Council which advocates for no fines for industry pollution, no regulation of financial institutions, and no public education.

According to the many statements made by themselves and their created organizational advocates, their agenda includes the destruction of: National health care, social security, Medicare, Medicaid, labor unions, minimum wage laws, unemployment benefits, disaster relief, desegregation, public education, and public transportation. They work to repeal campaign finance laws, the Departments of Energy and Transportation, the Environmental Protection agency, the postal service, worker safety laws, global warming initiatives, emission regulations, and anything that regulates free enterprise. This is not surprising since their industries are reported to be one of the major environmental polluters in America.

Their ultimate goal is to have the states call for a Constitutional Convention the intention of which would be to change every aspect of the constitution that allows for regulation of business and intends the support of the common good. In brief, the aim is to remake the constitution into a document supportive of economic despotism.

They claim that all such goals are designed to create a free society which means to eliminate anything they perceive to restrain economic enterprise. In their view the only legitimate purpose of government is to protect individual rights which means business rights. In brief, they are committed to doing away with any governmental agency or program that restrains business or contributes to the common good.

This agenda just happens to reflect the agenda of economic imperialism—to reduce American democracy to a utility for unrestrained capitalistic profit making. Libertarianism's devotion to the personal freedom of individualism is the mask behind which they attempt to hide this ultimate despotic goal. And in this pursuit the only legitimate ethics are behaviors which are supportive. Here is just one example among many of the destructive end result of unregulated free enterprise of the Koch Brothers variety. In the September 24, 2014 issue of Rolling Stone appeared this statement:

According to the University of Massachusetts Amherst's Political Economy Research Institute, only three companies rank among the top polluters of America's air, water and climate: Exxon Mobil, American Electric Power and Koch Industries.

Libertarian philosophy offers no historical working institutionalized models that hint of democratic intent. However, economic imperialism finds itself emphatically modeled by the Koch Brother's Industry and all the attendant organizations and causes they support. And this model, while allowed by American democracy, is actually devoted to the destruction of all three of democracy's intents.

165

Conclusion

The bottom line is that the economic imperialist politician, party, and prototype will vote any measure that enhances their financial benefit. It is a quid pro quo transaction between them and their political and corporate sponsors. This is not a difficult transaction because their primary commitment is the same as the economic imperialist—personal profit and social empowerment above the common good—an assured comfortable economic future irrespective of negative impact on the citizenry.

Democracy is committing suicide when politicians, parties, and prototypes convert its purpose into profit making decisions—when they become the Mini-Me of economic imperialist leaders and corporations.

OF, BY, AND FOR

Democracy was not created to elevate the economic well-being of politicians, political parties, or prototype imperialists. It was created of, by, and for the common good of every citizen of the nation.

PART IV

THE BATTLE ENJOINED

17

A TALE OF TWO GOVERNMENTS

Two of the primary driving spirits throughout human history have been competition and cooperation. Here is a comparative list of a few of their opposing tendencies:

Competition	Cooperation
Self-centered	Community centered
Exploitative	Nurturing
Utilitarian	Relational
Secretive	Open
Divisive	Inclusive
Individual goals	Common goals
Exclusive power	Shared power
Individualism	Communityism
Imported worth	Innate worth

In terms of the combined governmental outcome of these tendencies, competition tends toward despotism while cooperation tends toward democracy. The outcome of these tendencies and their appeal has been that despotism has dominated human history with democracy being a politically struggling latecomer.

Democracy as Problematic

Democracy has been a problematic governing style which suggests that humans have far more difficulty cooperating than competing. This difficulty may stem from acquiescence to imported worth motivations and the nurturance of individualism. And it may be reinforced by the universal modeling of cultures characterized by such competitiveness. Spurred by despotic tendencies, the spirit of competitiveness continues to assert itself in interference with the spirit of cooperation.

However, in western civilization, there has been a growing interest in the benefits the cooperativeness of democracy brings to community life. But the experiments around the globe have continued to be problematic. The problematic issue is the unyielding spirit of competitiveness and all it exemplifies in the negative. This does not mean that competitiveness is inherently bad. It only means that, up to this point in history, the human enterprise appears to favor it over collaboration. Cooperation has been unable to harness competition's potential for good in a manner primarily beneficial to democracy.

The Character of the American Battle

It is this tension between the competitiveness of despotism and the cooperativeness of democracy that is the hallmark of American governmental history. This tension finds its symptomatic focus in innate human worth versus imported human worth; communityism versus individualism; and capitalism as a means versus capitalism as an end. This is the character of the battle between democracy and economic imperialism.

By the People

America's democratic government emerged from the American Revolution. It is government of the people, by the people and for the people. It sees through the eye of the equal worth of all citizens, a government designed to maximize the common good, and the citizenry being in charge by virtue of its voice and vote. It is exemplified in the intents of the Declaration of Independence, the Constitution, and the

Bill of Rights. Two of its triumphs are:

Engaging the Civil War that kept the nation united and which acknowledged the equal worth of the black population.

Overcoming the Great Depression of the 1930s that initiated programs affirming the common good and regulated corporate power.

By the Economic Imperialist

The competing government is the despotism of economic imperialism which existed for centuries prior to the American Revolution. It is government of the wealthy, by the wealthy, and for the wealthy. It sees through the eye of the inequality of wealth worth and a government designed to create maximum profit for the wealthy whatever the cost to the rest of the citizenry. It is exemplified in international colonialism. Two of its triumphs are:

The takeover of America by Robber Barons during the late 19th and early 20th centuries and the subjection of the middle and lower classes to the brutalities of their economic goals that inspired the Great Depression of the 1930s.

The control of the modern Robber Barons of Wall Street during the late 20th and early 21st centuries that led to the national and world economic crisis of 2008.

Manifest Destiny

While the citizenry waves the banner of democracy with enthusiasm, it equally gives its allegiance to economic imperialism without understanding their opposing natures. This dual commitment is apparent throughout American history.

The Renaming

The nation was born from the womb of European economic imperialism which attempted to exploit the resources of the new world through military enslavement by various nations. Through this colonialism Great Britain ultimately dominated the eastern part of what is now called America. While the American Revolution and our country's independence were intended to liberate our emerging nation from this imperialist exploitation we continued the same tradition in pursuing our own new future. We simply renamed it as Manifest Destiny – the notion that such exploitation was a divine right given to the new nation because of its white male European Christian cultural superiority.

The Imperial March

We began our own imperial march immediately following the success of the American Revolution, gaining all the territories that now fly our flag, through purchase, suppressive annexation, encroachment, or war – whatever was necessary and with no regard for the worth of non-white skin color. Purchase examples are the Louisiana Purchase, the Gadsden Purchase, and Alaska. A suppressive annexation example is Hawaii. An example of settlement and military encroachment is Florida. War examples are the deliberate destruction of Native American Indian cultures and the taking of their territories and the conquest of a great deal of the southwest and western territories via The Mexican American War.

How the Ute Indians were treated during this Manifest Destiny expansion is an example of economic imperialism's total disregard for the welfare of non-whites in its pursuit of greater wealth. The Ute tribe was made up of seven different bands occupying a territory that encompassed large sections of what is now Colorado and Utah, including smaller sections of northern New Mexico and Arizona. These bands migrated back and forth across this territory according to seasonal need and available resources. This was their lifestyle defined by their relationship with the land.

Two things radically changed this lifestyle. The first was the indiscriminate killing of the Ute population that stood in the path of the nation's migration westward. The second was the deliberate shrinking of their original territory. Beginning in 1868, a series of treaties with the United States government gradually decreased the size of this territory into three small isolated reservations occupying what was perceived as worthless land. This decrease was due to the consecutive breaking of these treaties by the federal government in order to accommodate the white population's pursuit of gold, silver, and land ownership. The greed of this individualism smothered any concern for the worth of this Indian tribe. Whatever the European population did to the Indian population was justified by the superiority of the white skin color and its mode of living over the red skin color and its mode of living.

The Monroe Manifesto

President James Madison issued what came to be known as The Monroe Doctrine in December of 1823. It warned other world countries not to interfere with American meddling in the politics of countries in our hemisphere. Its purpose was to reserve the hemisphere for American trade and influence. We sought to expand this control beyond the Americas through the Spanish American war by which we acquired control of Puerto Rico, Guam, and the Philippines. We strengthened this control by imperial schemes in Central America that led to the construction and control of the Panama Canal.

America has never hesitated to engage the devious plots of economic imperialism under the guise of Manifest Destiny.

The Civil War

In the midst of our economic imperialist expansion we engaged in the internal conflict of the Civil War. This was the first highly visible and decisive military battle between democracy and economic imperialism in American history beyond the American Revolution. Devastating and unimaginatively costly, it was a war for the nation's heart that showed how unrelentingly destructive economic imperialism is in its determination to make democracy a utility for profiting making. The focus was unity and slavery. Unity was about retaining our geographic national integrity and slavery was about acknowledging the black population's equality of worth.

Even though democracy won the Civil War it has gradually and insidiously lost the long-term battle to economic imperialism. Often disguised as the so-called American Dream, this imperialism has uncannily posed itself as the measure of the nation's success—replacing the relational scale of democratic intent with the achievement scale of economic success.

The irony of this war was that it was fought to simultaneously retain our unity and to do away with the most cynical and debasing form of economic imperialism that exists - slavery. However, the Union's winning of the Civil War was not the end of economic imperialism. Its continuation is symbolized by the southern states celebration of its Confederate legacy. This celebration is the historic symbol of America's on-going contest between economic imperialism and democracy for control of both the nation's heart and its government.

Symbolic Tenacity

The primary success of pre-Civil War economic imperialism in the south was built on the back of slavery and the cotton crop. After the Civil War the southern states continued their imperialistic enslavement by exploiting the black population through forced forms of social bondage such as share-cropping, menial labor, and other demeaning methods of servitude that announced their inferiority as a race. Some visible means of this forced bondage were violent intimidation by the Ku Klux Klan, executions, lynching, tar and featherings, castrations, false imprisonments, public humiliations and Black Code state laws which guaranteed that the black population would remain in economic and social slavery to the white population. Any attempt by members of the black community to express their sense of human worth beyond being servants to the white population was vilified, severely punished, and often ended with violent death.

A significant segment of the white population of the south has diligently sought to keep the imperialist spirit of this conflict alive—announcing their continued devotion to exploitative racism and libertine capitalism. The construction and adoration of statues of confederate heroes have become primary symbols of this tenacity of spirit. These statues are largely an early 20th Century phenomena constructed to celebrate the legacy of southern economic imperialism sustained by the suppression of the black population. They are monument masks be-

174

hind which are hidden a devotion to state's rights above the national good and white racism above citizenry equality. They are symbols of an American sub-culture that has yet to acknowledge being part of a unified nation or of vowing allegiance to the equality/common good platform of democracy. They thumb their nose at the law and the constitution.

A current irony is that many of these southern states, such as Mississippi and Louisiana, are in the top ten of those most dependent on federal money to sustain their state budgets. There is a gross inability to see how the United States of America makes it possible for the disunited states of America to exist and maintain a brag-able low economic lifestyle.

The Total Nation

However, this legacy of economic imperialism is a cultural inheritance of the entire nation and is not limited to the Civil War or the southern states. It was also manifested by the Robber Barons of the late Nineteenth and early Twentieth centuries in their brutal and indifferent economic exploitation of men, women, and children in northern factories and our country's westward expansion. And it continues through all manner of social and economic exploitation of people of color in states outside the south.

Economic Imperialism in Modern Times

Economic imperialism perseveres in pursuing its goal of taking over the government of America and enslaving its structures for profit taking. It has done so primarily through the commitment of large corporations, the bribing of elected political leadership, and the hoodwinking of an unsuspecting public through all manner of obfuscation.

In the first part of the Twenty First century this persistence has paid off in a highly visible manner. Economic imperialism has converted the Republican party into its own image and elected its own president by disguising nationalism, nativism, and populism as democratic imperatives and posing itself as the economic savior of the nation. Through

175

such deviousness it has been able to stack the Supreme Court and the federal judgeship with its devotees so that it can violate the constitution and suppress democratic opposition. The Republican party has become so subservient to economic imperialism it no longer has the ability to distinguish between imperialist political empowerment and democracy. It confuses the use of democratic structure and process with devotion to democratic purpose.

Thomas Carlyle, Scottish historian and essayist, avows that:

In the long-run every government is the exact symbol of its People,
with their wisdom and unwisdom; we have to say,
Like People Like Government.

I take this to mean that who we citizens elect as our political leadership is a reflection of ourselves. Consider two contrasting back to back presidential elections as examples of the citizenry's divided loyalties to democracy and economic imperialism.

The Obama and Trump Mirrors

Barrack Obama was elected president in 2008 and 2012. During these years he painted a visible self-portrait of concerns through words and actions of: Truth-telling, fairness, tolerance, empathy, family, public health, ethics, listening, humor, collaboration, pragmatism, humility, integrity, hopefulness, respectfulness, honesty, community, compromise, law observance, loyalty to country, diplomacy, equality, common good focus, fact theorist, and democratic allegiance.

Donald Trump was elected president in 2016. During his electoral campaign and first years in office he painted a visible self-portrait of concerns through words and actions of: Sociopathic lying, paranoia, intolerance, vindictiveness, sexism, white male racism, historical ignorance, hate mongering, hypocrisy, obfuscation, vulgarity, manipulation, bullying, avariciousness, theft, deceit, callousness, impulsiveness, corruption, utilitarianism, self-centeredness, perfectionism, being above the law, loyalty to self, illusions of grandeur, top-dog-ness, conspiracy theorist, and despotic admiration.

Never, in modern history, has back-to-back national leadership so glaringly and succinctly portrayed the differences and tensions between democratic intent (Barack Obama) and economic imperialism (Donald Trump) as it has in these two radically different presidential leadership styles. And if Thomas Carlyle is correct then the citizens who voted them into office can find their own devotions mirrored in the president they helped elect — as have all who have worked on behalf of their administrations. The legal system calls such support abetting.

These two different administrations graphically illustrate the current state of the historical conflict between democracy and economic imperialism in America. And what it mirrors is that present America faces a democratic crisis equal to that which initiated the Civil War. While the social focus is different the peril is the same and the outcome will be as decisive. Recognized or not, we are already in America's second Civil War. And it is with the same opposing forces and motivations as the first one. The only difference is that it is being fought with ballots rather than bullets. But its outcome will be as decisive in determining the nation's destiny.

Conclusion

That we were birthed of imperialism and expanded geographically through its Manifest Destiny label does not make it right or warrant its continuation. We could have expanded both southward and westward through more democratic means. However, whatever it's perceived past benefits, economic imperialism offers nothing for the future except the suicide of American democracy—just as it has from the nation's inception.

The choice we face is between an economic slavery that requires the suppression of citizenry worth and its common good over a democracy that elevates citizenry worth and its common good. They can continue to exist in embattled form as they have since America's birth. However, all the indications are that the longer the contest the more devious and powerful economic imperialism's control becomes. And its empowered hand beckons toward democracy's open grave.

Here is the reason: It remains true, as it has throughout history, that one cannot serve two masters. Sooner or later one will prevail over the other. As Abraham Lincoln understood:

A house divided against itself cannot stand.

For over two hundred years we have struggled with an economic despotism in our attempt to have a real democracy. It is time to end the struggle and institute the dream. The real American Dream is democracy. And it is obvious that this will not happen without a citizenry revolution.

OF, BY, AND FOR

If the government of America was founded of, by, and for the people then it is the people who are responsible for demanding that democracy become the reality of national life —even if it requires a citizen revolution.

18

THE ROAD NOT TAKEN

At the conclusion of World War II, America emerged as the most powerful nation on earth. Prior to this event the world had been largely shaped by the economic imperialism of the European nations—through nation subservience enforced by military power. With this emergence, America had an opportunity to replace European economic imperialism with the model of democracy.

And we have given aid to emerging democracies when it was in our political and economic interests—especially in Europe during the immediate post war era. We celebrate ourself as the world's premier democratic model. However, our actual long-term record is quite different. It has often been an expression of our own style of economic imperialism. This has caused us to become despised by those we have exploited. Yet, our self-image remains flattering because of hidden information and a selective history. We do not seem to be a nation open to our own story except when it favors such flattery.

Devious Designs

During those times since World War II when economic imperialism has been in control, foreign policy has been a devious design to increase the wealth of corporations. It has been a mask behind which exploitation was hidden in its march toward economic enrichment. Intelligence agencies and armed forces have been the ultimate tools of economic aggression in this game of exploitation. Policies have been reported as reality rather than their end results. In addition, other ideological devices have been used to further hide the goals of our brand of imperialism.

179

Mantras and Slogans

Exceptionalism is one such ideological device. It is the mantra of economic imperialism. It is a perception of national superiority. Exceptionalism is a perspective without a democratic heart. It is national arrogance. It is evidenced in Donald Trump's attacks on national leaders of European countries and his attempt to undermine the sense of equality inherent in collaborative partnerships and treaties.

America First is another example. As a slogan it has been around for over a century and been given different meaning and used for different political purposes. It was used as an isolationist slogan prior to World War I by President Woodrow Wilson to keep America out of that war. It was used as a slogan by his successor, Warren Harding, as an appeal to return to pre- World War I normalcy. Prior to World War II it was the slogan of the America First Committee in its attempt to keep the nation out of that war. Such isolationism translated into foreign policy is decisions made in total disregard of the welfare of other countries in the global community or how one's own country is affected by this community.

Donald Trump and Imperialism

America First is the slogan chosen by Donald Trump to kick off his presidency. He has endowed it with the character of economic imperialism. As such, it is individualism expressed as American nationalism. It assumes the posture of being the most worthy among nations. It is global swagger. It uses power to intimidate for the sake of undemocratic goals. It closes the door of immigration to those who do not fit a white European stereotype. It is an expression of national conceit and racism. It is disguised Nazism.

Donald Trump, the supreme economic imperialist, understands himself to embody America and, as such, is the first good. The second good are those who remain loyal to his leadership. Everyone else is a pawn or an enemy in the achievement of his ego needs and economic goals. All decisions made by Trump will be made in accordance with this prioritized scale of good. This is individualism played out through the nation's highest office. It is despotism with the flair of god-likeness.

What Trump represents is a graphic boldness of economic imperialist leadership without any pretense of democracy.

Foreign Policy Impacts

Prior to Trump, the pursuit of economic imperialism often converted American foreign policy into an aggressive suppression of the rights of other countries in order to profit America's libertine capitalists. The end result has been a continuous smothering of democratic intentions in other nations and the support of brutal despots – done with deception and deliberate hiddenness.

This been particularly apparent in South and Central America and the Near East. These economic aggressions are normally disguised as democratic reforms and protective programs for the purpose of precluding American public outrage. Following are two transparent, undisputed, and legendary examples that took place immediately following America's emergence as the most powerful nation on earth. They set the model for the global function of the new powerful America.

Guatemala

The United Fruit Company, an American corporation, was organized in 1899 and quickly began seeking to control the production and sale of bananas in Central and South American countries such as Columbia, Honduras, Costa Rica, and Belize. Nations where this happened were nick-named Banana Republics.

Guatemala was one of these countries. By the early 1930s The United Fruit Company was the largest landholder in Guatemala. The country's populace referred to this company as El Pulpo (The Octopus) as a description of its tentacled stranglehold on the nation's life. It was brutal and suppressive in its treatment of workers and totally corrupt in its relationship with government. It literally owned the country as long as it partnered with the current dictator—no matter how brutal or suppressive. Its only ethic was profit.

Pablo Neruda, Chilean poet and Noble Prize Winner, published a poem in 1950 which named this company's profiteering role in degrading the population's quality of life. He says in a descriptive verse about American corporations that exploited the southern hemisphere for profit-taking that Jehovah's trumpet blew and by this sound the delicate waist of America was reserved for the United Fruit Company. The delicate waist to which Neruda refers is Central America which houses Guatemala. He ends the poem by naming the suppression, persecution, and death of the laboring class inhabitants by the partnership of The United Fruit Company and the nation's dictators.

In 1951, Jacobo Arbenz Guzman helped overthrow Guatemala's vicious dictator with the goal of establishing a democratic form of government. He became its first elected president. He immediately sought to initiate common good programs that modeled democratic ideals. But this included a massive program of land reform that would undercut the United Fruit Company's control of the economy. The United Fruit Company began a derogatory public relations campaign, labeling him as a communist sympathetic to The Soviet Union and a threat to American domination in the Americas.

In actuality, Guzman was a committed nationalist who admired and was devoted to democratic reform. He believed communists had a right to publicly air their views but none held high office during his administration. If there was an opportunity to democratize Guatemala it was under his leadership.

Nevertheless, the Eisenhower administration (1953-61), using the CIA, initiated a coup (called Operation PBSUCCESS) that unseated Guzman and in his place established an American puppet dictator that brutally crushed all of the reforms and reinstated the United Fruit Company in the economic catbird seat in Guatemala. This was a blatant and aggressive act of American economic imperialism. It was a brutal corporate form of colonialism.

The brothers, John Foster Dulles, then Secretary of State, and Allen Dulles, then head of the CIA, both had special ties to the United Fruit Company. Allen Dulles was a board member of the UFC and John Foster Dulles's old law firm had represented the United Fruit Company's legal endeavors. In addition, President Eisenhower's personal secretary was married to the United Fruit Company's principle congressional lobbyist. And the United Fruit Company published a book called Report on Guatemala which claimed Guzman's reforms were planned in Moscow and circulated it in the US congress. This was an economic imperialist propaganda campaign that took advantage of America's fear of communism to promote its own brutal behavior for the sake of corporate profit-taking.

Marcelo Bucheli is a professor in the Gies College of Business at the University of Illinois. He has written or co-written multiple articles on government and business in Central and South America and often serves as a consultant in conflicts between governments and corporations in developing countries. He has authored a book entitled: Bananas and Business and is an expert on the role of the United Fruit Company in the region. He suggests:

The US multinational United Fruit Company has been considered the quintessential representative of American imperialism in Central America.

Unfortunately, the United Fruit Company's attempt to control a government for the sake of profit is not an isolated incident in America's intrusion in the affairs of Central and South America. But it does illustrate how historically and nakedly aggressive our support of American corporate interests has been in the area and how we have used obfuscation to cover this brazenness. This support has usually trumped all democratic considerations.

Iran

America has also constantly interfered in the politics of near eastern countries to avail itself of oil and control its pricing in disregard of their desires or well-being. Iran is an example.

During the years leading up to 1953, Mohammad Mosaddeq, an Iranian politician and reformer, championed Iranian nationalism with a strong perspective on ethics, fair play, and justice. It was obvious that if Iran were to actually experiment with democracy, it could be under his leadership. He admired democracy and fought corruption and British economic imperialism. In particular, he spent years trying to correct an unfair oil agreement with Great Britain which stemmed from World War I, without success. Through his influence, in 1951, Iran's oil industry was nationalized. Immediately following, he was named as the Premier of Iran. In 1952, Time Magazine named him Man of the Year.

But this did not suit either American or British economic imperialists in the oil industry. In 1953, the American CIA (Operation AJAX) and British M16 (Operation BOOT) initiated a plan to restore control over Iranian oil production. The plan involved the use of deceit, bribes, and mobsters with the goal being to replace Mosaddeq with a western puppet, Mohammad Reza Pahlavi. The plot succeeded with American and British oil companies gaining control of a large percent of the Iranian oil fields for their exploitation.

This deliberate act of economic imperialism set up the political turmoil and domino effect which eventual outcome is present day Iran – one of America's avowed enemies. When an operation has a long-term negative outcome the CIA calls it blowback. This 1953 plot is a prime example of American created blowback destructive to both an individual nation and world democracy. While our present focus is on what an evil player Iran is on the world stage, we totally ignore the fact that she is as much an American creation as her own.

Leadership Hypocrisy

Both of these imperialist subversions occurred during the political reign of Republican President Dwight D. Eisenhower. Eisenhower was an admired and respected World War II hero with a global image. As such, he had the opportunity to establish America's post-war image of world leadership. Ironically, when he was leaving office in his farewell address to the nation he warned America of the dangers of the military industrial complex – which was a joint alliance of defense contractors and the armed forces—a profit making activity of economic imperialism. In January 1953 he closed his Inaugural Address with these words:

Whatever America hopes to come to pass in the world must first come to pass in the heart of America.

In brief, he suggested that America must model whatever it hopes will happen in the world.

Yet, the not so hidden legacy of his presidency was the support of an economic imperialism that was destructive of democracy in other countries with the end result of a long-term downside for international democracy. It makes no difference the rationale conjured to justify these acts of aggression. They were deliberate attempts to unseat democratically elected leadership of other countries for the purpose of profit for American corporations. And they modeled American foreign policy.

Unfortunately, President Eisenhower is not a presidential leadership exception. This has been an irony of America's international politics since World War II. We have helped dethrone the democrats and enthrone the dictators for the sake of economic imperialism. This was glaringly obvious in Guatemala and Iran. The historical listing of America's support of vicious dictators for no other reason than economic gain includes: Chile (Pinochet), Cuba (Bautista), Saudi Arabia (House of Saud), Mbasogo (Equatorial Guinea), Idriss De'by (Chad), Manuel Noriega (Panama), Islam Karimov (Uzbekistan), Berdimehamedov (Turkmenistan). Among the long list of dictatorships America currently supports are Saudi Arabia, Egypt, Philippines, Turkey, Jordan, Vietnam, and Thailand.

Our attempt to help dethrone leaders of other countries whom we claimed to be pro-communist has generated support for a multitude of the most depraved and oppressive dictators in global history—none of whom would have been a better alternative to a communist despot.

Citizen Hypocrisy and Ignorance

It is right for America to be outraged over the apparent cyber interference of Russia in the American 2016 election campaign – an interference that appears to have determined the election's outcome in favor of the despotic rule of Donald Trump. To lack outrage and corresponding protection is to invite further violation. But on the other side of outrage this interference should remind us how other countries feel when we violate their elections. It should cause us to examine our own history of interference in the democratic process of other nations. Recognizing our own hypocrisy is a first step toward modeling internationally what we aspire to model nationally. If we expect other nations to see us as a democratic model for the world's nations to admire we must acknowledge our own duplicity and strive for the high road of democratic integrity.

The Real or the Ideal?

To assume that nations of the international community will follow our example and take the high democratic road requires that we know our own road history. Such information can only come through a continued commitment to a free press, historians who insist on truth telling above national propaganda, and an education system devoted to teaching our whole history rather than a selective history. The question behind these statements is: Are our children being taught about the American suppression of democracy in Guatemala and the deliberate establishment of a puppet government in Iran and other democratic violations around the world as a part of their history education? Are they being taught about our treachery as well as our heroics? Are they being taught the real America or the ideal America?

Omission as a Lie

On June 4, 1989 a student protest movement in China came to a violent head. The movement had started the prior May in protest over government corruption, the impact of inflation, economic disparity, and the death of a reform leader. They wanted democratic reform. It culminated in Tiananmen Square in Beijing when a protest by hundreds of thousands of students was brutally crushed by an armed military force using assault rifles and tanks. No one knows how many were killed or executed but the estimates are staggering.

It is illegal in China to mention this incident. It has been wiped from the history books. And if a current student in China is asked to name a significant incident that took place in Tiananmen Square the probability is that they will have no idea what that might be.

Whether China or America, the omission of significant historical incidents in a nation's history is as much a lie as a lie's deliberate telling. It is an attempt to create a false history.

186

Failed Education and Failed Leadership

In an actualized democracy, America would be the champion of democratic reform in any nation making the attempt irrespective of its economic impact on American corporations. Such championship would seek to empower the success of democratic reform beyond all such considerations. This ignorance of the nation's history and the inability to be the globe's democratic model could only stem from an educational system that has failed to teach both the nation's actual history and the fundamentals of democratic civic commitment. We cannot insist on other nations taking the high road when they see us taking the low road. Being hypocritical is beyond being embarrassed. It is failed leadership. And it is a failure that is essentially unrecognized within our own nation.

The Training School

It is notable that America has no renowned institute to teach nations around the globe how to be a successful democracy. But we do have a well-known school that teaches international leaders how to be brutal despots. This fact is a significant revelation of national duplicity.

In 1946 the US created a military institute known as The School of the Americas. Its primary purpose was to train Central and South American military leaders in so-called counterinsurgency—the school's euphemism for psychological warfare, kidnapping, blackmail, assassination, torture, abusive interrogation techniques, the use of fear and bounties, and targeting the civilian population. As of this writing it boasts of over 64,000 graduates from all over the world. Supposedly, it was to enable countries to repulse communist incursions. However, it has produced a multitude of dictators who excel in human rights abuse such as Manuel Noriega of Panama and Roberto D' Aubuisson of El Salvador.

In 2000 it changed its name to the Western Hemisphere Institute for Security Cooperation (WHINSEC) in order to diminish its negative image. With minor changes it continues to pursue its goal of training in human rights abuse and brutal anti-democratic practices.

America not only helps install anti-democratic dictators, it trains them in horrific anti-democratic abuse. And there is no highly visible political leadership that has called our nation to task for this democratic perversion and publically sought to shut it down as anathema to democratic perspective. This is how deep and instilled our international economic imperialist hypocrisy has become.

Conclusion

Given all of this, it should be no surprise to the informed to realize that economic imperialists have taken over our country. Prior to American imperialism was the British economic colonial imperialism that birthed our nation. Along with Britain were the other European nations that controlled all the world geography they could conquer. This is what economic imperialists do—use their nation's power to expand capitalistic profit making across the globe. And some of our closest allies have been imperialist nations that have lost their power to dominate world affairs and wish to soar in the economic tailwind America creates.

Of equal importance, it is difficult to admit that our small brand of individual me first economic imperialism has encouraged those with a larger brand to become empowered. And, at this moment in history, our nation is on bended knee before the throne of economic imperialism —its soul an indentured servant—with the citizenry being responsible because in our democracy we are empowered to make government our reflection.

OF, BY, AND FOR

Democracy was not established of, by, and for the American corporation. It was established to bless the people of our nation with the fulfilled relationships of equality, the achievement of the common good, and the empowerment of voter rule—of, by, and for the citizenry.

19

DESPOTIC DEMOCRACY

Given the fact that democracy and economic imperialism have battled for control of the citizenry's allegiance since the nation's birth, the question is how is it possible that such opposing ways of being could inhabit the same culture? This can happen because the liberty democracy grants to its citizens makes it possible for them to give their allegiance to that which is not in their best interests and even to that which will suppress this very liberty in the name of what the citizenry has chosen. Walter Savage Landor was a popular eighteenth and nineteenth century British poet, novelist, and social activist. He once observed:

Despotism sits nowhere so secure as under the effigy and ensigns of freedom.

And Herbert Spencer, a British Victorian era sociologist, anthropologist, philosopher, and political theorist remarked along similar lines:

If men use their liberty in such a way as to surrender their liberty,
are they therefore any less the slaves?

This is the irony of liberty. It is designed to allow people to determine their own destiny even though the destiny chosen may be the conversion of liberty into enslavement. And no nation in history has exemplified how well a nation can espouse democratic ideals while enslaving both its own citizens and those of nations around the world as has America. The conclusions of Landor and Spencer rose from their nation's own history, that of Great Britain—one of the world's exemplars of economic imperialism.

The answer to how it is possible that democracy and economic imperialism could exist side by side as embattled enemies is that the citizenry has both allowed it and encouraged it. Whether this is by deliberate choice or blind ignorance makes no difference as to outcome.

The Importance of Boundaries

Boundaries make it possible to determine ownership and prescribe the limits of behavior. Everything that exists is defined by boundaries that express ownership and the nature of being. Consider the boundary differences between democracy and economic imperialism.

Democracy is owned by the citizenry and all behavioral boundaries are designed to honor citizenry equality and the achievement of the citizenry's common good through citizenry rule. Economic Imperialism is owned by a wealthy oligarchy and all behavioral boundaries are designed to maximize profit for the owners and anything is permissible in doing so no matter its despotic nature.

Corrupted Purpose

Democracy is government by all the people. An oligarchy is government by a few people. Economic imperialism is an oligarchy. It is despotism. Despotism is rule by absolute and unchallenged authority. In America, economic imperialism is a despotic oligarchy disguised behind the democratic façade of capitalistic freedom.

It is possible for a democratic form of government to become despotic. The means of this conversion is to retain the framework of democratic function of the Executive, the Legislative, and the Judicial branches while changing the purpose of the framework. It can happen when a president appoints cabinet and agency heads who will support economic imperialism in fulfilling their respective responsibilities. It can happen when a majority of the House or Senate become advocates for economic imperialism and block democratic action. It can happen when the majority of the Supreme Court makes interpretations that fit economic imperialism rather than the original intents of the constitution. The structure of democracy remains the same while its purpose is corrupted.

In America's case, the purpose is shifted from achieving the common good for all the people to achieving a maximum monetary profit for a few people. This allows despotism to wear the face of democracy. This makes it possible for the citizenry to assume they are still in a functioning democracy when they are actually in a functioning despotism. This is how despotism can capture a democracy and remain hidden in plain sight. And this is what has happened in America. Economic imperialism actually rules while the people go through the motions of ruling and maintaining the illusion that it is of, by, and for them. David Hume, eighteenth century enlightenment Scottish philosopher, historian, and naturalist summarizes the puzzlement of this reverse in this remark:

Nothing is more surprising than the easiness with which the many are governed by the few.

This ease is both encouraged and facilitated by the citizenry's devotion to a scheme of imported worth and the whims of individualism that make them inviting prey for the goals of economic imperialism. Where the worth con and individualism thrive, economic imperialism will thrive. They are mutually supporting perversions of democracy that invite despotism. And the power of that despotism currently resides in less than one percent of those who control the nation's wealth.

The Apparent Con

While imported worth and individualism seem to remain below the surface of the nation's awareness as destructive cons, there is a con that should be apparent. It is the notion of economic imperialism that all public good is measured by economics. This con is translated into the deception that the health of democracy is gauged by how well the citizenry's personal bank accounts are thriving. This measurement is generally called achieving the American Dream. When election time rolls around the primal focus is inevitably about how well the economy is doing or how well a politician can change it for the better. Thus, the people are likely to vote based on this premise or promise.

Here is the ultimate irony: In order to secure what they perceive to be their right to achieve the American Dream, a large segment of the citizenry is prone to elect the politician who will make the grandest promise about its economic fulfillment. Such a promise being kept rarely has anything to do with the efforts of the politician once voted into office. However, it is this dollar sign promise that blinds the eyes of the citizenry to the relational meanings of democracy and to those politicians who actually represent democratic intent. So the citizenry continues to vote into office promising economic imperialists detrimental to their own best interest.

Their own best interest is a government that is devoted to those democratic intents that always maximize the citizenry's economic benefits as a result of maximizing their relational benefits—that of mutual worth affirmation and mutual allegiance to the common good. Economic programs designed for maximum benefit of the people will realize maximum economic benefit for the maximum number of citizens. Focusing on the common good is the only way the entire citizenry is economically benefitted on any sustained basis. Fair and profitable relationships are what encourage fair and profitable economics.

The opposite of this in both pursuit and outcome is economic individualism that chases after private goals without regard to community benefit or fair play. Wittingly or unwittingly, this quest becomes the slave of economic imperialism.

Behind the Con

Richard M. Nixon became America's 37th president in 1969. He entered public office in 1947 in California. In his successful campaign for the United States Senate in 1950, he acquired the nickname of Tricky Dick because of his unethical campaign tactics. History has shown that throughout his political life he embodied this nickname in both attitude and action. He was a con man who grounded his career on lies and deceit. To hide this he postured himself as the opposite of his real persona, namely, The Law and Order politician. This sham finally caught up with him in 1974 when what became known as the Watergate scandal publically revealed his true character. He resigned from the presidency rather than being impeached for gross violation of his oath of office.

Nixon's entire life was spent hiding behind a mask of deceit and whose nickname suggested what was behind that mask. Yet, the citizenry put him into the highest office in the land knowing what this nickname implied. Why would they do so? The seeming reason is because the notion of law and order had greater appeal during the cultural chaos of the Vietnam War era than did the appeal of democratic intent. But if this reason touches the truth it can only be symptomatic of something deeper.

I suggest the deeper reason was because of a general lack of that generation's understanding of the nature and intents of democracy. Behind this lack was the nation's failure to teach that adult generation a civic awareness of the democracy that grounded their political existence. There seems to be no other reasonable explanation for a citizenry that betrayed its own best interests in favor of electing a president that used them for the political empowerment of his own naked self-interest.

The question that confronts this current generation is whether it has also failed in the same manner. Has it allowed an economic imperialist president to gain the highest office in the land because it cannot discern between democracy and the despotic nature of economic imperialism? Has the failure of prior generations to actually instill a sustained democratic civic education in its youth caught up with the nation again? Have we permanently lost our democratic eye to that of the economic imperialist eye? Does the dollar eye now supplant the eye of old glory?

Robert M. Hutchins was an educator, President of the University of Chicago, Dean of Yale University Law School, and head of the Ford Foundation during the first three quarters of the 20th century. He once suggested that:

> *The death of democracy is not likely to be an assassination*
> *from ambush. It will be a slow extinction from apathy,*
> *indifference, and undernourishment.*

Such apathy, indifference and undernourishment are the result of a lack of sustained and clearly focused civic education of the citizenry on the intents of democracy. If the citizenry is to devotedly practice democracy they must be inspired to do so—which means they must be emphatically taught democratic intent in a motivating fashion. If this were the case then the citizenry would have no difficulty knowing that

194

their American Dream bread was buttered on the side of democratic intent rather than on the side of economic imperialism's economic promises.

Conclusion

What presently exists in America is despotism masked as democracy. If the people are tired of being the slave of a few then all they need do is wake up to their state of self-imposed servitude and rebel. To rebel means to take back the structures of democracy for the sake of the total citizenry and their common good. And the people are the only agent capable of doing so. We can continue being duped by the lies of economic imperialism or we can become enlightened by our own discernment and exercise our voting power. We can re-convert the structures of democracy to their rightful purpose and glory in its benefits. It is our choice.

OF, BY, AND FOR

As citizens, we can remain under the illusion that so as long as the structures of democracy are in place, democracy is in place. But the reality was long ago expressed by Mark Twain, one of America's most insightful political humorists:

We have the best government money can buy.

And the only government money has ever bought is despotism —which is never of, by, or for the people.

20

THE FRANKENSTIEN MONSTER

There are three heads of the Frankenstein monster that has helped transform American democracy into a state of economic imperialism. They are corporations, corruption, and complicity.

Corporations

The first head is converting the common good into corporate good. It is equating the welfare of business with the welfare of the nation. It is making democracy a servant to capitalism. It is assessing national health by the state of its gross national product. It is elevating profit over people. It is the Supreme Court giving the corporation ultimate power by awarding it the same rights as the citizenry and inviting it to control elections and the government with its unmatched economic resources. It is permitting the phrase "of the people, by the people, and for the people" to be altered to "of the corporation, by the corporation, and for the corporation."

Essentially, the corporation has become the reason for the nation's existence rather than democracy. And the purpose of the imperialist corporation is to generate profit with the government and the citizenry serving as its cash register. Its strongest government ally in this democratic perversion, aside from congress, has been the Supreme Court. Imperialists have managed to alter the balance of power on the court from those devoted to democracy to those devoted to economic imperialism. Thus, the corporation owns the federal government by owning a majority of its people's elected and appointed representatives and its highest court. In owning the oval office this ownership is complete.

Corruption

The second head is corruption. The root meaning of the word corrupt is to falsify and destroy. It is to change a purpose. In the case of democracy, it is to totally corrupt its original intent of pursuing the common good into pursuing the individual good and the corporate good.

This kind of corruption is not new to politics. In the fifteenth and sixteenth centuries, Italian politician Niccolo Machiavelli wrote books that advised political leaders about how to govern in a manner that divorced politics from morality. He summarized this approach in his most famous book: *The Prince.*

Machiavelli asserted that humans are essentially evil and will behave in a manner consistent with their peculiar version. Given this assumption, he was concerned with how to govern humans with the best possible social outcome. He suggested that the wise ruler will make decisions based on pragmatism and expediency. He avowed that the greater the absolute power of the ruler the greater the possibility of achieving good government. This suggests that the ends justify the means. The only morality involved in Machiavellianism is achieving the goal of a stable government in which the people will gladly acquiesce. If this requires deception, murder, or destruction, then, so be it because it is for the sake of the entire nation's well-being. He also suggested that humans are so focused on their immediate necessities that they are easily deceived by the wise ruler.

While supposedly to achieve a good for the total citizenry, this is an approach to government that justifies all the perversions of despotic individualism. In the recent past we had a national administration unabashedly devoted to this corrupting principle of Machiavelli and which saw nothing wrong with plunging the nation into a costly and unending war motivated by deliberate deception.

The worth of the citizenry, as expressed in the democratic goal of the common good, isn't simply a political goal. It is a moral goal that affirms the citizenry's worth. Morality and democracy cannot be divorced except at the expense of both. To divorce politics from the morality of human worth, as recommended by Machiavelli, is to divorce governance from democracy. It is to totally corrupt its intents and open them to despotic usage.

Complicity

The third Frankenstein head is complicity—that of the three branches of the federal government in this converting and corruption. This means that the majority of all branches of government have been consistently selling out a large measure of their power to economic imperialism by making decisions that converts democracy into a utility for profit-making rather than a mechanism for affirming citizenry worth and facilitating their common good. When any branch of government sells its soul to economic imperialists, its owner's wishes will be the first priority.

There are two end results. One is a minimally-regulated domestic capitalism that empowers the rise of modern robber barons and their control of the nation. The other is an aggressive international capitalism that seeks control of the global economy in a manner divorced from democratic intent. Unless democracy is re-empowered, these results will only increase.

The Judicial Branch

The purpose of The Supreme Court is to make sure that all legal decisions, regulations, and laws – executive, congressional, and state— uphold the constitution and that the people's rights are protected. Essentially, this means to safe-guard democratic intent.

However, in their interpretations the justices have fluctuated between the politics of economic imperialism and democracy, depending on the majority's personal political alignment. In recent American history this focus has re-aligned itself with the appointment of representatives of economic imperialism. Their votes confirm this alignment. Because of longevity based terms, the Court's fluctuation changes slowly and one justice can change the Court's decisions for generations.

History makes it clear that the Court's interpretation of the constitution has been through political eyes. For almost a hundred years following the Civil War, the justices were devoted to upholding the economic imperialism of a de facto slavery that was one of the major focuses of that war – despite the constitution. For example, in 1896 they made the decision to uphold equal but separate laws aimed at suppressing the civil rights of the black population in their Plessy vs. Ferguson decision. The vote was by a majority of Republican appointees. Not until 1954 did the Court's posture shift to upholding the constitution in its Brown vs. Board of Education ruling against separate but equal laws. This Court was dominated by Democratic appointees. The recent ferocious battles over court appointees leaves no doubt that, however the appointees might see themselves, the politicians and citizenry see them as representatives of political perspectives and expect them to vote accordingly.

However, the only legitimate eyes the Court has are those provided by the constitution and its opening fifty-two word paragraph which focuses on the national community and its common good. The paragraph begins with We and ends with United States. In between are the enforcing words of union, common, and ourselves. This focus of community oriented common good can only be missed by those whose eyes are blind to democratic intent. Justices can remain totally oblivious to the focus of the constitution because their eyes have been captured by an economic imperialism that has no capacity to see with a democratic focus. However, the Supreme Court does not need any other eyes to make legitimate rulings irrespective of the nature of the issue before them. This first paragraph of the constitution is the only criteria of vision needed for interpreting everything else in the constitution, the amendments, and any other issue that might rise for their consideration.

Unfortunately, in recent years the Court's shift of political view interpretation reflects a diminishing number of justices devoted to democracy and an increasing number devoted to economic imperialism—with specific focus on individualism, imported worth, and how these are affirmed through devotion to economic imperialism.

A prime example of this shift is its ruling that corporations are persons in the Citizens United decision. In this ruling, the Court defined corporations as equals to individual citizens – thereby unleashing their economic power to influence government in a manner beyond

199

just bribing politicians but actually electing them—thus, essentially, purchasing control of government. This duplicity is the most devastatingly hypocritical joke the Court has played on American democracy. The Court perversely permits corporations to literally buy elections but, otherwise, refuses to hold them accountable for their actions as they do individual citizens.

Robert Reich is a respected economist and author who has worked with presidents Gerald Ford, Jimmy Carter, Bill Clinton, and Barrack Obama. He is the award winning Chancellor's Professor of Public Policy at the University of California in Berkeley. He summarizes the issue succinctly in tongue in cheek manner:

I'll believe corporations are people when Texas executes one.

This ill-advised Supreme Court decision permitted corporations to behave as humans in the electoral process while refusing to hold them accountable to the other laws of the nation governing criminal behavior. If they were held accountable our prisons would be full of corporations. It was a decision made through illogic and willful blindness.

Here is another reason why this ruling is an exercise in illogic. Society created institutions to fulfill its enduring needs—educational, health, political, financial, justice, religious, etc. Institutions are organizational tools for fulfilling social purpose just as is government. To declare financial institutions as persons without declaring all the other institutions, including government and religion, as persons is an exercise in spurious logic. It is a tunnel-vision decision birthed of a tunnel-vision political view. It is a perspective that fails to understand the nature and purpose of institutions in social living. It is a decision that totally ignores common logic. It is a tragic irony that reveals the commitment of the majority of the Court to economic imperialism over democracy.

In a democracy, the function of all institutions is to affirm citizenry worth and contribute to the common good. This is the only legitimate gauge of their behavior in reference to either privilege or justice. What the Supreme Court has done is devise a different set of rules for judging the financial institution's social behavior than either the individual citizen or the nation's other institutions. If this duplicity were not real then all other institutions would be granted the privilege of voting, contributing in unlimited fashion to political candidates, and given special exemptions when violating citizenry worth and the common good.

That some members of the Supreme Court cannot see this simple logic is because they have eyes that prevent such perception—the eyes of economic imperialism—eyes that see everything through the dollar $ign. Thanks to this perverted vision, corporations, rather than being organizational servants of democracy, have become the goal of democratic benefit. The common good focus is shifted from the citizenry to business. The watchdog of democracy, the Supreme Court, has become the guardian of corporations. It has fallen for the fallacy that democracy exists to serve economic imperialism. It has invited the nation to be ruled by corporate despots and, as a consequence, has brought democracy to the edge of its grave.

These inconsistent and political posturings of the Supreme Court reminds of an observation by Thomas Jefferson:

Our judges are as honest as other men and not more so. They have, with others, the same passions for party, for power, for privilege of their corps.

In brief, our judges are humans who will vote the view of reality they have adopted irrespective of how contrary it might be to constitutional perspective and will use this same view to justify their vote. They may be the Supreme Court but they are not supreme humans. But this does not excuse them when they betray the constitution they have sworn to defend and become advocates for economic imperialism.

Less visible than the Supreme Court is the entire system of federal court judges. When this system is purged of those with Old Glory eyes and replaced by those with Dollar $ign eyes then the capturing of the judicial system by economic imperialism is complete. This purge is presently in process by the Trump administration.

The Executive Branch

The Executive Branch is given the power to act with immediacy when faced with issues that confront the nation. For example, it can negotiate treaties. President Obama helped negotiate a treaty with Iran that limited trade sanctions in exchange for cessation of that nation's proliferation of nuclear warfare capability. President Trump, upon assuming office immediately reversed this treaty.

One problem with this power is that the president is often elected by money provided from the wealthy elite. Moreover, it usually subverts its own democratic intentions by taking direction from the so-called experts who represent the institutions of economic imperialism. Appointed cabinet members affirm this tendency. Thus, with or without deliberate intent, the Executive Branch easily becomes the pawn of economic imperialists—and usually does in some measure.

The dangers of Executive Branch anti-democratic decision-making are multiplied by the increasing power granted the President by a congress that is gradually abdicating its own power to be a balancing agency of government. Particularly is this the case when it comes to determining military action and war. Congress may simply accept the conclusions of the Executive branch without demanding proof or doing its own due diligence. This allows devious presidents to plunge the nation into disastrous military ventures that cost lives and mortgage the nation's future. An example is the George Bush administration's unchallenged lies that led to the Iraq war which expanded to the Afghanistan war. This war continues to inflame military aggression in the near east, and is responsible for a disastrous federal budget deficit. But whatever the cost to the nation, such actions inevitably create enormous profits for economic imperialists in the private sector—which may have been their original disguised purpose.

Donald Trump represents a political victory for economic imperialism—the actual capturing of the White House. He continues the tragic decision-making that characterizes the undemocratic vision of this eye. If he were forced to vacate the presidency would that effect the empowerment of economic imperialism? The answer is: Very little. Here are supportive reasons for this answer:

- Trump is as likely to be dethroned for personal dementia as for subversion of democracy. Beyond being a committed economic imperialist, he is psychologically bent toward social destruction.

- Even if Trump vacates the Oval Office the Republican party

202

that elevated him to that position remains devoted to using democracy to empower economic imperialism.

- The federal judicial system, to a great extent, has been converted into an advocate for despotic economic imperialism. Many current appointees are totally lacking qualification for this office and are devoted to undemocratic right-wing views about race, ethics, law, and justice.

- That segment of the citizenry which voted Trump into office is still a part of the nation and blindly remains supportive of the subversions of economic imperialism.

- Trust in American diplomacy and democratic vision in the world community has been severely eroded and will require transformative leadership for correction.

- The wealthy elite that fuels and sustains economic imperialism with its political purchasing power is committed to a game plan of national takeover that Donald Trump only represents as a momentary phenomenon.

That his removal from office would not greatly affect the game-plan of economic imperialism to take over American government does not mean it makes no difference whether or not he stays in office. Because of his ego instability he is a grave danger not only to American democracy but to the entire world order – both politically and physically. He must be ousted before his damage to national and international stability shoves the global community over the brink of chaos where despotism and destruction always wait with open arms.

The Congressional Branch

Over the past thirty years the national congress has grown increasingly polarized beyond the normal distinctions between the Republican and Democratic parties. This polarizing is a reflection of the historical battle between democratic intent and economic imperialist goals. And it foreshadows the final showdown of a battle between opposing ways of governing that have persisted from our nation's birth. Whatever subtleties may have indicated party differences in the past are now plainly revealed in unapologetic fashion.

The Democratic party largely retains its emphasis on human worth, the common good, and the right to vote. It expresses concern for racism, sexism, voter suppression, environmental violation, citizenry health, and global warming. These issues find focus in its attempts to pass progressive laws and programs that address such issues.

The Republican party continues to expand its embrace of the character and goals of economic imperialism. Its focus is on whatever is believed to aid the economy and which diminishes restraint on business endeavors. It is devoted to converting all common good programs into capitalist profit making ventures. It approves of the presidency as a dictatorial power. It demands allegiance to Donald Trump as the criteria of loyalty to both the Republican party and the nation. It has no concern for democratic intent and insists that economics is the only valid measure of democratic success.

Both parties claim that the nation has arrived at a moment of historical crisis. But their claims are based on opposing rationales. And eventually one of these rationales will win the heart of the nation's citizenry. The winner will determine the nation's destiny. At this moment, economic imperialism, in the guise of the Republican party, has the upper hand.

The Company Store

In 1946 Merle Travis wrote a song called Sixteen Tons. It was about coal miners and was inspired by lines written in a letter from a coal miner relative: I can't afford to die. I owe my soul to the company store. The company store was established by the coal corporation. It provided all the necessities of living for the miners and deducted the cost from the miner's salaries. The cost of living was deliberately higher than the salaries and very quickly the miners were deep in debt to the company store. Soon the miners became economic slaves to this store which was the company's economic imperialist intention. The refrain in Travis's song is that the coal miner cannot afford to die because he owes his soul to the company store. The soul reference was to the coal miner's total existence.

Selling one's soul to the company store is a cultural euphemism for being so indebted to corporate business that you become its slave. One's soul is the essence of one's being. So it is being that is being sold. When being is sold the eyes of being are reframed to see through the lens of the buyer.'

In America, the company store is economic imperialism. When any branch of government commits to economic imperialism they have sold their soul. They have become its slave. Whether this is witting or unwitting is irrelevant to the slavery. The same is true of the citizenry as a whole. When one grows up in this system of slavery it may seem natural and may not be questioned. When it becomes a piece of the culture's fabric in which the slaves wrap their being, this selling is complete. It has become the norm-all.

Complicity and the Wealthy

There are many wealthy people and corporations in America that are committed to democracy and national and global human improvement. They should be applauded for the nobility of their commitment. However, it is difficult to believe that economic imperialism could dominate and control the nation's three branches of government without a majority of the wealthy elite and their organizations subscribing to its goals.

If this is true then wealthy imperialists outnumber wealthy democrats. It is doubtful that the generosity of many wealthy democrats toward national and international common good causes will change this outcome. The root problem is lack of political leadership commitment to the common good rather than the symptoms that reflect this lack. If wealthy democrats wish to defeat wealthy imperialists then they must devote themselves to electing democratic leadership.

Equally important, there must be a corresponding decrease in the number of imperialists who have an economic choke-hold on the nation's democratic structures. How to contribute to the election of devoted democrats seems obvious— investment of adequate resources in their election campaigns. But how do wealthy democrats contribute to decreasing the number of economic imperialists?

An Entrepreneur's Analysis

In the July 2019 issue of The Atlantic there is an article by Nick Hanauer entitled: Education Isn't Enough. Hanauer is an entrepreneur, venture capitalist, founder of an organization on public policy called Civic Ventures, co-founder of the League of Education Voters, and the host of a podcast called Pitchfork Economics. He is knowledgeable and committed to democratic intent.

His stated concern is that the billions of dollars being contributed by wealthy democrats to what he calls educationism is a tragic waste. By educationism he refers to the belief that higher education levels automatically translate into higher income levels. Behind that belief is the notion that if poor families were better educated they would be better paid and a consequence would be that a lot of the negative sociology of lower class living would be turned into positive sociology. This belief motivates wealthy democrats to invest heavily in making educational achievement available to the lower classes.

Hanauer provides statistics that he believes shows this thesis to be misguided. Here is one of the statistics he cites. Between 1979 and 2017 the income of the top 10% of the nation's wealthy population rose 156%. The income of those in the top .01 % rose 343%. The rest of the population's income level has remained relatively stagnant for this past almost forty-year period. This stagnation occurred despite the fact that the proportion of Americans attaining a college degree has more than tripled since 1970. Thus, while Americans have never been as highly educated as today, only those at the top of the income ladder have stepped upward financially. He also predicts that the largest growing category of available future jobs will be those that pay the lowest wages and would need no degree diploma for engagement – the food and service industries.

He concludes that schooling is vital but does not necessarily address the basic issue of income inequality that promotes depressed sociology in the lower classes and particularly the lowest class. His assumption is correct that simply investing in acquiring diplomas for the lower classes is not the answer. He suggests that the most direct way to address economic inequality is to increase the minimum wage, restore labor's bargaining power, and instate higher taxes, especially for the wealthy. The question is: What would inspire the nation to engage such remedial action?

A Different Kind of Education

The answer is still education, although, not of vocational focus and degree achievement which are important but do not address the issue of income inequality as Hanauer so aptly points out. But there is a type of education that addresses all citizenry inequalities. It is the civic education of the people that instills in them a profound commitment to the intents of democracy. Commitment to equality and the common good and their application to living is the only way to adequately address the inequalities that plague the nation. This is ideological and a taught value. Education is society's social means for both value transmission and transformation. Only a citizenry committed to equality of worth will be committed to economic relationships and structures that reflect equality of worth.

When a business owner believes that everyone in the shop is of equal worth there is a motivation to create the best possible work environment and pay the highest possible wage. The answer to economic inequality is growing a cadre of civic minded citizens and entrepreneurs more dedicated to democracy than to economic imperialism – a cadre that wraps the work place in democratic principle and is committed to lifting the lower classes out of negative sociology simply because it is the right thing to do.

This means doing more than improving work environments and income levels. It involves training employees in civic mindedness and modeling the attitudes of equality so that it characterizes relationships beyond the workplace. It must be devoted to making the nation's entire social system, including formal education, a class in democratic civics. It must ground the nation in its democratic vision by making its education eye the Old Glory eye.

Economic imperialists will not be interested in such goals because they have no concern for democracy except as a utility for profit-making. However, decreasing the number of economic imperialist entrepreneurs and politicians through civic education, while increasing the number of democratic entrepreneurs and politicians through the same means, can make this happen. It will reverse the trend of the last forty years. This is the long-term answer to the inequities that result from depressed social environments caused by depressed income levels. It is civic education that informs how vocation education should be lived democratically irrespective of its degree focus. It is to motivate all vocations to facilitate democratic intent as their first goal.

This assumes, as Hanauer suggests, that all those present and future wealthy democrats ensure that their own workers are paid compensations that make for a present and a future free of depressed social living and encourages them to support democratic politicians. If wealthy democrats would dually invest in electing civic-minded democrats to high office and raising civic-minded democrats in the national educational and social environment, America could be gradually transformed toward its democratic promise. Where would the nation be if that had been the focus of wealthy democrats over the past forty years?

The Power of the Wealthy Democrats

We should have profound appreciation for Hanauer and all those wealthy democrats who are investing economically in so many different ways to raise the quality of living of those of the lower classes. The wealthy have had enormous influence in shifting America from democracy to economic imperialism. With the same kind of commitment they can help empower the shift back to democracy. When wealthy democrats outnumber wealthy economic imperialists and contribute to this empowerment then the character of America's attempt at democracy will radically change for the better.

Citizenry Consent

If democracy is of, by, and for the people then the corruption of democratic purpose and the complicity of the three branches of government could not happen without citizenry consent. This consent has been given in three ways:

- We have not insisted that the people we elect vote for the intents of democracy.

- We have continued to reelect those who betray these intents.

- We have continued to elect those who have appealed to our momentary interests rather than those who envision a democratic future.

A major reason for this consent is that we citizens have fallen for the lie that the measure of success of democracy is how well our personal bank accounts are doing rather than how well the common good is being fulfilled. We have been persuaded to vote the lie.

Conclusion

All three branches of government are required to work in check-and-balance unison if a democracy is to both emerge and be sustained in healthy fashion. This form of government was devised to guarantee that the intentions of democracy would prevail. Unfortunately, contention rather than cooperation seems to be how it has worked throughout most of the immediate past. At this moment in history economic imperialism essentially has taken control of these three branches. Henry Clay was an American statesman who represented Kentucky in both the house and senate during the 1800s. His wisdom has been drowned out by the clamor of economic imperialist propaganda:

Government is a trust, and the officers of the government are trustees, and both the trust and the trustees are created to benefit the people.

If we are concerned about the Frankenstein monster that confronts us as government in present day America we should remind ourselves that it has been cobbled together by power hungry economic imperialists. It does not reflect the democratic intentions of our founders. And it is we, the people, who have empowered the creation of this beast.

OF, BY, AND FOR

It is we citizens who have allowed our government to become of, by, and for economic imperialism rather than of, by, and for ourselves.

PART V

HOW DO WE KNOW?

INTRODUCTION

GUIDEPOSTS

To guide means to show the way. A guidepost is a sign or marker that indicates direction. Usually set at a crossroad or a place of possible confusion it indicates to the traveler the appropriate direction to a destination.

It is imperative that we have distinctive gauges as guideposts that tell us the actual extent to which we are moving toward democracy or economic imperialism. One reason for this urgency is that the norm we have been raised in may be called democracy but is, in actuality, a hybrid of economic imperialist perspectives and democratic intents. The two have been so intertwined during America's history they can easily be mistaken for each other – even by those committed to what is perceived to be an actual democracy. The norm for democracy has become so perverted by economic imperialism that an actualized democracy appears to be extreme, even by devoted democrats.

A simple example of this perversion is that the word progressive has come to denote that which is extreme in implementing democracy rather than that which is a natural evolution in its application. This perverting is one of our primary dangers in seeking to measure these two opposing governing ideologies.

How do we know the real state of American democracy? What is the actual measure of the extent to which America is engaging the three intents of democracy? What legitimate tools do we use to ascertain this state? Following are some guideposts that indicate our nation's location on its contentious journey toward an actualized democracy.

Economic Imperialism Guideposts

Economic imperialism has many guideposts for measuring its success. These guideposts are normally very visible in their social expression. One set can be summarized in the Koch Brothers goals for achieving their vision of totally replacing democracy with an uninhibited free enterprise that is structured to empower individualism and imported worth without any ultimate concern for the common good. It is measured by the lack of laws restraining capitalists in their profit making ventures. This goal is masked behind citizenry acquiescence to the notion that the success of democracy is gauged by how well the economy is doing. However, this is one of the major deceptions of economic imperialism—a deception that the American citizenry finds difficult to grasp because it is so fully geared to our individual sense of financial well-being and the achievement of the American Dream.

Related is the guidepost of the status of the Gross National Product. Robert F. Kennedy understood both the difference and the importance of the difference to democratic success. Robert was the brother of John F. Kennedy and served as his Attorney General. During a 1968 speech at the University of Kansas, he stated this succinct perception of the limitation of using the Gross Domestic Product as a measure of democratic success:

It measures neither our wit nor our courage; neither our wisdom nor our learning; neither our compassion nor our devotion to our country: it measures everything, in short, except that which makes life worthwhile.

It is obvious that Kennedy understood that you cannot measure the success of that which is relational by that which is financial. And the question Kennedy's observation raises is: What is the benefit of having a strong economy if the real blessings of democracy are suppressed under the weight of capitalistic despotism? Democracy can survive bad economics but it cannot survive bad relating.

Joseph E. Stiglitz of Columbia University's Department of Economics, one time Chief Economist of the World Bank, Noble Prize winner, and prolific author has been speaking to the same issue for years. He suggests that the state of the economy does not address critical issues that portend the future like environmental destruction and depletion of natural resources. Nor does it focus on what causes people to be fulfilled and the role of education and health in their living. Essentially, we are measuring the wrong thing when we rely on the GDP to indicate the state of a nation's well-being. And, as he notes:

If we measure the wrong thing we will do the wrong thing.

The implication is that a nation and a global community that continues to rely on this economic measurement to determine its state of well-being may be in for a rude awakening when all its real environmental and social issues come home to roost. It's the essence of putting all one's eggs in a single basket. What do you do when the bottom drops out of that basket? What is your state of well-being then? That should have been at least one of the lessons America learned from the Great Depression.

The GDP only measures the strength of capitalism at any given moment. It measures nothing about democratic strength. It is a false guidepost. This does not mean that economic strength is unimportant. It is vital and it is imperative for a nation to have a strong GDP. But it is only a symptom of well-oiled economic machinery. Any despotism is as easily measured. So, it is a false issue when seeking to measure the success of democracy. The two do not equate. When the citizenry uses the GDP as its guide during an election campaign it shows its inability to distinguish between economic imperialism and democracy. It expresses civic failure. It models the attempt to see through both the eye of Old Glory and the eye of the Dollar $ign at the same time—with the consequent incapacity to see very far beyond the nose length of immediate financial status. A question that follows is: Of what benefit is a decent financial living if the possibilities offered by that status are suppressed by racism and sexism—limitations of freedom? A jail cell that offers a good bed and good food is still a jail cell.

Democracy Guideposts

Democratic guideposts are geared to how well the three intents of democracy are being fulfilled. Is the citizenry being treated with equality of worth? Is the citizenry's common good actually being achieved? Is the right to vote being upheld and sustained for all the citizens irrespective of ethnicity, class, religion, or gender? The problem with taking the measure of these guideposts is that the citizenry is impacted in significantly different ways in measuring each of these three criteria of intent. A corporate CEO might measure these differently than a worker at McDonalds.

The following chapters are intended to enable us to get past our susceptibility to the enemies of democracy—the whims of individualism and the unfairness of imported worth—and to measure success in more socially and visibly holistic ways.

21

THE ECONOMIC IMERIALISM GAUGE

There is no doubt that our nation divides itself between those devoted to the common good and those devoted to economic imperialism. American history is a record of the battle between these two devotions.

Calvin Coolidge became the United States 30th president in 1923 during a period of economic growth. He opposed all regulations that protected the citizenry from financial speculations and insider trading. He advocated unrestrained capitalism and an invisible federal government. He suggested that:

If the federal government were to go out of business, the common run of people would not detect the difference.

Coolidge was an advocate of economic imperialism who believed business structures were temples to democracy. In brief, unrestrained business was the heartbeat of democracy. He is a past president who believed democracy was the servant of capitalism. He represents those moments in American history when the citizenry, seduced by good economic times, falls for the false story line that democracy and capitalism are synonymous. What they fail to see is the aftermath of putting this story line into practice as a national policy. The aftermath was that Coolidge's policies invited the Great Depression which was largely due to failed business regulation and he was absolutely wrong. The people did detect the difference when the federal government failed in its financial oversight and the Great Depression became the nation's plight – they detected it in in the bitter and destitute economic circumstance imposed upon them to physically survive.

As is often exemplified by national political leadership, the battle for control of the nation between democracy and economic imperialism shifts back and forth. The focuses that dominate the cultural drama tell the story of when democracy or economic imperialism is prevailing in the social order—and to what extent.

Indicators of Economic Imperialism's Triumph

Here are primary indicators that measure the degree of economic imperialism's triumph in a democracy's government:

- **Expertise and Devotion:** The federal government will be run like a big business because that is economic imperialism's devotion and expertise.

- **Maximum Profit:** The purpose of big business is to create profit from free enterprise and all policies and legislation will be designed to maximize such profit irrespective of harm to the citizenry or environmental health.

- **Compatible Leadership:** The political leaders of the nation will be drawn from big business and those attendant agencies, both private and government, that profit from alliance with big business.

- **False Equation:** Capitalism will be equated with democracy – the end will be subsumed under a means with business good becoming the common good.

- **Unregulated Empires:** The largest businesses will be permitted to become empires unto themselves, transcending and ignoring government domestic regulations and foreign policy and monopolizing industries.

- **Capitalization:** All common-good social programs will be gradually capitalized for the profit of big business because that is a primary goal of economic imperialists.

- **Minimized Rights:** All human rights that do not facilitate business profit such as the ability to vote and a free press will be minimized, suppressed, or eliminated.

- **Skewed Policies:** Both domestic and foreign policy will be what benefits big business, howsoever subtle or disguised may be its declaration or enactment.

- **Labor Servitude:** The common citizenry will be viewed as laborers working for the profit of big business.

- **Subverted Goals:** All branches and departments of government will submit to the goals of big business because they will be run by the advocates of big business.

- **Gauge Shift:** All vital national and international concerns will be gauged by economic concerns.

- **Oligarchy Rule:** An elite economic oligarchy will rule the nation and all within it will become subservient to this rule.

- **Ally Shift:** Who are America's allies and how they are treated will be determined, not by democratic values, but by economic concerns.

- **Leadership Perversion:** The leaders of America will either collude or clash with the economic imperialists who control and dictate the governments of other nations.

The aggregate degree to which these indicators dominate the government is the degree to which economic imperialism rules the nation in triumph over democracy.

Individual Business Assessment

While these larger criteria are indicative of whether a culture is primarily governed by economic imperialism, what about individual business? The common good is the major goal of democracy. The common good has to do with the whole of the citizenry.

The lower class is part of the common good of the whole. How it is treated by business is an indicator of the rule of economic imperialism. The ultimate issue is not how well the middle class is doing but how well the lower class is doing. If the lower class is doing well the same will be true of the middle class.

Fair Compensation

Assessment question: Is the business's laboring class making a comfortable economic living—inclusive of health care and retirement? A major indicator of democratic success is when the poor are empowered to live without economic stress because all the citizenry is profiting from economic policies devoted to citizenry equality and the common good.

If the common good is being served, then everyone associated with a business will be receiving a just compensation that guarantees a just economic future. However, when corporate chiefs make millions while workers just scrape by, this may be successful capitalism but it is failed democracy—a violation of the common good.

Fair Prices

A second measurement is whether or not the business's product is being sold at a fair price. If the price to the public is excessive beyond cost, then it can only be at the expense of the common good. The function of capitalism within a democracy is to serve the common good. If business is making excessive profit it is in violation of this function. A fair profit will adequately reward everyone in the business and assure future viability. Excessive profit indicates the worst virtues of individualism and unrestrained capitalism.

Gearing profit to supply and demand may be a capitalist principle but it is not necessarily a democratic common good principle. The issue is which is serving which? This raises a demanding question: Can a business make billions of dollars annually by grossly inflating its profit margin be serving the common good? For economic imperialism the answer is yes. For democracy the answer is no.

Fair Play

A third criterion is: Do business transactions evidence the collaboration of moral intent and ethical outcome. If so, fair play will drive the relationship.

Democratic behavior and ethical behavior are the same because both depend on relational transactions being motivated by mutual worth affirmation. This affirmation will endow all transactions with the intentions of honesty and trust. On the other hand, dishonesty and distrust will dominate the business life where economic imperialism prevails.

Fair Worth

Here is a fourth criterion: Does the business honor the worth of every employee? If business is honoring this obligation there will be an avowed commitment to:

- Fair compensation.
- Safe working conditions.
- Ample provisions for health care.
- Gender and ethnicity equality attitudes and practices.
- Equality of opportunity.
- Ethical relationships and treatment.
- Promotions based on merit.
- Retirement Benefits.

There will be no need for labor unions because democratic capitalists will provide for employee well-being out of their commitment to the relational goals of democracy. Businesses that are invested in destroying the power of labor unions are unconcerned about the well-being of their workers and identify themselves as advocates of economic imperialism and enemies of democracy.

Fair Laws

A fifth criterion is the relationship of a business to lobbyists. Any business devoted to democracy would have no need to hire lobbyists to bribe legislators to enact laws that would increase their business profits. Businesses invested in democratic intent will promote themselves without the deceit of political bribery. Businesses that invest in lobbyists who seek unfair laws to elevate their profit evidence a commitment to economic imperialism and contempt for democracy.

The Measurement

Where economic imperialism prevails, every aspect of government and its programs will be subverted to serve the benefit of the economically empowered. And these empowered will be willfully blind to citizenry worth. The manufacturer of the toilet bowl will be held in high esteem while the cleaner of the toilet bowl will be held in disregard if not contempt.

The bottom line in a democracy is that the measure of the common good is the measure of all success—whatever the issue. It is commitment to the common good that evidences both the motivation for and the allegiance to democracy. The reason is that devotion to the common good is the ultimate measure of equality and equality is a statement of mutual worth. The extent to which the cleaner of the toilet bowl and the manufacturer of the toilet bowl are held in equality of worth is the true measure of the extent to which democracy prevails.

The New Normal

Here is the norm that economic imperialism has produced:

Crisis: In order to create greater wealth, the large corporations push the profit making envelope beyond its democratic limits and an economic crisis cripples the national economy.

Bailout and Pillage: Congress bails out the perpetrators while the middle and lower classes are pillaged and left to fend for themselves.

Invitation: Congress refuses to let perpetrators fail, to appropriately punish them, or to enact and sufficiently sustain laws that will prevent similar future fiascos. Or, they will enact such laws because of citizenry demand and then dismantle them as unobtrusively as possible.

Soul Selling: Politicians sell their soul to the company store which rewards them with economic benefit both during their tenure and beyond.

Repetition: It happens again and the scenario continues to repeat itself —all for the profit of economic imperialists and at the expense of the middle and lower classes.

Misnamed: Democracy has been misnamed for this drama which is actually an economic oligarchy.

Such a norm is produced by un-democratic political leadership. It is the kind of leadership that has been described in past historical moments this way:

We hang the petty thieves and appoint the great ones to public office.

This kind of perverted norm will remain the norm until one of two things happens: Either we citizens decide to elect political leadership that will represent our common good interests rather than the interests of economic imperialists or the nation will complete its plunge toward democratic suicide. There are no other options. The imperative question is: What is the point of no return and have we reached it?

Conclusion

The foregoing analysis poses a dilemma in reference to patriotism. As previously indicated, it is possible to confuse love of democracy with love of culture when the two may be in conflict. Thus, it is easy to confuse what one is patriotic about: democracy or culture? If the two are not compatible, then what might patriotism be about? If the common good is the bottom line of democracy, then, it is taking actions to bring the culture in line with democracy's intents as opposed to blindly following the leadership of economic imperialists. There are no democratic patriots among economic imperialists. There are only capitalist patriots.

Aristotle once commented:

The real difference between democracy and oligarchy is poverty and wealth. Wherever men rule by reason of their wealth, whether they be few or many, that is an oligarchy, and when the poor rule, that is a democracy.

He also stated in the same light that:

Democracy is when the indigent, and not men of property, are the rulers.

Aristotle believed that since there were far more poor people than wealthy people in a democracy the poor would rule by virtue of numbers. He was claiming the right of every citizen to be a part of the decision making of the nation state. He was announcing the essence of one of the three primary intents of democracy—total citizenry rule.

Implied in Aristotle's remarks is the notion that the gauge of democratic success is when the lower class is elevated to the same measure of worth as the upper class. This suggests that any valuation about democratic success must include their status of well-being. Economic imperialism could care less about the lower class's well-being other than their availability as a cheap labor force.

OF, BY, AND FOR

Democracy was not established of, by, and for the maker of the toilet bowl. It was established of, by, and for the maker, the cleaner, and everybody in between.

Evaluating Question

Given the foregoing criteria about the success of economic imperialism, to what extent does it rule over democracy in America?

22

THE ACUTUALIZED DEMOCRACY GAUGE

We humans are imperfect and live imperfect lives within imperfect communities. We create ideals to encourage our nobility—to empower the best that is within us. None of us live up to these ideals either as individuals or as communities. We commit to them and hope for as high an attainment as possible. There is often failure and always room for improvement. And either one can have an escalating result.

A Democratic Model

A model is an example, a standard, a representation, an archetype. Models empower us with a vision of what is not but can be. They inspire our devotion. They keep our eye on the prize. They remind us of the boundaries of appropriate attitudes and behaviors. They tell us where we are in our pursuit of the ideal and what we need to do to realize success. They mark out milestones and recommend celebration. We create them and they guide us. When we commit to them we pursue becoming the model we created.

Democracy is a creation that idealizes the grandest possibilities inherent in community government. It grounds itself in mutual affirmation, collaboration, and benefit. While being unattainable in wholeness it is attainable in measure. And whatever it might become in actuality reflects the devotion of its community adherents.

Here are the essential characteristics of an envisioned democratic model:

- **Multi-faceted Flavor:** There would be a profound commitment to the equal worth of every citizen that transcends ethnicity, gender, wealth, and social status. The culture would be dynamically interactive with a multifaceted relational flavor.

- **United Loyalty:** There would be a united citizenry loyalty to the common good that is the goal of every facet of government and every social and economic institution. All private goals would be willingly subservient to this loyalty.

- **Revered Responsibility:** There would be an honoring of the citizenry's rule and obligation to shape democratic outcome through their voice and vote. Laws and customs would encourage and protect this rule and responsibility.

- **Free Press:** There would be a free press viewed as sacrosanct to the health of the democratic body. It would be upheld as inviolable to that openness to truth required for democratic success and provocative of the issues needing to be addressed.

- **The Government:** The branches of government would be dedicated to the three intents of democracy above private or political party agenda. They would aspire to a true democratic servanthood to these intents for the sake of the common good.

- **Bridging Dialogue:** There would be a constant dialogue in every facet of social life attempting to bridge ideological and cultural differences, to embrace compatibilities, and to promote commonalities. Communities, small and large, would seek uncommon encounters in order to enlarge common benefit.

- **National Education:** There would be a free education system from kindergarten through graduate level that would be grounded in the three intents of democracy, citizenry civic responsibility, and American and world history. This civic education would be pervasive of every course of study irrespective of its nature or level.

- **Justice System:** The justice system would be devoted to rehabilitation and the social redemption of reentry into society as a productive citizen. It would model and be programmatically grounded in civic consciousness and the meanings and rewards of committing to the intents of democracy. It would be pervasive of every facet of the system from pre-entry to post-exit.

- **Law Enforcement:** Enforcers would be trained in applying their vocation in a manner that reflects the intents of democracy and would seek to exemplify these intents, only using force when required to keep them from violation.

- **Truth Evolution:** There would be an ardor to apply the evolution of truth in every area of human endeavor to the specific mission of every cultural institution. Institutions would posture openness and collaboration toward achieving the most noble human possibilities.

- **Health System:** The health system would be freely available to every citizen. It would have two primary devotions: The promotion of healthy living, both physically and mentally, and the capability of dignified dying through willful choice.

- **The Arts:** The arts community would dramatize the struggles of the nation toward democratic achievement. It would hold high its ideal intents, its failures, and its successes as a national reflection. It would be both the exposing and teaching arm of social media.

- **Tax Funding:** The national community would be funded through an uncomplicated fair share system of taxation that embraced both citizenry and business. No group would be favored over another and evasion of responsibility in any way would be maximally punished.

- **Financial System:** Free enterprise would be the means of the sustenance of wealth production and distribution. Whatever its usage for business, its ultimate goal would favor the community's common good.

- **The Military:** The function of the military would be the safeguarding of the nation and the aid of emerging democracies in the global community. It would limit its activity to democratic protection and promotion.

- **International Relations:** There would be a devotion to

democratic intent when dealing with other nations. Every attempt would be made to make decisions that would model democratic principle and encourage democratic conduct. Economic decisions would be subservient to this devotion.

- **Stealth Industry:** There would be a diligent application of America's democratic ideals to the work of the intelligence community. They would perform their mission with the intent of upholding the common good of both the nation and the global community.

The Challenge of International Democracy

It is difficult enough to sustain a significant measure of democratic achievement within a nation committed to its ideal. Applying democratic intent to international relations in a world full of despotic governments is to swim in murky and dangerous waters. It requires a forced reliance on democratic ideals, the wisdom of past experience, the data of present relationships, the capacity to envision outcomes, and a large element of risk. Often, only a dim hint of a desired outcome can be seen in making profound decisions.

There may be circumstances that require actions that appear undemocratic. War is an example. Difficult decisions may need to be made that honor the welfare of the community over the individual. Being an actualized democracy in such a world may necessitate undesirable action to protect the nation. What must be guarded against is using such necessities to justify deliberate violations of democratic intent. Mistakes may be made but unjustified violation remains unjustified.

It is up to elected officials to make the judgments. And it is one of the functions of the free press to call out violations and hold the nation accountable. When both are doing their job unjustifiable violation can be held to a minimum. In such interactions the nation will never be guiltless but it can be self-aware and self-correcting. It can never be perfect but it can be nobly responsible.

Conclusion

The global community is changing radically. Democracies are failing and chaos and despotic de-civilization is beginning to posture itself as a possible future. Unless something is done to model a different and inspiring reality than what we have had since the mid-twentieth century, a new world dark-age could emerge. This may be the greatest international challenge that faces America. And the nation can only be a saving leader if it is a democratic leader.

OF, BY, AND FOR

Democracy does not exist to serve those at the top of the economic food chain but to serve every citizen in this food chain in the spirit of equality and the goal of the common good.

Evaluating Question

Given this ideal face of democracy, how does the face of present day America compare?

23

THE CLASS GAUGE

Nothing measures lack of democratic reward like the working class living in destitute social and economic circumstance. *Hillbilly Elegy* is J.D. Vance's autobiographical story based on life in the city of Middletown, Ohio and the Appalachian town of Jackson, Kentucky. This area, at one time called The Industrial Belt, had become known as the Rust Belt. The reason for the name change was the negative economic decline due to the exodus of the industries that had once sustained it. These areas declined socially as they declined economically.

The story is about Vance's growing up experience in this culture of a declining white middle class into a lower class community characterized by poverty, social and educational ignorance, welfare cheaters, joblessness, physical and emotional violence, drug abuse, ill health, laziness, distrust, paranoia—the despair of helplessness and hopelessness.

Vance struggles with parallel issues: How to remain prideful of his cultural past where he experienced loving support and at the same time address the circumstances that created the terrible downsides that surrounded that love with degrading and destructive behavior. The former question requires an individual answer and Vance avows respect for his cultural legacy despite the downsides. The latter requires a social answer and Vance is not sure what this might be other than a change of attitude toward class differences. However, the very chain of events that led to his personal rise out of this debilitating cultural milieu hints at some answers.

Government Support

After High School graduation he chose to enter the military as a Marine instead of immediately going to college. He affirms that this experience led to his personal transformation into adulthood.

- It was motivated and guided by government employees and at government expense.

- His subsequent higher education achievements were subsidized in various ways by forms of government aide—an extended event that led to his social and economic transformation.

In brief, concrete government intervention and support was critical to empowering his rise into an alternative cultural and economic reality. He did not accomplish this on his own.

Economic Class Equality

His assertion that there must be a change of class attitude may be the foundation of any permanent cultural alteration. In this assertion he is onto that which is bedrock for a successful democracy to exist—an acknowledgement of the equality of every citizen which means an equal worth valuation of economic classes. It is not difficult to see this necessity. What is difficult is making it a reality in a nation that has sold its soul to a scale of imported artificial worth.

In interviewing for jobs, Vance discovers the superficial social signals of externalized worth that were required for success in the law world such as the quality of the suit you were wearing or whether you selected the proper utensil when you ate. These mannerisms are akin to what signaled the worth pretensions of eighteenth century European royalty. Serious progress will have been made when the worth of every citizen is simply accepted and the issue of job hiring is based on expressed skills and potential rather than contrived and meaningless fashion and demeanor that denotes a contrived superior worth.

Not much of the snobbish attitudes of upper class superiority Vance describes will change until the base line for class relating is acceptance of innate mutual worth. It is the bridge over which all democratic social change must cross. Investing in the intents of democracy is the key in the same manner that divesting the nation of the intents of democracy has led us to this present moment of devout class prejudice.

Genetic Gifts

It is apparent that Vance's birthed mental capacity was a consequential aid in his liberating journey. But this was a genetic endowment and not something he earned. Genetic inequality has no concern for class. What his story affirms is that while individual initiative is certainly an imperative, no one pulls themselves out of lower class blight into higher class blessing by their own bootstraps. Such is an illusion born of the arrogance of individualism which ignores the role of multiple social, economic, and physical factors in every individual's experience—the role of chance. Fundamental to Vance's success was the aid of government in both his employment and education in the use of his gifts.

Social Responsibility

In an actualized democracy, the government, business, and the citizenry would all feel and assume responsibility for providing remedies for the kind of environment in which Vance was raised. They would do so from the perspective of human worth, the common good, and their assumed obligations. They would do so because it is ethically and morally right. They would do so because they understand that the social and economic health of all the classes is integral to a democracy's well-being. However, such perspectives are counter to economic imperialism where big business often sees workers and environments as utilities for profit making and may abandon both when no longer useful to this purpose.

The question is: In a democracy of, by, and for the people, who is obliged to help those in economic and social distress? Certainly there must be a commitment by those in distress to help themselves in whatever way is possible. However, while acknowledging the primary role of personal initiative, can such environments be altered toward betterment without the empowering support of both business and government? If it is business withdrawal which has contributed to the economic plight behind the community's plunge into despair then the business world is obliged to address concretely the circumstance they have helped created. Offering courses that help workers who have lost their jobs to transition to some other work environment is only an insufficient nod in the right direction. Such may help a few who are highly motivated but it does not alter the suppressed environment left by the business's absence. Business must do more than shout instructions for how to swim to those who are drowning in the sink-hole they have created. It must offer more concrete ways of remedy.

Government is the agency most responsible for citizenry well-being. It is the people's agency that is created and sustained for this well-being. History assures us that, primarily, if the government does not demand rectification then big business will not engage it. Moreover, as the people's agent, government has a direct obligation beyond insisting on the rehabilitating actions of causing business. It must make its own investment in corrective action. It must aid the community as it aids the individual. Imperative to this aid is a quality education system, a renewing vocation service, appropriate health care, and a social service system that addresses the lacks Vance's story illustrates. If the government were to truly commit to democratic intent with appropriate community focus, then many of the issues faced by the lower class would find a significant measure of recuperation.

It is when democracy becomes a utility for profit making and the culture becomes defined by economic imperialism that the middle and lower classes are left to fend for themselves. The reason is that they, like democracy, are viewed as utilities and their worth is correspondingly measured by the wealthy oligarchy.

What I believe Vance is describing in his book is the final circumstance of the lower class when both social ignorance and economic imperialism prevail. By social ignorance I refer to all the suppressed learning that sustained the perspectives of Vance's family and community life styles. I refer to all the social deficits that he was required to address and overcome in order to help climb his way out of the hindrances that environment created.

When strong government, insisting on the responsible assistance of business and individual initiative, creatively tackles the issue of those circumstances described by Vance, this will be a sign that democracy is being successful.

Democratic Intents

There is no ultimate answer to the plight of the lower class except government instituting the primary intents of democracy. When this happens the entire culture will be transformed. The issue of living will no longer be about upward mobility. It will be about the common good. The American Dream will not be an individual achievement. It will be a democratic achievement and every class will participate.

Gore Vidal was an American essayist, playwright, novelist, and political commentator of the 20ᵗʰ and early 21ˢᵗ centuries. He saw only subtle differences between the Democratic Party and the Republican Party when it came to supporting economic imperialism, which he called laissez faire capitalism. He succinctly describes the situation of the poor when economic imperialism reigns:

> *In public services, we lag behind all the industrialized nations of the West,*
> *preferring that the public money go not to the people but to big business.*
> *The result is a unique society in which we have free enterprise*
> *for the poor and socialism for the rich.*

According to the Washington DC newspaper, The Hill, in a report by Michael Lambert of August 24, 2017, around twenty billion dollars annually is spent on government farm subsidies. And keep in mind that most of that goes to those already making outrageous profit—big farms and agribusiness. Those farmers who need it the most get the least and often barely survive natural disaster. This is congress using government for the private benefit of their corporate sponsors—it is selling their soul to the company store. It is congress abetting economic imperialism which is the same as abetting the suicide of democracy.

Farming subsidies are only the tip of the iceberg when it comes to government abetting corporate profit. It is important to keep in mind that government is not some obscure faceless entity but the nameable representatives that we vote into office. It is those politicians who promise they will empower democracy for the benefit of the American people when they are running for public office but, once elected, betray that promise for the economic benefits of becoming lackeys for economic imperialists. Or, they are already economic imperialists who disguise themselves as champions of democracy but revert to being champions of economic imperialism once elected.

Conclusion

The only way the lower and the middle classes can lay claim to the economic and social benefits of democracy is for such a democracy to actually exist. If this were to happen the nation would be transformed and all the classes would reap a satisfying measure of economic well-being. This is not to suggest that utopia would exist but it is to suggest that something would happen relative to a total citizenry well-being that America has yet to experience in its history.

Nelson Mandela was the black South African revolutionary who led his country out of apartheid toward democratic reform in the last half of the twentieth century. He spent 27 years in prison for expressing his views on equality. In the following remark he was speaking about the prison population but, as an avowed democrat fighting for the equality of a suppressed black lower class, his assessment applies across the class spectrum:

A nation should not be judged by how it treats its highest citizens, but its lowest ones.

One apparent gauge of the success of a democracy is the state of the well-being of the lower class. Equality of class treatment will only happen with profound commitment by the citizenry and a demand that those elected invest in democracy rather than being willing lackeys of economic imperialism.

The bottom line when it comes to measuring the success or failure of democracy is that it cannot exist in fullness until all citizens are declared to be of equal worth and every agency of government is devoted to their common good. When it is apparent that every class is treated in this manner then it is apparent that common good democracy exists. Until that time it only exists for those who are viewed as being at the top of the social worth-omoter scale.

When the lower class is treated with the same measure of worth equality as the upper class, then democracy has finally found a comfortable home in America. Here is one common occurrence scenario that would exemplify this achievement: Upper class citizens living in $2,000,000 houses would invite lower class citizens living in $20,000 houses over for dinner and conversation and treat them as equals—and vice versa.

OF, BY, AND FOR

Democracy is of, by, and for the people which means all the people which means every economic class.

Evaluating Question

Given the current state of the lower class in America, what is the nation's measure of actual democracy?

24

THE PRESS GAUGE

Unlike other measurements, the state of the press as a gauge of democratic health is apparent. Since the electronic communications revolution the term press refers to all media that is devoted to the goal of reporting news and baring the truth.

As the First Amendment of the Constitution states:

The people shall not be deprived or abridged of their right to speak, to write, or to publish their sentiments, and the freedom of the press, as one of the bulwarks of liberty, shall be inviolable.

There can be no democracy without a free press. The more robust this press the greater the possible health of the democracy. The less robust this press the less the possible health of the democracy. How the press is viewed and treated is a primary measure of the vitality of a democracy. It is one of the critical gauges used in measuring the success or failure of nations attempting to institute and maintain democracies. Its importance as a gauge is its high visibility.

The suppression of the press is the same as the suppression of the citizenry's voice. The sacredness of the press is about the people maintaining the sacredness of their right to know the state of the nation and their ability to express their view about this state and influence its direction.

First Amendment Test

In 1971 America had a major test of the state of the free press. Richard Nixon was president. The nation was in a deeply troubling turmoil over its involvement in the Vietnam War.

Robert McNamara, President Lyndon B. Johnson's Secretary of Defense, had commissioned a secret review of America's engagement in that war spanning the presidencies of Harry S. Truman, Dwight D. Eisenhower, John F. Kennedy, and Lyndon B. Johnson. It was originally intended to preserve the history of America's involvement. However, the results revealed serious questions about the motivation's and conduct of the war—awash with despotic political underhandedness, constant lies to the American public, and presidential egos that kept it going with a horrendous waste of both lives and resources and a negative reflection on democratic values. The report, constituting forty seven volumes and 7,000 pages, spanned the twenty-two years between 1945 and 1967. It became known as The Pentagon Papers.

The Rand Corporation, a private research and analysis company, possessed copies of the McNamara report. Daniel Ellsberg, one of its employees, after reading this report became convinced that America's involvement in the war was highly unethical and even unconstitutional. Without Rand Corporation knowledge, he provided the New York Times with a copy. The Times verified its conclusions and decided to publish excerpts. Alerted to this possibility, the Nixon administration, concerned about harmful political revelations, asked a lower federal court to restrain the Times from publication on the grounds of national security. The court complied with Nixon's request and the Times complied with the court.

During the meantime, the Washington Post procured a copy and decided to publish its own excerpts despite the lower court ruling. Ellsberg sent copies to other city newspapers which also began publishing excerpts. This drama eventuated in a ruling by the Supreme Court in favor of the newspapers based on the first amendment. Justice Black, in his brief on the ruling, states the intent of the amendment:

The press was protected so that it could bare the secrets of government and inform the people. Only a free press and unrestrained press can effectively expose deception in government.

He summarizes with this statement:

The press was to serve the governed, not the governors.

Dana Priest is an investigative reporter for the Washington Post.

She is the recipient of two Pulitzer Prizes. The first of these prizes, awarded in 2006, resulted from her expose' of secret CIA black site prisons located in a number of European countries along with other controversial features of the US government's counterterrorism campaign. The second was awarded in 2008 as part of a team reporting on the mistreatment of wounded veterans at Walter Reed Army Medical Center.

In an article about the importance of the Pentagon Papers and why freedom of the press is so vital, she says:

All governments lie and all use secrecy to cloak their wrongdoing and their poor judgment. Our protection exists to uncover this.

The word Our refers to the free press and its reason for existence.

The Bulwark of Freedom

Obviously, freedom of the press serves our nation in many ways aside from the expose' of government secrets that are not in the interests of democracy. As suggested by the First Amendment, it serves as a bulwark of our freedom. Basic to that freedom is our right to be informed citizens.

There need be no concern about protecting government agencies from a prying press. Government agencies are over protected by laws that allow them to declare most any document or action they wish as a national security secret and, therefore, unavailable to the public. Unfortunately, these laws are used to hide anything an administration wishes not be exposed, especially that which is against settled law—both national and international. As often as not, such laws are grossly abused to keep undemocratic government actions hidden from the public. It is this abuse that the free press is beholden to expose.

But it is more than government machinations. It is anything that threatens the intentions of democracy. An uninhibited free press is democracy's great ally because it promotes an informed citizenry. No democracy will survive without a determined press that is devoted to truth without qualification.

Pressing Concerns

A profound communication revolution has occurred since the Nixon era. Companies claiming that their job is the function of the free press have proliferated. They compete for resources to maintain a net profit. Companies who have devoted time and resources in the past to finding and reporting the truth are under pressure to use their resources to have something to say on a 24/7 basis. News often becomes repetitious and boring. Instead of deep reporting of real issues, it is easy to focus on the shallow entertainment of symptom exploration and exposure. There are multiple concerns that rise from this revolution. Following are two of immediacy.

The Concern of Political Profiles

How is the public to navigate all that is coming at it in order to vote for politicians with democratic intent? The last thing that can be relied upon to find out their real commitments is campaign ads or the false press. Moreover, there is need for a long term profile of candidate voting that will reveal real character as opposed to a temporarily created persona at citizen voting time. This would also expose the hypocrisy and lies that politicians get by with because of the citizenry's short term memory. If citizens spent a lot of time accessing and reviewing voting records, they could come up with their own legitimate voting profiles of political candidates. However, it is obvious in our busy world that only a small percentage of the citizenry has the time or will to make such effort.

Could this be a major function of the free press? It has immediate access to the required information. Could the local, state, and national segments of the press devote time each month to educate the citizenry about the voting profile of their representatives and parties and do so in prime time? Why not make creating such profiles a constant media focus so that they could not be air brushed at election time? Some media are diligent about reporting and analyzing the result of political polls. Why not be as diligent about how politicians actually vote? This would be a public service of constant expose' that would make it difficult for politicians to hide their real motivations behind soundbites and ads.

The Concern of Truth Crisis

At our moment in history, something has happened that threatens all that we cherish about a free press and its sustenance of democracy. Economic imperialism has decided to create its own false press and declare the democratic press as fake. It has been a sly move based on an old devious notion: If you cannot defeat them then join them. This false press has no respect for truth as confirmed data. Like its sponsor, economic imperialism, truth is a utility created to manipulate public opinion and to elect and keep despotic leadership in power. It has no concern for democratic intent. This new creation has spawned a truth crisis in the nation. This is compounded by the multiple media communication outlets open to all citizens for their usage that remain unregulated in respect to democratic principle, factual data, or despotic propaganda.

Thus, we must add another consideration to how we evaluate the state of the press beyond attempts to suppress its existence. We must figure out how to deal with the new false press in a manner that honors freedom of the real press. And we must determine how to regulate communication outlets to protect the viability of truth. This may require more stringent laws governing the use of data and public character degradation. It may require the real press to dig into the background of the false press and disclose both its nature and source so the citizenry can name it as an enemy of democracy. And it will certainly require a greater reliance on the nation's education system in teaching how to discern the nature of truth so that the false press will simply commit suicide by being itself. But however we decide as a nation to deal with this issue, we must do so for our own sake because our destiny as a democracy rides on the health and commitment of a free press which we can trust. Trust has become the critical issue.

Conclusion

Leon Gambetta was a politician and Prime Minister of France in the last half of the 19th century. He avowed that:

Despotism and freedom of the press cannot exist together.

241

He has stated what must be absolute where an actualized democracy exists—a free press that is not only unhampered by government but given unqualified support by government.

There are two obvious media indicators that relate directly to the possibilities and health of a democracy:

- A major hallmark of despotic leadership is contempt for the free press and attempts to suppress it, control it, or destroy it.

- A major hallmark of democratic leadership is admiration for the free press and attempts to champion it, empower it, and safeguard it.

When either of these hallmarks is obvious, so is the character of the leadership and the direction of the nation. Democratic leadership will protect and value the free press. Despotic leadership with degrade or control it. Thus, the health and stature of a nation's free press is a dramatic indicator of the health of a nation's democracy.

OF, BY, AND FOR

The press was created to keep truth information open and available to the citizenry so they can self-rule with clarity and confidence. It is the tool of, by, and for the people.

Evaluating Question

When looking at the state of the free press in current America, how does is stack up against dictatorship versus democracy?

25

THE JUSTICE GAUGE

The meaning of the word justice has been debated throughout history. Inevitably, the definition is tied to the community's system of government. It reflects both the mission and goal violations of that government. Justice in a despotism is radically different from justice in a democracy because their mission and goals are radically different.

What is viewed as a crime and its degree of violation is measured by how that crime affects the capacity of the government to accomplish its purpose. This means that what is a crime in one government might be an asset in a different one. Saudi Arabia is an example of a dictatorship while America is an example of a democracy. To criticize the government in Saudi Arabia is to risk imprisonment for committing a crime. To criticize the government in America is viewed as a civil right.

Retributive vs. Restorative Justice

In reality, there can be no such thing as justice. The closest humans can come to such a system is geared to the biblical notion of "an eye for an eye". This is called retributive justice. This means that if a citizen murders another citizen then that citizen is murdered by the government. But that is punishment not justice. Real justice would be for the life of the murdered to be restored. But that is not possible. The same would be true of any physical or psychological violation. While property loss might be measured and fully restored, even this is not normally viewed as sufficient because it does not address the psychological violation inflicted by the theft on the individual and the community. This means that any form of retributive justice is inadequate to address either the crime or the criminal. It is punitive in nature with minimal restorative focus.

There is a growing awareness of the value of restorative justice in the international community. Its focus is a redeeming relationship between the offended and the offenders. It is interactive and seeks processes for restoration and transformation and is endowed with a spirit of repentance and forgiveness.

These are polar justice models. And while the retributive model is as old as human history the restorative model is emerging as a possible alternative in countries that have a deep sense of democratic values or where there has been catastrophic racial division and violence.

Retributive Justice

Whatever else retributive justice might be it is the use of fear and an attempt to force some form of sustained pain upon the offender as both punishment and a warning message of restraint regarding similar future behavior. It is an attempt to protect society from disruptive and violent people by limiting their freedom.

Once such justice has been served the system has supposedly fulfilled its obligation. If viewed as appropriate, offenders are then released back into society with the notion that punishment has been positively educational. If this system actually worked, then there would be few repeat offenders. And fear of its punishment would deter those who are tempted to become first time offenders. Unfortunately, the opposite of this positive outcome seems to be the case for nations that use this system.

The assumption behind this model is that humans can be forced to change. It is individual based.

Restorative Justice

Restorative justice seeks to rehabilitate the offender. It approves adequate punishment for lesson learning but it wishes for more. It wants the offender to move past lesson-learning punishment and become a productive citizen. It is focused on the well-being of both the offender and the community. It specifically seeks a restored and productive relationship with society. Its goal is to enable the offender to prepare to re-enter society successfully and facilitates all the possibilities of such a re-entry including the post jail or prison experience.

Thus, it is an educational experience focusing on knowledge and relationships. It is an immersion in the meaning of citizenship. If it succeeds, every aspect of the justice process will model this goal, beginning with initial incarceration, moving through the court system, serving jail or prison time, and only ending with a meaningful re-entry into society. Such success would be evidenced by a decrease in the need for incarceration facilities.

The assumption behind this model is that humans can be motivated to change themselves. It is community based.

Justice in a Despotic Government

Despotisms come in many forms. In reference to justice, what they all have in common is using justice as a mechanism to enforce the goals of the despot. Whatever the size of the culture, the system of justice in the west has, with some exceptions, been retributive in character and modeled after colonial economic imperialism.

Goals

There are two primary goals in this system. The first is to use it to silence opposition to the despot's rule. The second is to create monetary profit through the expansion of inmate population, enforcement personnel, and incarceration facilities—and, when possible, use inmates as a cheap labor force.

Approaches

The approaches used to facilitate these goals are to corrupt the processes of justice and violate citizenry rights. In doing so it is impersonal and retributive in character. It cares nothing for the life of the violator which is viewed as a tool to achieve other goals. Neither does it care for the cost since it will be paid for by government.

Justice in a Democratic Government

What defines a democracy is its focus on equality of worth, the common good, and citizenry rule. This means that every facet of the justice system in a democracy—from its beginning to its concluding—will model these goals in significant measure. No consideration will be given to gender, ethnicity, religion, or class. No part of the system will be excluded.

Goals

The goal is to instill remorse in the offenders, inspire hope for a better future through education, and restore them to society as productive citizens. It is to reduce the size of the entire system by reducing the size of the inmate population. It is personal and restorative in character.

Approaches

From its inception, the entire system is geared to personal redemption. Processes and programs will facilitate the growth of a healthy personhood and the meaning of citizenship. Inmates will be treated with the democratic intents of birthed worth with a view toward the common good of the facilities population. Released inmates will have all their rights fully restored.

The American Justice System

Justice in America is modeled after European colonialism which gave the nation birth. It is a retributive form of despotic economic imperialism with the bottom line being profit-taking. Here is a current profile. According to a May 21, 2018 report from Smart Asset entitled The Economics of the American Prison System, America is currently spending over 74 billion dollars annually on the prison aspect of its justice system. Basically, this part of the justice system is being capitalized by turning it over to private enterprise which is the goal of economic imperialism for all public programs. What impact does this have on the justice system? It converts the purpose of the system from either retribution or rehabilitation to profit-making. Following are a few of the ways this is done.

- **By increasing the number of inmates:** The larger the prison or jail inmate population the greater the corporate profit. America consistently has the largest inmate population of any country in the world.

- **By increasing the number and size of facilities:** The larger the number of inmates the greater the need for more facilities and the more demand for facilities the greater the construction and maintenance profit.

- **By converting offenses:** Making minor offenses into major offences increases the number of jail and prison inmates. Those states and cities devoted to unnecessary incarceration swell the cost of the system and, thus, the profit for those who run the system.

- **By reducing services:** The less the services and the level of their quality the greater the profit for the corporation. In addition, decreasing comprehensive rehabilitation programs encourages the possibility of repeat offenders which adds to the system's cost and profit.

- **By hiring unqualified personnel:** Unqualified personnel who are not devoted to rehabilitation are less costly to hire and increase system profit. They may also model perspectives and behaviors that violate the system's rehabilitation purpose and could even harden the offender's perspectives.

For the economic imperialist despot, the larger the incarceration system the higher is the profit both economically and politically.

Restorative Focus

There is little to find in the American justice system that is highly supportive of the restorative model other than isolated areas where justice representatives seek to diligently apply the intents of democracy to decision-making that reduce prison populations and enable offenders to re-enter society in a more prepared fashion. While there are isolated examples, systemic ones are difficult to find.

The TRUE Experiment

There is a restorative democratic justice system experiment happening in Connecticut at the Cheshire Correctional Institute, a maximum security facility. It is run by the Vera Institute of Justice and is called TRUE—standing for Truthful, Respectful, Understanding, and Elevating. Its focus is on 18-25 year old offenders, an age range viewed as developmental in terms of mind capacities.

The program, with modifications, is facilitated by trained professionals and mentoring older inmates and is modeled after a successful one in Germany which has rehabilitation as its goal and which has resulted in a prisoner recidivism rate half that of the United States.

The focus of the TRUE program is developing life skills, resolving conflict, accepting responsibility, mutual support, and social empowerment with emotional growth and personal potential the goal.

It is too early to tell what the success rate might be from this program. However, that it is focused on rehabilitation and is viewed as an experiment, speaks to its novelty in our American system that uses the economic imperialist system as its playbook.

The Bard Prison Initiative

There is another program started in New York state that is beyond the experimental stage. It is successful and growing. It was created by Bard College which is an accredited four year co-ed liberal arts college at Annandale-on-Hudson with around 2,000 students. The program is called The Bard Prison Initiative (BPI). It is a regular college education program offered to prison inmates with degree possibility. To become enrolled an inmate must indicate serious commitment. As high as 97.5% of its graduates, once released from prison, do not return. They become absorbed into the community of their choice as contributing members of society. Some businesses welcome graduates into employment. It is so successful it has been expanded into a consortium of colleges across the nation.

Some professors, who teach in the BPI, claim that the prison inmates are more seriously devoted students than many of their regular college students. What this program proves is that, when given the opportunity, many prison inmates will devote themselves to self-transformation with a diligence. It models what the restorative prison system program should be totally embracing.

Justice as a Mirror

The question confronting American democracy is what its system of justice reflects beyond incarceration? To what extent is it retributive or restorative? If democracy is restorative in honoring equality of citizenry worth and their common good while despotic imperialism is utilitarian in accomplishing its goals without interest in equality or the common good, how is this reflected in the nation's cultural life? Following are a few examples.

Racial Example

ABC news, in a November 2017 report by Erica King, indicates that black men serve sentences over 19% longer than white men for similar crimes. A more detailed study by The Sarasota Herald Tribune in December of 2016 about racial discrimination in Florida's justice system supports this conclusion:

The investigation revealed that blacks are more likely to be found guilty; their sentences are usually longer; and they are not given as many opportunities to avoid incarceration through pre-trial diversion.

Almost all responsible major news services make similar reports. Obviously, there is gross racial discrimination in the American justice system that dishonors citizenry equality of worth and, in doing so, the common good.

Every attempt has been made in American history to keep the black citizenry in lower class suppression. Such discrimination serves three apparent purposes for the economic imperialist. Since the lower class, whatever its racial make-up, is more likely to vote in favor of democratic common good issues, it diminishes that class's numerical strength in the voting booth when its members are incarcerated. On the other side of incarceration, due to the social stigma of criminal conviction, it ensures there will be an economically depressed class available as a cheap labor force for greater profit making. The third purpose is to satisfy white racial prejudice and superiority.

Political Example

Representational discrimination is another form of apparent injustice. While there is gradual improvement in overcoming both racial and gender discrimination in politics, no study is needed to confirm its pronounced existence. A look at the skin color and gender of those who make up the congresses of both the nation and its respective states is sufficient.

The racial make-up of a congress will determine the bias of its laws. American voters have obviously been inclined toward a dominance of white males—a reflection of white European male racial superiority. And such leadership is prone to favor the goals of economic imperialism goals over democratic goals – as is reflected in the voting history of American government.

Class Example

Laws often discriminate against the average citizen while favoring the wealthy. The Chapter 11 bankruptcy law is an example. It makes it possible for a corporation to liquidate its debts, restructure, and continue paying its executives outrageous salaries and bonuses. It's the law that Donald Trump used repeatedly as a business tactic to survive bad decision-making. As a result, those smaller businesses, which are a part of the corporation's indebtedness, are often forced into hard financial times or failure. This is a gross economic class discrimination against small business owners. But if the wealthy own congress then congress will pass laws that favor economic imperialism over democracy which is, generally, what the Chapter 11 bankruptcy law accomplishes.

A Deduction

All of these examples speak to economic imperialism using the American justice system as a profit-making enterprise and to reinforce the white male superiority bias it represents.

Chapter Conclusion

A look across the spectrum of the entire American justice system will reveal whether democracy or economic imperialism is triumphing. Economic imperialists would have citizens believe that the measure of democracy is how well the economy is doing. While the economy is important it does not measure the success of its justice system. Only how well the intents of democracy are fulfilled tell us about the health of this system. Whether this system is retributive or restorative and the state of its mission fulfillment is the state of its health.

OF, BY, AND FOR

In a democracy the purpose of the justice system is to restore offenders to a lifestyle commitment to the intents of democracy which is the same as honoring a government of, by, and for the people.

Evaluating Question

If retributive justice primarily reflects despotism while restorative justice primarily reflects democracy, what is the American justice system reflecting?

26

THE EQUALITY GAUGE

As previously indicated, the new world colonies, which eventually became America, were established by the European form of economic imperialism called colonialism. This was a form of despotism that had little concern for the worth of the colonized people. Economic gain was the focus.

America was born out of a desire for a more democratic relationship but Great Britain refused and a successful revolution for independence resulted. However, this birth was characterized by competing governmental visions with the new democracy and the old economic imperialism seeking to enlist citizenry allegiance.

Throughout America's history this competition has been exemplified by how two major segments of the new nation's population—black people and women—have been treated with respect to equality. For the black population, worth inferiority was expressed in permission given to whites to maintain slavery and, once it became illegal, to continue violently suppressing their democratic rights. For women, worth inferiority was expressed in a refusal of the right to vote and, beyond this granting, maintaining inequality of reward and pay for the same labor. Both expressions were for the sake of white male profit-making and the elevation of white male social worth. Both are expressions of economic imperialist despotism.

Racism

The contention between democracy and economic imperialism continued from the nation's birth into the mid-eighteen hundreds when it contributed to the eruption of the Civil War. One issue of this war was whether a major part of the black population would be allowed to enter into the nation's democracy or remain as slaves. As a result of the war, in 1870, the 15th Amendment to the constitution granted black males the right to vote.

Despite this amendment, de-facto slavery continued in the form of civil rights suppression, social and physical brutalities, murder, and legal manipulations intended to keep the black population in a state of submission to white social and economic interests.

This battle raged through the civil rights movement of the nineteen sixties and seventies until laws were passed in 1965 that outlawed racial discrimination. While the democratic status of the black population increased in the following years it remains a social struggle. And given the gradual rise of the Republican party's wholesale embrace of economic imperialism, its leadership's open racism, and the Supreme Court's repeal of protective voting laws, the ugliness of hate and civil rights suppression has visibly re-emerged in the culture. The battle for democratic embrace of the black population continues into the 21st century.

Dual Purpose

Racism in America has always served the dual purpose of profit-making and worth elevation for white racists. It is this purpose of artificially upgrading the worth of white citizens by demoting the worth of black citizens which has made it possible for the black citizenry's economic exploitation to last so long. And particularly has this been effective in southern states where it was integral to an economic way of life grounded in racial superiority and a disposition for a genteel lifestyle at the expense of the black population.

From our nation's beginning, white male racism has been a primary ally of economic imperialism's attempt to suppress democracy in favor of its own rule. Racism and the exploitation of economic imperialism in America are two sides of the same coin.

Together, they are committed to making democracy a utility for profit-making so that economic imperialism can run government as its subsidiary. They have sought to suppress the freedom of people of color so they could be used as a cheap labor force and an artificial prop to the social worth of white people.

Black Lives Matter

In recent years the phrase Black Lives Matter has become a slogan to raise cultural consciousness and counter white racism. The political importance of the phrase is that it dramatizes the historical battle between democracy and economic imperialism. The struggle of the black population to be empowered with the same equality of worth as the white population—from its original slavery, through The Civil War, through the civil rights battle, up until this current moment—portrays the history of democracy's struggle to overcome the despotism of economic imperialism. This despotism exploits people for profit.

The measure of the black citizenry's elevation to a status of equal worth to the white citizenry is a visible gauge of democracy's triumph over economic imperialism. When black lives matter as much as white lives matter then so will brown lives, yellow lives, and red lives matter. When black lives are viewed as of equal worth to white lives then democracy will have arrived in America in triumph over economic imperialism.

Sexism

As indicated in the introduction to these comments, women were not originally empowered with equality of worth to men at our nation's birth. Male sexism dominated the culture. The original historical focus of this issue was the right to vote. Suppression of this right was symbolic of the suppression of other democratic rights for women such as equality of pay and recognition for social and business contribution. To gain such a status of equality would require diligent and courageous action on the part of women. Exemplars of this diligence and courage are people like Mary Wollstonecraft, Elizabeth Cady Stanton, Susan B. Anthony, and Emmeline Pankhurst. This right to vote was finally granted in 1920 by the 19th Constitutional Amendment—144 years after the American Revolution proclaimed the nation as democratic.

But male sexism continued to dominate the social order despite this granting of the right to vote. It prevailed in every area of American culture from home life to work life. Women were kept in their place for the same reason that the black population was kept in its place—as a cheap labor force and as an artificial elevation of men's social worth. Democracy threatens both of these purposes.

The fight for women's rights was dramatically aided by the advent of World War II which required the elevation of both women's work place leadership and their social status. As a result, the notion that women were inferior to men could no longer be justified except as a male bias. Despite this inability male sexism persists. But women also persist. Modern feminists advocate equal rights. Exemplars are Ella Baker, Betty Friedan, Angela Davis, Gloria Steinem, Ruth Bader Ginsburg, Alice Walker, Oprah Winfrey, Emma Watson, Beyonce' and Tarana Burke. The list is long and these are only representative. This social and historical taskforce of modern women continues to push for equal rights beginning with strength and organization in the 1950s up to this present moment. And significant progress has been made. But like its twin, white male racism, white male sexism is inordinately stubborn and the battle continues.

Despite all the feminist advances made since women were accorded the right to vote, men continue to award themselves better positions and higher compensation than women. In brief, men have been determined to stay the hand of equality when it comes to including women. The apparent reason is that they continue to rely on the compensation of imported worth rather than engage the innate worth offered by democratic intent. Imported worth is more socially visible when built into social structures, which white men have created. Men also desire the economic imperialist's larger profit of cheap labor over the lesser profit of fairly compensated labor and women, as a suppressed rights group, help fill this goal.

The Alternatives

In America, both racism and sexism are synonymous with economic imperialism. Both non-white ethnic minorities and women of all colors have been kept economically deprived to ensure two things: That white male capitalists will have a cheap labor force for profit making and so their egos can be artificially inflated.

Because economic imperialists have largely held the wealth of the country they have also set the rules and controlled the social, political, and economic game board to their own advantage. Thus, if the total citizenry is to ever be treated with equality of worth and opportunity one of two things will have to happen: Either women and people of color must be empowered by gaining control of at least half the nation's wealth or democracy will have to prevail.

Conclusion

If we look at the history of America from the moment of its revolutionary triumph over British colonialism, and we look at the gradual empowerment of both the black citizenry and women with democratic equality of worth, we can measure where we are in terms of actual democratic rule. There is no more socially visible measure of our success and failure in instituting a democracy than these two factors. An actualized democracy will embrace every citizen in its democratic intents.

Here, then, is another tool for assessing the true nature of our national character in the battle between democracy and economic imperialism: The actual relational equality of worth of people of color and women as compared to that of white men.

To assess correctly we must take the long look at our history while also refusing to validate the concept of gradualism. There is no inherent value in the notion that slow social change is better than fast social change. Our own revolutionary birth denies this claim. The call for gradualism is usually intended to facilitate the agenda of status-quoism. It invites resistance to change and the illusion that our nation has existed as a democracy since 1776. However, being something in name and being something in actuality are often totally different.

OF, BY, AND FOR

American democracy was not created for the exclusive benefit of white males but for the benefit of, by, and for the entire citizenry irrespective of ethnicity or gender.

Evaluating Question

Given the present state of white male racism and white male sexism in America, to what extent does democracy or economic imperialism reign? Or, to state this question differently: To what extent is the black population and female population as esteemed in worth as the white male population?

27

THE ULTIMATE GAUGES

When gauging the impact of the economic imperialism model and the democratic model it is important to keep in mind two ultimate differences that drive motivation and determine character.

Mission Statement Versus Actual Behavior

Every institution is created with a mission whether it is one of democracy or economic imperialism. However, that mission and the institution's behavior may not be on the same page. For example, a business may pose itself as the benefactor of the common good while being destructive of that good.

An Example

A prime example of this duplicity is the fossil fuel energy industry. It will often pose itself as focal to the nation's well-being while simultaneously poisoning the environment in irreparable ways. Duke Energy headquartered in Charlotte, North Carolina is an example. Here is its mission statement:

At Duke Energy, we make people's lives better by providing gas and electric services in a sustainable way—affordable, reliable and clean.

But how does the clean part match up to reality? It turns out that the company has been dumping the toxic waste of coal ash into unlined pits which has allowed water from other sources to flow through them and pollute the environment—with arsenic, lead, mercury, and chromium among these pollutants.

258

In 2014 water from ash pits overflowed into the Dan River in North Carolina containing over 20 million gallons of contamination and 39,000 tons of coal ash. Duke Energy resisted all legal attempts to require it to clean up the sources of this pollution. Instead it lobbied the North Carolina legislature to lower restrictions on polluting. In 2015 Duke Energy was fined 102 million dollars for clean water act crimes. But it continued to resist environmental care-taking.

In April of 2019 Duke Energy was required by the North Carolina Department of Environmental Quality to remove the coal ash from all of its unlined leaking sites. According to a Sierra Club February 2019 article by Mary Anne Hitt, Duke Energy is trying to force its customers to foot the bill for this cleanup. What Duke Energy will do about complying with clean water regulations and governmental actions requiring it to keep the environment clean is unclear since it has resisted all prior efforts to fulfill its mission of supplying its customers with clean energy.

Duke Energy serves around 7.6 million customers in seven different states. According to a February 14, 2019 report in the Charlotte Business Journal, its profit for 2018 was 2.7 billion dollars – a drop from its 2017 profit of over 3 billion. Its profit margin provides ample resources for cleaning up its own mess.

It is a company's actions rather than its statements that tell us its real mission. It is the action rather than the mission statement that tells us if a business is committed to democracy or economic imperialism.

The same is true of the democratic institution. A congress, whether state or federal, will reflect a primary devotion—as will all its representative agencies. And, irrespective of the stated mission, it is actual behavior that reflects the institution's real devotion. The primary focus of its energy is usually the focus of its mission. Consider the radical differences between the focused energy of the Republican party and the Democratic party as examples.

The Bottom Line

Before making an assessment of any institution's motivations, compare its mission statement with its actual behavior. It is its behavior that states the real mission. It is action that makes a mission statement real or false.

Assumptions and Outcomes

There is an assumption behind everything humans create. This assumption is a reflection of the creation's mission.

Economic Imperialism

A baseline assumption of economic imperialism is that the planet and its resources are marketable for the profit of the entrepreneur and, thus, available for destruction. Its devotion is to economic good over all other considerations. The well-being of the citizenry is measured by economics and the environment is a utility. The economic imperialist will seek to control government in order to facilitate this basic assumption.

Democracy

A baseline assumption of democracy is that the citizenry is sustained by its physical environment which must be nurtured and protected. Thus, the well-being of the citizenry and the well-being of the planet are inseparable. Devotion to the citizenry's good is synonymous with devotion to the planet's good. This baseline assumption about citizenry and planet worth will translate into every decision made by a democratic government.

The Bottom Line

These bottom line assumptions underscore a primary difference between economic imperialism and democracy. The distinction is between a utilitarian society and a relational society.

Conclusion

The ultimate mission of economic imperialism is to convert state governments and the federal government into profit-making agents of business. This mission has no concern for the common good welfare of the nation of people.

The mission of democracy is to use the power of government to increase the citizenry's common good. This mission is vitally concerned that all decisions and actions promote this purpose.

The outcome of these two diametrically opposed missions and their inherent assumptions will manifest themselves in the visible drama of a culture. The conflict cannot be hidden because they are in constant battle for social and governmental control and one will inevitably dominate a culture's character and behavior.

There may be transition periods of dual domination between these two perspectives that cause an analysis such as the best of times and the worst of times. However, such periods will only prevail until either despotism or democracy ascends to a new dominance through citizenry commitment.

From the beginning of human history, whatever the culture, views of human worth and mission focus have been transparent. These two polarities will dictate whether the resulting cultural governance will be despotic or democratic or some in-between struggle. And one or the other will be visibly displayed in how the government is given focus.

OF, BY, AND FOR

All governments are created to facilitate a specific mission. In a democracy that mission is the common good of, by, and for the people.

Evaluating Questions

If the real mission of America's government is revealed by actual behavior, what would that mission statement be? And what assumption would be supportive?

PART VI

WE THE PEOPLE

28

WHO IS RESPONSIBLE?

Whatever the style of government, all nations are made up of people. We call these people the citizenry. Edmund Burke was a respected 18th century Irishman, member of the British parliament, and supporter of the rights of the American colonists. He understood that the citizenry made choices that determined their destiny. And he believed that the basic outcome of these choices was one or the other of what we usually call bad and good. Here is one of his comments about this ultimate struggle:

When bad men combine, the good must associate; else they will fall, one by one, an unpitied sacrifice in a contemptible struggle.

As a group, the citizenry decides what it will be—weak or powerful—fallen or risen. Individually the citizenry may easily succumb to social pressure. But as a group they can combine into that which creates a larger collaborative power. And if they do not do so they will become the victims of those who do.

We, the Vote

The takeover of democracy by economic imperialism could not happen without the consent of the citizenry. If there is a problem with the nation's democratic health it is the people who are responsible. Despite capturing the allegiance of politicians and the judiciary by the wealthy oligarchy, the mechanism for sustaining a true democracy remains in place and available to us citizens. We can still vote. All the power to actualize democracy is concentrated in our vote and consecrated by our vote. This vote makes us citizens more powerful than any other social agent. We can stop our wholesale exploitation whenever we choose. We remain the ultimate power in democracy. But such is only true when I and Me become Us and We. Democracy never happens until community happens.

We, the Cause

Why, then, would we willingly remain enslaved to an economic imperialist oligarchy? The simple answer is that we have submitted to the lie of externalized worth and the self-interest of individualism. We have become their modelers. We have become the game play of worth contention and competitive one-ups-man-ship. We have become the conscience of Me First. We have become that which exploits ourselves and are co-conspirators in our own servitude. We have converted democracy from a community affair to a private affair. We have allowed the tail of capitalism to wag the body of democracy—confusing it with the so-called American Dream. We have made the success of democracy about economics rather than relationships. We have become the lifestyle of our own democratic suicide. It is we, the citizenry, who are empowering economic imperialism.

The problem with American democracy is the same problem that has caused many prior attempts at people rule to fail. We, the citizenry, capitulate to the death-dealing enemies of democracy. We become the formulae of economic slavery. And we continue to elect those who are owned by the company store and fall for the ruse that the failure of democracy is because of the size of government.

It is obvious that democracy is not just about elections. It is about promoting equality of worth and the common good and all those means that make this happen. It is attitudinal as well as behavioral. It is relational. It is about national character and destiny. It is about international modeling. However, whatever its actual face, it will be publicly modeled by those we citizens elect. This electing is where it all starts. Therefore, nothing is as important because nothing is as causal.

We, the Power

We remain responsible for our own plight. We can change whatever needs changing when we assume our power as voters. If congress is broken then it reflects a broken citizenry. We must mend ourselves so we can mend that for which we are responsible.

An August 9, 2018 report by Brittany Short in Fortune shares a study for the Pew Research Center about the 2016 election. It reported that 55% of eligible voters did not cast a vote in this election. These potential voters were primarily young, non-white, less educated, and less affluent. They were also prone to vote democratic. Certainly a large number of these citizens had their voting right suppressed by political skullduggery. However, had even half of them voted the election would have been notably different in out-come. One way of saying this is that the non-voting citizens elected Donald Trump to the presidency. They elected a president that sees them contemptuously as nothing more than economic pawns. By not voting they empowered the election of their worst enemy and promoted their own economic destitution. By not voting they affirmed how much their vote actually counts.

We, the Choice

We have freedom of choice when it comes to living in a democracy. And we will make some choice in every election that empowers or disempowers our citizenship – both individually and as a citizenry body. The government we elect will reflect our choosing. It does not stand apart from we who create it.

The Choice to Lose

There are three ways we can choose to lose by allowing economic imperialism's ultimate triumph:

- By voting for the supporters of economic imperialism. In the 2016 election the citizenry deliberately voted into the presidency the model economic imperialist, Donald Trump,

and a Senate that would assure his success as an undemocratic despot.

- By not voting. Voter registration restrictions play a significant role in low voter turnout but it is primarily driven by
  assumptions that motivate indifference.

- By voting for fantasies such as Mickey Mouse—anybody that
  is not on the ballot. It is to vote to make one's vote inconsequential.

Any of those three is a vote for economic slavery. The citizenry
always decides how long it will be enslaved. Fredrick Douglas was a free
black social reformer and abolitionist of 19th century America. Here is
his understanding:

The limits of tyrants are prescribed by the endurance
of those whom they oppress.

The Choice to Win

Behind the choice to win are three assumptions:

- That my vote counts and I have a social responsibility to
  cast it.

- That I must carefully study both the candidates and the
  ballot measures to prevent being hoodwinked by the ads that
  deliberately create false and misleading images.

- That I must know the difference between democracy and
  economic imperialism and recognize the character of the
  candidates for whom I vote.

All available data shows that critical elections are often won by a
narrow margin of votes. In the 2018 election some of the margins were
so narrow that the winners and losers were required to wait days for
ballot recounting to be sure the vote was accurate. And many seats,
especially in the House of Representatives, were won by the smallest of
margins. There is no doubt that my vote counts.

Attack ads and lying have become acceptable by both parties. One
must access reliable sources to get a truthful picture of the candidates

and the ballot measures. Obfuscation has become a primary political tactic for those who represent economic imperialism because they have no concern for truth, ethics, or democracy.

To win I must rise above the deceits of political campaigns and gain the truth about both the issues and the candidates. I must rise above my immediate self-interest concerns, grasp the bigger picture, and make my decisions that invest in a future beyond now. When I have done this then I am ready to walk into the voting booth and vote to win.

Conclusion

One can vote for Mickey Mouse out of disgust over the lack of satisfying available choices but doing so only cancels one's vote. But the ultimate act of cynicism is to not vote which is to indicate that voting is irrelevant to outcome. Bill Vaughn, 20th century American author and entrepreneur, makes a comment that describes the ironic nature of this view:

A citizen of America will cross the ocean to fight for democracy but won't cross the street to vote in a national election.

Why fight if one will not vote? Voting is a far safer way of preserving democracy and the freedoms it offers. And if one votes for the candidate that prefers peace then fighting wars may become unnecessary.

Voting for Mickey Mouse or not voting is a betrayal of all that democracy represents. It is to relinquish one's own power to others. As Thomas Jefferson reminded the citizenry at the beginning of the American experiment in democracy:

We in America do not have government by the majority.
We have government by the majority that participate.

By participating he meant more than voicing one's opinion. He meant voting one's opinion. Whatever the issue that might challenge a rewarding democracy it can be overcome by an enlightened and self-empowered citizenry. Plato stated the bottom line hundreds of years ago:

If you do not take an interest in the affairs of government then
you are doomed to live under the rule of fools.

Abraham Lincoln was a bit more picturesque in saying the same thing:

Elections belong to the people. It's their decision. If they decide to turn
their back on the fire and burn their behinds, then they will
just have to sit on their blisters.

And Edward R. Murrow sums it up:

A nation of sheep will beget a government of wolves.

OF, BY, AND FOR

The citizenry becomes its devotions and those elected reflect these devo-
tions. It is always of, by, and for the people.

29

WE DESERVE WHAT WE GET

Louis Brandeis was a Supreme Court justice between 1916 and 1939 who fought against corporate corruption and advocated for citizenry rights. He penned this democratic insight:

The most important political office is that of the private citizen.

Democratic fulfillment ultimately rests in the hands of the citizenry. We can whine or win.

Here is a graphic example from American history. Our nation rose out of the ashes of a revolution against one of the world's most powerful and brutal economic imperialist nations. Great Britain ruled the colonies with the intention of exploiting a maximum profit. Colonial leadership sought a more democratic kind of relationship. But it became apparent that the colonists would never be viewed as anything other than servants of the British monarchy's company store. Weary of being treated with worth contempt, this leadership incited revolution.

The revolution was a statement of worth that demanded an equality of relationship. It was a bitter and bloody war that was won only through the commitment of great sacrifice, perseverance, and luck. And its chance of success was precarious. Only a third of the colonists were in support of the revolution while the rest were either opposed or were in a wait and see posture. Nevertheless, the visionary minority made revolution happen.

Ironic Present

Here is the irony. The American citizenry currently has willingly allowed itself to be ruled by an economic oligarchy contemptuous of its worth. This oligarchy is a wealthy libertine capitalist elite that has taken ownership of the ship of state via its corporate purchasing power. Its intentions and attitudes are the same as those of the earlier economic imperialists of Great Britain—exploitation of the citizenry for maximum profit. That this oligarchy is home-grown does not change the historical parallel. The issue of demeaned citizenry worth is the bottom line for both the nation's original economic slavery and its present economic slavery.

How could the citizenry have allowed democracy to be taken over by libertine capitalists – by the very kind of suppressive leadership that prompted the American Revolution? There are two symptomatic reasons.

The Coattail Lie

The first is that we fell for the lie that the citizenry rides on the coattail of big business success—that economics and the common good are synonymous—that capitalism and democracy are equivalents. We have fallen for a grand deceit. As historian Will Durant perceptively asserts:

It may be true that you can't fool all the people all the time, but you can fool enough of them to rule a large country.

We bought the lie and now we must undo it. We must restore democracy as a common good focus and place capitalism where it rightfully belongs—as a means to an end and not an end to itself. While economic health of the nation is vital it is not the measure of democratic health. A strong economy does not mirror a type of governance. Examples are replete around the world. Many despotic governments have a strong economy. China, Saudi Arabia, Russia, and Turkey are examples.

The Nose-Length Lie

The second reason is attendant to the first reason. The common good is the big picture of democracy. Our individual good is the little picture. As citizens our tendency is to see only what is at nose length, which is the little picture. We erroneously assume that our little picture and the big picture are the same. But they are not. We can vote for our immediate short term economic interests without realizing it might be a vote against our long term economic interests. It is the common good that ultimately defines our individual good.

For instance, because of the Great Depression, laws were instituted to curb the behavior of corporations that would keep them from acting in ways economically dangerous to the common good. However, our politicians have gradually rescinded and weakened these laws. This produced irresponsible and unethical corporate behavior that eventually resulted in the 2008 economic meltdown. To correct this disaster, we voted to bail out most of the businesses that caused the meltdown, falling for the false propaganda that they were necessary to our immediate economic survival.

Our congressional leadership voted in partial regulations that would supposedly curb future abuse and demand corporate responsibility. But since then we have elected politicians who see these laws as restricting capitalism and favor reducing them to meaningless safeguards. We voted in this leadership because we citizens were unable to distinguish between our own short-term and long term best interests. We fell for the false rhetoric of economic imperialists that claimed our best interests are tied to their totally uncontrolled profit making interests. Until we can shift our focus from the economic imperialist eye to the democratic eye we will remain the prey and victims of libertine capitalists.

Citizenry Choice

As colonists, our forefather's sense of self-worth demanded the choice of revolution. And this choice required an extended blood bath for victory. In present day America the citizenry is confronted with the same choice of worth enslavement or worth revolution. Here is the difference: The vote for revolution that fueled the birth of the nation posed no alternative but violence or submission. The vote that confronts modern America need not be bloody. It need only re-empower the citizenry as controllers of the nation's destiny via the election of political leaders that honor the people's worth and their common good.

One of the grand promises of democracy is that it can bring about consequential change in a peaceful manner. BR Ambedkar was an early to mid-twentieth century Indian jurist, social reformer, member of Parliament, and principle author of India's constitution. In describing democracy he said it was:

A form and a method of Government whereby revolutionary changes in social life are brought about without bloodshed.

Michael Moore is an American documentary film maker, journalist, and advocate for democratic citizenry involvement. He put his finger on the power of the citizenry to create social revolutions when he said:

I realized that this was the big secret of democracy—that change can occur by starting off with just a few people doing something.

The only other option is to remain the demeaned economic servants of the wealthy oligarchy and watch democracy further diminish toward suicide. Somewhere along this path there is a point of no return when democracy's power is gone and despotism's power becomes absolute. The present means of accomplishing this goal by economic imperialists is voter suppression and gerrymandering tactics—which are rapidly increasing.

The economic imperialist Robber Barons who control present day America cannot be beaten with violence except of the bloodiest kind because they inevitably control law enforcement and the military as they have in the past. They must have this control in order to stay in power. Winston Churchill, as England's Prime Minister, led the country through the darkest hours of World War II when it appeared that Germany might win. He understood the psychology of war with its populace anxieties and its leadership foibles. He once observed:

Dictators ride to and fro upon tigers which they dare not dismount.

Our choice must be a voting revolution. And to succeed it must be uncompromising and doggedly determined. What must be kept in mind is that if the advocates of economic imperialism do not yield to a peaceful revolution then there is only one alternative. As John F. Kennedy understood:

> *Those who make peaceful revolution impossible*
> *will make violent revolution inevitable.*

To begin a peaceful revolution we must quit deceiving ourselves that big government, greedy corporations, and special interest groups are responsible for our plight. Again, John F. Kennedy makes the issue clear:

> *We, the people, are the boss, and we will get the kind of political leadership, be it*
> *good or bad, that we demand and deserve.*

Briefly, if there is an enemy of democracy it is we citizens who vote for our own worst destiny.

Conclusion

The success or failure of democracy rests in our hands. We either empower it or allow its suicide. Benito Mussolini, fascist dictator of Italy during World War II, says it with succinctness:

> *The struggle between the two worlds (Fascism and Democracy)*
> *can permit no compromises. Its either Us or Them.*

The Us is democracy: Of, by, and for the people. The Them is economic imperialism: Government and business married. Us and Them are deadly enemies. Ultimately, one will conquer the other. It's our choice.

As Plato said:

> *Those who are too smart to engage in politics are punished*
> *by being governed by those who are dumber.*

Studs Turkel's life spanned the 20th century. He was an author, historian, actor, radio program host, and Pulitzer Prize winner. Here is his wisdom about the citizenry's desire to be liberated from despotism:

> *We are the ones we've been waiting for.*

OF, BY, AND FOR

If there is to be a return to the promise of democracy invented by our forefathers, then we the citizens must acknowledge that we are the ones who will make it happen. We are the of, by, and for.

PART VII

THE CHOICE

30

CLARITY OF CHOICE

Given the difficulties of trying to reclaim democracy from its despotic enemies, why go to all the trouble? Winston Churchill probably answered this question as well as anybody in history:

Democracy is the worst form of government except all those other forms that have been tried from time to time...

The choice is clear. It is between some form of democracy or some form of despotism. And in American democracy, we will either allow its continued descent into the suicide of economic imperialism or we will engage a revolution that installs ourselves as its owners. As 19th and 20th centuries Irish playwright, political activist, and Nobel Prize Winner, George Bernard Shaw concluded:

Democracy is a device that insures we shall be governed no better than we deserve.

The Three Questions

The means for recapturing ownership is voting assessments based on a positive answer to the three primary questions of democratic intent:

- Does it promote the equality of every citizen?
- Does it promote the common good?
- Does it promote the rule of the citizenry?

The answer to these questions offers a political profile of voting and policies.

There are three major steps in securing such a voting revolution:

- **Change the Leadership:** The first is electing and appointing officials devoted to democratic intent to house the three branches of government – otherwise, nothing will change.

- **Alter the Laws:** The second is to alter the constitution or enact laws so the nation rids itself of the out dated and counter-productive Electoral College. This will also require establishing election processes that are reasonably time-limited, funded by government, and based on a democratic majority – otherwise, the wealthy elite will continue buying elections.

- **Affirm the Intents**: The third is demanding that the criteria for all governmental decision making be an affirmative answer to the three primary questions of democratic intent—otherwise, economic imperialism will continue to reign.

To accomplish such a revolution will require a devotion to democratic possibility that enlists courageous commitment. It will demand the ability to distinguish between the politician devoted to democracy and the one devoted to assuring a self-centered economic future. It will require seeing through the democratic eye.

Following are examples of the kind of patriotic commitment necessary to engage such a revolution.

Example of Choice: The Politician

Ralph Lawrence Carr was governor of Colorado from 1939 to 1943. In 1942, President Roosevelt's ill-advised Executive Order 9066 caused over 120,000 Japanese Americans to be interred as a danger to the war effort, costing them their homes, businesses, and futures. One of these sites, Ameche Japanese Internment Camp, was located in a desolate area of Colorado.

Governor Carr not only condemned such incarceration as blatant racism but also demanded these Japanese be treated humanely and fought to help them retain their citizenship. Having the Ameche camp established in Colorado gave him an opportunity to fight for the civil rights of the Japanese who would be interred there.

Carr was a rising star in the Republican Party. However, during the hysteria of the war his attitude toward Japanese citizens was not looked upon kindly by the majority of Coloradans. He suggested that *We the people of the United States* referred to all the people of America and not just English, Scandinavian, and French descendants. The reaction was so negatively vehement that he was threatened with both impeachment and death. Despite all urgings to back down from this stance, he held firm. He refused to sell his soul to the company store.

Some had believed him to be a potential candidate for high national office. But he fell into disfavor and lost his bid for reelection. Ironically, his democratic integrity cost him a promising political future. However, he remains a model of the political embodiment of democracy's intents.

A democratic revolution demands the election and appointment of Carr-like politicians whether it is to local government, Congress, the White House, or the Supreme Court. This will require a self-educated and discerning citizenry that relies on social postures and voting records rather than the lies and distortions of media advertising to determine candidates. It will require a citizenry that knows that its best long-term economic interests lie in elevation of the common good above individual self-centeredness.

Example of Choice: The Judge

Louis Brandeis was one of America's greatest Supreme Court justices. He served in this capacity from 1916 to 1939. Brandeis' appointment to the court was highly contentious. The reason was his concerns about the power of bankers, corporations, and monopolies. He was further concerned with corruption, insurance fraud, and social justice issues. He was known as The People's Lawyer. His philosophy was that the law needed to address the common good. Those who opposed his appointment feared him because they saw him as incorruptible.

These opposers knew he was not up for purchase by the company store. The company store was the leaders of the giant corporations of the early twentieth century whose goal was to gain a monopoly over their segment of business, utilize the lower class as economic slaves, and use government as its subsidiary. Anti-Semitics and pro-economic imperialists added their weight to this opposition. They mobilized all their resources and influence against his appointment. Yet, he won.

What Brandeis understood was that the corporations were doing everything possible to control the government for the explicit purpose of profit making. Here is the choice as he saw it:

> *We can have either democracy in this country or we can have great wealth concentrated in the hands of a few, but we can't have both.*

If democracy is to be restored the citizenry must elect politicians who will see that the Supreme Court and other judicial positions are housed by justices of Louis Brandeis' insight, courage, and incorruptibility. Otherwise, these bodies will continue to make decisions that favor the subversion of American democracy into an instrument of economic imperialism.

Hidden In Plain Sight

Despotism comes in many forms. It need not be economically based. There are those who work for it simply for the sake of its ego inflation. There are those who permit it for the sake of efficiency or misguided fear.

Consider Ego. There are those who aspire to political position because it gives them the opportunity to exercise power over others. It is this empowerment that raises their sense of self-esteem. Lacking a sense of innate worth, they seek compensation by assuming their position elevates their worth over others. It is an artificial transaction grounded in the assumption that roles and positions are stations of worth status and that human worth is a social commodity of achievement.

Consider efficiency. Both the House of Representatives and the Senate give inordinate power to their basic leadership in the name of efficiency. This leadership can choose agendas, grant or suppress bill voting, limit debate, speak for the party, appoint leadership positions, and enforce the party platform. With this power, consideration of that which the country might desperately need can be blocked. Efficiency is often despotism's cover and can stifle democratic process.

Consider fear. Since World War II the nation has gone to war, without official congressional approval, in Korea and Vietnam at the behest and whim of presidents for their own reasons using threats to national security as a fear based rationale. In order to rein in the power of presidents to act on their own in a war-like manner, congress passed the War Powers Act in 1973. But this act has had little effect on presidential actions.

One reason is that when presidents violate this act congress does nothing or acquiesces. Following the destruction of the twin towers in New York City, President George W. Bush declared a War on Terror. Terrorists are individuals and groups that have no specific geographic identity. This is a war against the obscure that has found no definable end and continues to be sustained by fear—a fear often used by presidents to pursue private agendas which can be acts of despotism.

Another reason is that congress may vote measures in support of war without actually declaring war. The Iraq War (2003-2014) is an example. It was initiated deliberately by the lies and deceit of the George W. Bush administration claiming the presence and potential usage of weapons of mass destruction in Iraq that posed a threat to national security—an appeal to fear without supportive evidence—then or now.

Consider threat. Some presidents in the past have engaged war using the concept of emergency power when they perceived threats to America's democracy. Abraham Lincoln understood the Confederacy and slavery to be such a threat. He used his power as president to undertake a war intended to preserve the union and eventually to abolish slavery. And he did so with great reluctance. He framed this decision in light of the nation's constitution:

> *We the people are the rightful masters of both congress and the courts,*
> *not to overthrow the constitution but to overthrow*
> *the men who pervert the constitution.*

Without doubt, the Confederacy and slavery were gross perversions of constitutional intent. But so was the Vietnam War and Donald Trump's war on immigrants. Smaller despotisms invite larger ones. And together they capture governmental power.

While this book is focused on the despotic threat of economic imperialism to democracy it acknowledges that it is not the only despotic threat that might put the nation in harm's-way. Lack of citizenry insight and courage allows the enthronement of all kinds of despotisms.

Conclusion

Alexis de Tocqueville was a French diplomate, historian, and activist of the 19th century who traveled to America to study the successes and failures of the country's democracy. He interviewed people of all walks of life and all geographic areas. He wrote a two-volume book entitled Democracy in America about his conclusions which is still relevant in the 21st century. Here is one of his conclusions:

The health of a democratic society may be measured by the quality of functions performed by private citizens.

OF, BY, AND FOR

Democracy is of, by, and for us, the people. Our control of democracy is our authority to elect those who represent us. When we elect representatives who reflect democratic intent the nation will reflect democracy. Until then the nation will continue its descent into the suicide of despotic economic imperialism.

CHAPTER 31

THE REVOLUTION

A revolution is a turning toward an opposite. Revolutions are created by devotees to such turning. Revolutionaries are not compromisers. Compromise slows down or stops the turning. The question is: What causes the turning? The answer is raging, rallying, and regulating.

Raging

Most revolutions begin with outrage over violation of respect for human worth. This raging is normally the last straw in a series of events which pushes the population toward its unwillingness to abide by the growing volume of disrespecting behavior. The perpetrators of such behavior are usually those who establish and enforce community laws and customs. Thus, the rebelling interaction is inevitably between the ruled and the rulers; between the common citizen and the empowered authority. But however it gets expressed it is provoked and sustained by a We Won't Take It Anymore form of raging.

Rallying

This rage is a response to perceived worth abuse and suppression of the common good. If the rebellion sustains itself it must translate this outrage into a means of correction. This statement of means must be clear and inspiring of a continued motivation for rebellion until correction is achieved. It must provoke continued rallying.

If revolution is to happen a mass of the citizenry must take up civic arms. There must be an overpowering citizenry demand that creates the turning—a mass that either causes authority to acquiesce to the demands or step down from power. Numbers become critical in a non-violent revolution. Those who lead and inspire such a revolution may be small in numbers but that leadership is only effective if it elicits the response of the populace. Those in power will not bow to a peaceful turning unless they are compelled by the numerical strength of the people they rule.

A few people may be able to capture a government if such a revolution is provoked by armed force. However, a democratic revolution requires that a majority of the people must agree with the turning and rally support till it happens. Small may be inspirational as a protest but is impotent as a peaceful revolution. The larger the numerical rally the greater the political force for correction.

Regulating

The revolution is not a revolution until its demands are regulated. Regulating means that its demands willingly become the guidelines for the behavior of the citizenry, the government, and its organizational agencies. It must become laws and order that are translated into instinctive behaviors and customs. It must become the new willing obedience. It must become embedded in the structures that carry and implement democracy. It must become the accepted norm. Essentially, it must become institutionalized which means to become organized into social carriers. And the citizenry, who are the revolution, must be the watchdogs that guarantee this institutionalization.

Revolution calls for the intents of democracy to become regulated through being institutionalized—becoming the cultural way of life.

Compromise and Progressive

If there is need for a revolution in a so-called established democracy, it is because its very soul has been compromised. If acknowledged equality of worth is the soul of democracy then every compromise of this soul is an act of defeat that opens to despotism.

286

Compromise

In the drama of compromise there is a point at which democracy ceases to exist and the spirit of compromise becomes enthroned in its stead. Every compromise that demotes the citizenry's worth announces this enthronement. With such demotions the soul of democracy becomes only a ghost that can be called forth from documents. A nation can exist for decades on the illusion that its democratic documents are the same as their embodied intentions.

Progressive

In America, compromising democracy by making it a servant of economic imperialism has become the norm. Thus, when new citizens are introduced into the culture they assume this is the face of real democracy. But it is not. And this is why calls for an actualized democracy seem radical. The phrase that is often used to imply this radicalness is: It is too progressive. Progressive stems from the Latin for forward movement and was early used to refer to gradually meeting the goals of a journey. When it was eventually applied to politics it denoted those who invested in forward progress toward the meeting of a larger vision. It was the assertive posture of anti-status-quoism.

Unfortunately, in recent years the term progressive politics has come into vogue as a label for those who want to go too far in the political journey. Going too far in America means to actually apply the intents of democracy. It is viewed as too far because it would go past what presently exists and require capitalism to become the servant of democracy. It would go too far because it would disempower economic imperialism. In America, being progressive means actually instituting democratic intent. It means a political revolution. All revolutions are progressively too far. It is the jaded democrat or the economic imperialist who sees democratic progressiveness as a journey too far. It is the citizen who has confused economic imperialism and democracy who sees real democracy as too progressive.

Conclusion

Revolutions are instituted by those who know the difference between documents and the reality the documents intend. Revolutionaries are totally uncompromising in their goal that documents must be embodied in attitudes and actions before they become reality. They will not sell their soul to the company store for any reason of compromise. They will accept defeat before accepting the loss of democratic integrity.

If we wish to restore democracy to the nation, it will only be done through the kind of uncompromising commitment to the sine qua non of democracy of former Colorado governor Ralph Carr and former Supreme Court justice Louis Brandeis—the equality of citizenry worth. In regard to democratic intent, the art of compromise is the art of failure. It is both the first and continuing down payment to the company store that gradually enslaves in unending fashion.

Langston Hughes was a highly respected black and white mixed race American poet, novelist, playwright, and author. His life spanned a little more than the first half of the 20th century. He was an early initiator of what came to be known as jazz poetry. He lived amid racial prejudice and suppression. He was devoted to an America of democratic intent but felt that he, among those who were not the privileged white, had never been permitted the experience. This was what Hughes had in mind when he wrote a poem entitled: Let America Be America Again. Here is a defining verse from this poem:

> Out of the rack and ruin of our gangster death,
> The rape and rot of graft, and stealth, and lies,
> We, the people, must redeem
> The land, the mines, the plants, the rivers.
> The mountains and the endless plain —
> All, all the stretch of these great green states —
> And make America again!

The purpose of these words is not the egotism of a false national greatness. It is the grandness of the institution of the citizenry's commitment to democratic intent. What Hughes understood was that

America was a relationship of worth acceptance that also embraced the land that sustained the citizenry. It was the total embrace of all that defined the nation. This worth acceptance is what makes for true national identity. It is an identity he recognized as having been lost to prejudice, hate, and utilitarianism. Such identity re-institution will only happen with a profound commitment of the citizenry to the intents of democracy and particularly to its grounding tenet.

OF, BY, AND FOR

The revolution that successfully institutionalizes the intents of democracy will be of, by, and for the people or it will not happen.

32

WHEN DOES REVOLUTION HAPPEN?

Just as the purpose of a government may take time to deteriorate, so may it take time to restore. Revolution is what is required to restore. In creating a revolution it is easy to get trapped in illusions that seem to imply actual success but which really only imply the possibility of success. Here are two such illusions.

Illusion One

We citizens adore the notion that all we need do is flex our muscle of dissent and our elected officials will pay heed. This is an illusion.

Paying heed to the citizenry requires a commitment to democracy. Economic imperialists have no such devotion. They only pay heed to self-interest economics. Thus, polls, protests, and petitions have no meaning to them except as it might significantly affect money making empowerment.

While it is true that public servants committed to democracy will pay heed to polls, protests, and petitions, they may be a minority and not in control. Thus, the only guarantee for revolution to happen is for the citizenry to replace corrupted politicians with those who are uncorrupted.

This means that, while there is merit in polls, protests and petitions because they declare the mood of the citizenry, state its demands, and enlist additional citizenry support, they will not compel a revolution if they fall on deaf political ears. The only assured means is representative replacement. And representation is what American democracy is all about. Thus, committed and knowledgeable voting becomes the critical issue in a peaceful revolution.

Here is an example. Following the election of Donald Trump and the Republican control of both houses of the nation's federal government, in 2016 there were enormous protests in cities in America and European countries. These protests indicated public outrage but did not provoke any measurable change in the nation's negative politics. In fact, these politics have only increased. However, at the midterm election of 2018, the citizenry took concrete action and elected a majority of democrats in the House of Representatives. This election initiated the possibility of governing change. It permitted one half of congress to act with democratic integrity.

The lesson is clear. It is important to express the nation's mood through protests and other means. This makes visible both the need and the support which helps sustain the energy of citizenry outrage. However, peaceful change will only come through electing those who represent the nature of the desired change.

Illusion Two

Our tendency is to assume that revolution happens when good laws are instituted that uphold democratic intentions. This is an illusion. Laws are only kept by those who believe in their validity.

Laws are symptoms of what ought to be but are not the causes of what ought to be. This is why the constitutional changes following the Civil War that affirmed the equality of the black citizenry were only minimally honored for almost a hundred years. It is belief in validity that causes compliance with law. This constitutional law of equality did not accord with a large segment of the citizenry's beliefs and particularly those in southern states. It was not until the 1950s when the Supreme Court had a belief change that it began making decisions that upheld these constitutional rights. It was not until a large segment of the white citizenry changed its belief about the worth of the black citizenry that it lent its support to the civil rights movement of the 1960s and 1970s.

It was not until political leadership changed its belief about the right to vote of the black citizenry that it passed enforcing laws.

Social Change is Heart Change

This was the primary message of Martin Luther King, Jr. He understood the necessity of the restraining and teaching value of good laws that allowed blacks and whites to eat in the same establishment. He wanted such laws to be passed and enforced. But what he wanted far more was a change of the heart of the citizenry that would make the necessity of such laws irrelevant. He knew that all sustained culture change results from sustained citizenry heart change. And heart change was change of belief. It was to see differently. It was to see people and not their skin color.

As he affirmed:

A social movement that only moves people is merely a revolt. A movement that changes both people and institutions is a revolution.

His method of inducing revolutionary change was love oriented non-violent attitudes and actions that demanded such heart change from those who harbored hate. The ground of love is the embrace of equality. Everything he worked for was rooted in the desire for the social heart to be transformed so that all citizens would be mutually embraced in democratic community.

When democracy exists in reality it does not require supportive laws because it dwells in the heart of the citizenry. When the citizenry believes in worth equality there will be worth equality.

Lack of Heart Change

The reason why the issues of racism and inequality remain in contention today is because a significant number of white citizens have never allowed their hearts to acknowledge the worth of non-white citizens. The nineteen sixties began a consequential social revolution that is far from complete because it stopped short of a dominating national heart change.

As a result of the civil rights movement, in 1965 congress passed The Voting Rights Act. A part of that act was a section that forbade laws that denied citizens the right to vote based on race. For almost fifty years the formula for judging such laws has held firm and staid the hand of voter discrimination. In 2013 the Supreme Court ruled this formula to be outdated and unconstitutional. According to a report in September 2019 by Common Dreams, since the court's ruling, almost 1700 polling places in America have been shut down, most in black and Hispanic communities. Texas closed 750 and Georgia 214. These have basically been Republican party actions intended to suppress ethnic votes. If democracy is not a core belief of those in political power then there will be an attempt to suppress the vote of those for whom it is a core belief.

The work the nation has left to do is to bring the total of the citizenry's social vision into accord with the vision of democratic intent. And such is heart-belief change. Vision transformation is the same as heart transformation.

The Lesson

This is the lesson of the victory dance the nation did in the latter part of the twentieth century when voting rights laws were enacted due to the Civil Rights Movement. The dance was pre-mature. This is what documentary film-maker Michael Moore was implying when he said:

Don't do the end zone dance on the fifty-yard line.

Social revolution only occurs when both the social law and the social heart change in agreement.

The Transforming Conclusion

If we citizens wish to be transformers of the nation then we must first be transformed. We must:

* Accept our own innate worth. This will liberate us from the cultural con of imported worth that empowers libertine capitalism.

293

- Commit to the common good as the ground of democracy and behave and vote accordingly. This will free us from the selfishness of individualism that robs us of profound relating.

- Acknowledge that we citizens determine whether despotism or democracy rules us. This will release us from blaming corporations, big government, and bad politicians for our destiny.

When our heart is transformed our way of seeing is transformed.

The Way We See

Each of us views our world through a particular eye. Through this eye we interpret and give meaning to our entire experience. Through it we create reality and give focus to our devotions. We determine the nature of our relationships and shape our destiny. It is our way of seeing. We can adopt a different eye if we choose. This capacity is called freedom and this freedom is our birthright.

The dollar $ign is a metaphor for seeing through the eye of economic imperialism. It is the eye that birthed the original colonies—that of European colonialism. Its motivating vision is to translate everything seen into monetary profit. It assigns worth according to this capacity to profit from what is seen whether such is human or environment. It is a utilitarian eye. It sees government as a means to facilitate this motivation and acts accordingly. It becomes an oligarchy because it is of, by, and for the wealthy.

Old Glory is a metaphor for seeing through the eye of democracy. It is the eye that motivated our ancestors when they rebelled against Great Britain and birthed the nation. It is the vision of the tattered flag that still waved after the British bombarded it with every destructive device in its arsenal. This eye is motivated by seeing every human as born worthy and by a devotion to their common good. It is a relational eye. It sees government as a means to facilitate this worth and common good. When it is in control the people are in control because it is of, by, and for them.

These are our choices of governing vision. We must finally choose one or the other. Otherwise we will continue languishing toward national suicide. The Russians have a proverb to describe the outcome of choice indecision:

If you chase two rabbits, you will not catch either one.

The Challenge

Our challenge is simply stated: We are in the most critical crises the nation has ever faced. It is a crisis more profound than that of the Civil War. This crisis is about whether economic imperialism will control the entire nation rather than just the southern states. The difference is that during the Civil War the president was Abraham Lincoln, who was devoted to democracy, while at this moment in history the president is Donald Trump, who is devoted to economic imperialism. It is eye to eye combat. It is America's moment of destiny. And whichever way the majority of the citizenry chooses to see will translate into this destiny.

The Power of Hope

In voting we must allow ourselves to be energized by hope despite all opposition. This hope must persist in action until it becomes reality. As 18th century British poet Percy Bysshe Shelley exhorted:

To defy Power, which seems omnipotent;
To love, and bear; to hope till hope creates
From its own wreck the thing it contemplates.

Ursula K. Le Guin was an American 20th and 21st century author and master of speculative fiction and the science genre. She has stated the issue with clarity:

You cannot buy the revolution.
You cannot make the revolution.
You can only be the revolution.

This means we must be the embodied transformation and the embodied hope which will make us the embodied revolution.

OF, BY, AND FOR

All peaceful democratic revolutions are of, by, and for the citizenry.
And this understanding provokes critical questions:

- *Where is my heart when it comes to affirming the equal worth of every citizen irrespective of their religion, gender, ethnicity, or class?*
- *Does my own modeling of democratic intent invite hope and social transformation?*
- *Do I have double vision or single vision?*
- *If I have single vision, is my eye that of the dollar $ign or that of Old Glory?*

EPILOGUE

IF WE REMEMBER

In the middle of the century following the Revolutionary War, the conflict of the Civil War threatened American democracy's very foundation. This war cost over a million lives in total casualties. And, not counting property devastation, its minimal economic costs totaled around 8 billion dollars—translatable in 2019 as 144 billion. This was a staggering price in life and property to preserve the union and its focus on equality of worth. And this was on top of the cost of the revolutionary war. A mammoth price has been paid by our ancestors for our present democracy.

In the midst of the Civil War, following the Battle at Gettysburg, President Abraham Lincoln delivered a speech dedicating the cemetery at that site where the Union casualties were buried. He could not have known that we, in this present moment, would be continuing the battle to preserve the democracy he was addressing. Here are the last few sentences of this address:

> *It is for us the living, rather, to be dedicated here to the unfinished work which they who fought here have thus far so nobly advanced. It is rather for us to be here dedicated to the great task remaining before us—that from these honored dead we take increased devotion to that cause for which they gave the last full measure of devotion—that we here highly resolve that these dead shall not have died in vain- that this nation, under God, shall have a new birth of freedom—and that government of the people, by the people, for the people, shall not perish from the earth.*

Despotic rule again challenges our commitment to sustain the democracy for which so many have paid so dearly. Our heritage is to both preserve and mature that which they began. It is to see that their sacrifice was not in vain. And there is ample hope that we can do so. All we need do is remember that the revolution that birthed America was started by approximately one third of the citizenry who were willing to give their lives for the blessings of a potential democracy. We have tasted of those blessings but we are being driven toward suicide by an economic imperialism that cares nothing for them. It is time for us to rise up in empowered hope and engage a revolution that will return us to democracy. And we will succeed if we remember that democracy is:

OF THE PEOPLE

BY THE PEOPLE

FOR THE PEOPLE

(Democratic Unity)

E PLUIBUS UNUM

(Out of many, One)

UNUS PRO OMNIBUS,

OMNES PRO UNO

(One for all, all for One)

In the final analysis, a democratic government represents the sum total
of the courage and the integrity of its individuals.
It cannot be better than they are.
~ Eleanor Roosevelt

Not everything that is faced can be changed:
but nothing can be changed until it is faced.
~ James Baldwin

If you do not change direction, you may
end up where you are heading.
~ Lao Tzu

ABOUT THE AUTHOR

Robert T. Latham grew up in a fundamentalist religious and conservative political environment characterized by white male privilege and patriotic swagger. Through the exposures of education and a tour of duty in the Vietnam War these views of reality were transformed. As a result he has been motivated to explore the purpose of being human, the meaning of democracy, and why America's attempt to institute democracy has been so contentious and problematic. He is a writer and consultant. His organization is The MythingLink. Website access is mythinglink.com.

CPSIA information can be obtained
at www.ICGtesting.com
Printed in the USA
FSHW020125090220
66775FS